KU-713-478

King Alfred's
Winchester

Martial Rose Library
Tel: 01962 827306

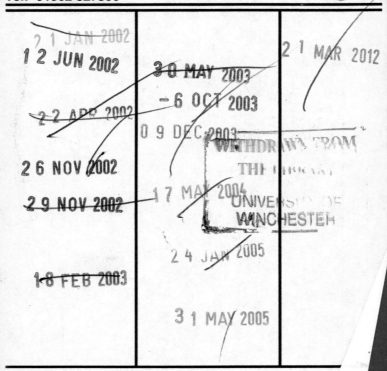

2 1 JAN 2002
1 2 JUN 2002
3 0 MAY 2003
2 1 MAR 2012
2 2 APR 2002
- 6 OCT 2003
0 9 DEC 2003
WITHDRAWN FROM
THE LIBRARY
26 NOV 2002
2 9 NOV 2002
17 MAY 2004
UNIVERSITY OF
WINCHESTER
2 4 JAN 2005
1 8 FEB 2003
3 1 MAY 2005

To be returned on or before the day marked above, subject to re

KA 0258014 4

MASKS
FACES OF CULTURE

MASKS
FACES OF CULTURE

JOHN W. NUNLEY · CARA McCARTY

HARRY N. ABRAMS, INC., PUBLISHERS

in association with The Saint Louis Art Museum

To my son
Avery James Nunley
J.W.N.

To my parents
Martha and Perry McCarty
C.M.

Published on the occasion of the exhibition, MASKS: FACES OF CULTURE, organized by The Saint Louis Art Museum, St. Louis, Missouri

Exhibition Itinerary:
The Saint Louis Art Museum, October 9, 1999–January 2, 2000
The Field Museum, Chicago, February 19, 2000–May 14, 2000
Museum of Fine Arts, Houston, June 25, 2000–September 17, 2000

This exhibition and catalogue are made possible by a grant from AT&T. Additional generous funding was provided by the National Endowment for the Arts, a federal agency; the Whitaker Foundation; the Jordan Charitable Foundation; The Rockefeller Foundation; the Helen Clay Frick Foundation; and Jefferson Smurfit Corporation

For Harry N. Abrams, Inc.:
Project Director: Margaret L. Kaplan
Editor: Nicole Columbus

For The Saint Louis Art Museum:
Editor: Mary Ann Steiner
Designer: Alex Castro

KING ALFRED'S COLLEGE
WINCHESTER

731.75
/NUN

KA02580144

Library of Congress Cataloging-in-Publication Data

Nunley, John W. (John Wallace), 1945–
    Masks : faces of culture / John W. Nunley, Cara McCarty : with contributions by John Emigh,
Lesley Ferris.
        p.   cm.
    Published to accompany an exhibition held at the Saint Louis Art Museum, St. Louis, Mo.,
Oct. 9, 1999–Jan. 2, 2000 and the Museum of Fine Arts, Houston, Tex., June 25–Oct. 1, 2000.
    Includes bibliographical references and index.
    ISBN 0-8109-4379-4 (Abrams: cloth)
    1. Masks. 2. Masks—Exhibitions. I. McCarty, Cara. II. Emigh, John. III. Ferris, Lesley. IV.
Saint Louis Art Museum. V. The Field Museum, Chicago. VI. Museum of Fine Arts, Houston. VII. Title.
GN419.5.N85 1999
391.4′34—dc21   98-53973
    ISBN 0-8917-8078-5 (museum: pbk.)

Copyright © 1999 The Saint Louis Art Museum
Published in 1999 by Harry N. Abrams, Incorporated, New York
All rights reserved. No part of the contents of this book may be reproduced without the written permission of the publisher

Printed in Japan

Harry N. Abrams, Inc.
100 Fifth Avenue
New York, N.Y. 10011
www.abramsbooks.com

Title page: Hockey goaltender's mask, 1964; Ernest C. Higgins, Co., United States; fiberglass; h: 10½ inches (26.7 cm); The Museum of Modern Art, New York, Emilio Ambasz Fund

Contents

LENDERS TO THE EXHIBITION

All-Star Sporting Goods, Massachusetts

American Museum of Natural History

The Art Institute of Chicago

Barbier-Mueller Collection, Dallas

Bibliothèque nationale de France. Bibliothèque-Musée de l'Opéra

Bread and Puppet Theater

Bulgarian National Ethnographic Museum

The Cleveland Museum of Art

Collection of Ralph T. Coe

Collection of Pearl and Daniel Crowley

Collection of Charles and Kent Davis

Denver Art Museum

Collection of Geraldine and Morton Dimondstein

Walt Disney Theatrical Productions

Don Post Studios, Los Angeles

General Counsel of Dordogne

Gent, Oudheidkundig Museum van de Bijloke, Belgium

Collection of William Greenspon

Collection of W. and U. Horstmann, Zug

Collection of Mr. and Mrs. Richard Palmer Hoyt

Institut für Ethnologie der Universität Göttingen, Abteilung Völkerkundliche Sammlung

The J. Paul Getty Museum

Jackalope, Inc., Santa Fe, New Mexico

Linden-Museum, Stuttgart, Staatliches Museum für Völkerkunde

Collection of Mr. and Mrs. Meredith J. Long

Collection of Alfredo MacKenney

Collection of Sam Merrin

The Metropolitan Museum of Art

Museo Barbier-Mueller de Arte Precolombino, Barcelona

Musée Dapper, Paris

Musée de la Civilisation, Quebec

Museo Ruth Lechuga de Arte Popular, Mexico City

Museum der Kulturen, Basel

Museum für Appenzeller Brauchtum, Urnäsch, Switzerland

The Museum of Fine Arts, Houston

International Folk Art Foundation Collections in the Museum of International Folk Art, a unit of the Museum of New Mexico, Santa Fe

The Museum of Modern Art, New York

Museum Rietberg Zürich

National Air and Space Museum, Smithsonian Institution

National Museum of African Art, Smithsonian Institution

National Museum of Ethnology, Osaka

Portland Art Museum, Oregon

Rijksmuseum voor Volkenkunde, Leiden, The Netherlands

Römisch-Germanisches Museum der Stadt Köln

Royal British Columbia Museum

Royal Museum for Central Africa, Tervuren, Belgium

Royal Tropical Institute, Tropenmuseum, Amsterdam, The Netherlands

The Saint Louis Art Museum

C. Raman Schlemmer, The Malabar Collection

Seattle Art Museum

Collection of Marielle and William Segal

Semitour Périgord

Staatliche Museen zu Berlin, Preussischer Kulturbesitz, Museum für Völkerkunde

Staatliches Museum für Völkerkunde, Munich

Collection of Mr. and Mrs. Michael Steinhardt

Collection of Allan Stone Gallery, New York

Theatre Estate Oskar Schlemmer (Bühnen Archiv), courtesy C. Raman Schlemmer, Oggebbio, Italy

Tiroler Volkskunstmuseum, Innsbruck

UCLA Fowler Museum of Cultural History

University of Cambridge Museum of Archaeology and Anthropology

Collection of Wolfgang Utzt

The Walters Art Gallery, Baltimore, Maryland

The Weston Collection

Collection of Thomas G. B. Wheelock

Zivkovic Modern Fencing Equipment, Inc., Massachusetts

Bait Al Zubair Collection, The Sultanate of Oman

Foreword

IT IS RARE AND EXCITING for a major art exhibition to be organized around so universal and appealing a subject as masks. In an age when large retrospectives and carefully culled thematic presentations are abundant, we take great pride in presenting *Masks: Faces of Culture*. The individual masks selected for exhibition, and the themes of human existence they relate to, are as accessible to the youngest visitor as they are to the most sophisticated museum-goer.

That said, however, it is important to note that the driving forces behind this exhibition have been concerned not only with the expression—indeed facial expression—of basic human themes, but also with a quality of visual aesthetics that exemplifies the highest culture of individual societies. The masks represented in these pages reveal some of the best craftsmanship, artistry, creativity, and design that we could expect in any art form.

The idea for this exhibition came from the collaboration of two curators at The Saint Louis Art Museum: Cara McCarty, Curator of Decorative Arts and Design, and John W. Nunley, Curator of the Arts of Africa, Oceania, and the Americas. Their early conversations in 1993 warranted the enthusiastic support of the institution; as the project grew in ambition and complexity, they carefully wove into this large effort the generosity of an extensive group of lenders and the expertise of scholars, writers, artists, and designers.

We are especially grateful to the individual collectors and institutions who have lent their masks and costumes to this exhibition. Their willingness to share these wonderful objects and their gracious flexibility in the complicated arrangements for photography and exhibition have made possible a presentation that could easily have been so much less than it is.

So large an enterprise as this can only succeed with the intelligence and energy of many. Cara McCarty and John Nunley's vision and perseverance have been commendable. We thank Peter Marzio, Director of The Museum of Fine Arts, Houston, who will welcome the exhibition to Houston in the summer of 2000. We gratefully acknowledge Alex Castro for his dogged brilliance in designing the exhibition as well as the book. Jeanette Fausz, Sidney Goldstein, and Rick Simoncelli have each had an important role in shepherding this project to reality. Mary Ann Steiner has attended the publication from inception, through manuscripts, to the book now in your hands. The many names in the Acknowledgments that follow have contributed so specifically to our final product that only space prevents the details. We are grateful to them all.

We thank AT&T, whose support truly makes possible both the exhibition and book. Additional generous funding from the National Endowment for the Arts, a federal agency, the Whitaker Foundation, the Jordan Charitable Foundation, The Rockefeller Foundation, the Helen Clay Frick Foundation, and Jefferson Smurfit Corporation has encouraged our efforts and enabled us to carry out our best vision of the exhibition.

BRENT R. BENJAMIN
Director

JAMES D. BURKE
Director Emeritus

Acknowledgments

A PUBLICATION AND EXHIBITION OF THIS MAGNITUDE could not have been realized without the support and assistance of many people and institutions. Throughout our six-year journey organizing this project, we have encountered new friends, collectors, and colleagues and have been gratified to be able to rely on the help and knowledge of many people already known to us. While no such list is ever truly complete, we hope that the following acknowledges each and every one of them. If we have omitted anyone, we apologize greatly.

Above all else, we are deeply indebted to our lenders, without whose very willing participation this book and exhibition could not have been assembled. During our travels and research we were continually met with great enthusiasm and tremendous good will towards our project. The following colleagues and institutions have been extraordinarily generous with loans, and to them we owe our sincerest appreciation: Carol Jurga, All-Star Sporting Goods, Massachusetts; Enid Schildkrout, Curator, and Belinda Kay, Registrar for Loans, American Museum of Natural History, New York; Richard Fraser Townsend, Curator, Ian Wardropper, Curator, and Jane B. Neet, Research Assistant, The Art Institute of Chicago; Jean-Pierre Angremy, President, Pierre Vidal, Director, Hélène Fauré, Exhibitions Coordinator, and Philippe Cousin, Bibliothèque nationale de France, Bibliothèque-Musée de l'Opéra, Paris; Elka, Peter, and Maria Schumann, Bread and Puppet Theater, Vermont; Nadezhda Teneva, Bulgarian National Ethnographic Museum, Sofia; Margaret Young-Sánchez, Associate Curator, The Cleveland Museum of Art; Nancy Blomberg, Curator, Denver Art Museum; Don Post, Don Post Studios, Los Angeles; Bennet Bronson, Curator, and Janice B. Klein, Registrar, The Field Museum, Chicago; André Van den Kerkhove, Curator, Gent, Oudheidkundig Museum van de Bijloke, Belgium; John Walsh, Director, and Karol Wight, Associate Curator, The J. Paul Getty Museum, Los Angeles; Sheryl Murchy, Jackalope, Inc., Santa Fe, New Mexico; Peter Thiele, Director, and Ingrid Heermann, Curator, Linden-Museum, Stuttgart, Staatliches Museum für Völkerkunde; Barbara Ford, Curator, Julie Jones, Curator, and Andrea Lee, Collections Management Coordinator, The Metropolitan Museum of Art, New York; Mr. and Mrs. Jean Paul Barbier, and Laurence Mattet, Secretary General, Musée Barbier-Mueller, Geneva, and Museo Barbier-Mueller de Arte Precolombino, Barcelona; Christiane Falgayrettes-Leveau, Director, Musée Dapper, Paris; Johanne Blanchet, International Exhibitions Service Manager, and Richard Dubé, Collections Manager, Musée de la Civilisation, Quebec; Ruth D. Lechuga, Director, Museo Ruth Lechuga de Arte Popular, Mexico City; Clara Wilpert, Director, and Christian Kaufmann, Curator, Museum der Kulturen, Basel; Rudi Alder, Director, Museum für Appenzeller Brauchtum, Urnäsch, Switzerland; Peter Marzio, Director, and Anne-Louise Schaffer, Associate Curator, The Museum of Fine Arts, Houston; Barbara Mauldin, Curator,

Museum of International Folk Art, Santa Fe, New Mexico; Matilda McQuaid, Associate Curator, Pierre Adler, Study Center Supervisor, and Mikki Carpenter, Director of Rights and Reproductions, The Museum of Modern Art, New York; Lorenz Homberger, Curator and Loans Coordinator, Museum Rietberg Zürich; Amanda Young, Early Manned Spaceflight Astronaut Equipment Loans, and Ellen Folkama, Registrar, National Air and Space Museum, Smithsonian Institution, Washington, D.C.; Roslyn Walker, Director, National Museum of African Art, Smithsonian Institution, Washington, D.C.; Kenji Yoshida, National Museum of Ethnology, Osaka; Bill Mercer, Curator, Portland Art Museum, Oregon; Ted J. J. Leyenaar, Honorary Curator, Rijksmuseum voor Volkenkunde, Leiden, The Netherlands; Hansgerd Hellenkemper, Director, and Friederike Naumann-Steckner, Römisch-Germanisches Museum der Stadt Köln; Peter McNair, and Martha Black, Curator, The Royal British Columbia Museum; Anne-Marie Bouttiaux, Assistant Curator, Royal Museum for Central Africa, Tervuren, Belgium; J. H. van Brakel, Collections Manager, Elisabeth den Otter, Curator, Josefine Boers, and Martha Persoon, Royal Tropical Institute, Tropenmuseum, Amsterdam; Manuela Fisher, Curator, Maria Gaida, Curator, and Wibke Lobo, Curator, Staatliche Museen zu Berlin, Preussischer Kulturbesitz, Museum für Völkerkunde; Mary Gardner Gates, Director, Pamela McClusky, Curator, and Lauren Tucker, Associate Registrar, Seattle Art Museum; Jean-Loup Rousselot, Deputy Director, and Helmut Schindler, Curator, Staatliches Museum für Völkerkunde, Munich; Herlinde Menardi, Curator, Tiroler Volkskunstmuseum, Innsbruck; Doran Ross, Director, and Fran Tabbush, Associate Collections Manager, UCLA Fowler Museum of Cultural History, Los Angeles; David W. Phillipson, Director and Curator, University of Cambridge Museum of Archaeology and Anthropology; Marianna Shreve Simpson, Curator, The Walters Art Gallery, Baltimore, Maryland; and Branimir Zivkovic, Zivkovic Modern Fencing Equipment, Inc., Massachusetts; Sarah White, Curator, Bait Al Zubair Collection, The Sultanate of Oman.

We give special thanks to Gundolf Krüger and the Institut für Ethnologie der Universität Göttingen, Abteilung Völkerkundliche Sammlung, for permitting us to borrow the extraordinary Siberian Shaman's mask and costume that is part of the University's Baron von Asch Collection of ethnographic art. They very graciously agreed to lend us this pivotal work in exchange for conservation and remounting, which was skillfully and respectfully executed by Gerry Barton. We also thank Kerstin Roggenbuck at the Institut for her assistance with the project.

We are exceedingly grateful to the following private collectors, who graciously admitted us to their homes and, because of their profound understanding and enthusiasm for our project, entrusted us with their works of art: J. Gabriel Barbier-Mueller; Ralph T. Coe; Pearl R. Crowley; Charles and Kent Davis; Geraldine and Morton Dimondstein; William Greenspon; W. and U. Horstmann; Mr. and Mrs. Richard Palmer Hoyt; Mr. and Mrs. Meredith J. Long; Alfredo MacKenney and Luz E. de MacKenney; Sam Merrin; C. Raman Schlemmer, U. Jaïna Schlemmer, and Assunta Trotta, Theatre Estate Oskar Schlemmer (Bühnen Archiv), for their considerable cooperation in overseeing the reconstruction of Oskar Schlemmer's mask "The Abstract" from *The Triadic Ballet*; William Segal and Marielle Bancou-Segal; Mr. and Mrs. Michael Steinhardt; Allan Stone and Claudia Stone, Allan Stone Gallery; Roger L. Weston; Wolfgang Utzt; and Thomas G. B. Wheelock.

During our visits to Bulgaria we were kindly welcomed by a number of people eager to share their culture with us. The United States Information Service helped us make the initial inroads, so we are particularly thankful to Lawrence I. Plotkin, Erik Holm-Olsen, and Ana Todorcheva. We especially want to thank Maya Avramova, Archaeologist, National Museum of History, Sofia, Bulgaria; Maya Kalimerova, Novecon; Albert Benbassat; Iglika Mishkova; and Anastasija Parovsheva. We are also grateful to Maya Bistrina and Dimitar Bistrini for making the wonderful Souvrakari masks and costumes. Paolo Piquereddu, Director of the Istituto Superiore Regionale Etnografico in Nuoro, Sardinia, graciously introduced us to Sardinian culture and masking traditions; he was most generous in overseeing the fabrication of four Sardinian masks and costumes. We are grateful to Sebastiano Brasu and Giannino Puggiani for making the Sardinian masks and costumes expressly for our exhibition. Without the tip from Beth and Michael Keyser we may never have discovered Sardinian masking traditions and carta da musica. For our travels and research in Guatemala, we would like to give particular thanks to Michael D. Orlansky, Cultural Affairs Officer, United States Information Service, Guatemala, and to Raymond Senuk for all their suggestions and for sharing with us their contacts in Guatemala. In Jamaica, Lloyd Jackson, Executive Director, Jamaica Cultural Development Commission, was most helpful in securing the commission of a Belly Woman mask and costume. We are very grateful to him and to the costume maker, Pansy O. M. Hassan, for making it possible to include this marvelous piece in our project. In the village of Urnäsch, Switzerland, we would like to thank several people who helped with loans and who eagerly shared their New Year's masking traditions with us on several occasions: Stefan Frischknecht, Mayor of Urnäsch, Bruno Aicher, and Elisabeth Baumberger. In France, Jean-Michel Geneste, Curator, Grotte de Lascaux, and Eric Dosset, Director, Semitour Périgord, could not have been more receptive to our requests for information about Lascaux and our desire to represent a facsimile section of it in our exhibition.

We are exceedingly grateful to Martha Frick Symington Sanger, through whose recommendation the Helen Clay Frick Foundation funded the commissions of four Sardinian masks and costumes and the reconstruction of Oskar Schlemmer's mask "The Abstract." Both commissions enhanced the exhibition and book.

Our warm personal thanks to Alex Castro of Castro/Arts, who deserves full credit for creating a book and exhibition that match the power, beauty, and dignity of the masks. Alex has not only brought to this endeavor his extraordinary gifts as a designer, but he provided intellectual insight and a number of suggestions that helped round out the project. Our collaboration with him has been a tremendous pleasure and learning experience.

At The Saint Louis Art Museum there are numerous individuals who have supported and assisted with this project. First and foremost, we would like to thank James D. Burke, Director Emeritus, for believing in this project from its inception and for giving us the time and financial support necessary to pursue a book and exhibition of this scope. We are equally grateful to Brent R. Benjamin, Director, for his immediate support of the exhibition and his willing direction of the project in the final months of its preparation. At the same institution we thank Rick Simoncelli, Assistant Director, and Sidney Goldstein, Associate Director, for their great interest and help in overseeing the management of the exhibition. Jeanette Fausz, Director of Exhibitions, coordinated the exhibition's overall planning with extraordinary enthusiasm and professionalism. As always, Judy Graves, Director of Finance, attended to all the financial concerns that sometimes became logistically complicated. Her expertise and advice were greatly valued.

The preparation of this ambitious book has been an enormous task for the Museum's Publications Department. They deserve considerable special recognition for their heroic efforts. The editing at The Saint Louis Art Museum was in the expert hands of Mary Ann Steiner. She has contributed countless improvements and is really the third author of this publication. Patricia Woods very skillfully assembled all the transparencies for the book and handled the daunting task of coordinating all the new photography in the United States, Central America, and Europe, and was on sight for all new photography at the Museum. Kate Weigand and Jill Henderson Heins have both done extremely noble jobs of coordinating the caption writers, preparing manuscripts for Harry N. Abrams, Inc., assisting with editing and proofreading, and arranging the photographers' travel schedules.

We could never have accomplished our research without the assistance of four terrific interns: Kimberly Patton, Meghan Barnes, Michael Murphy, and Samantha Krukowski. Among their multiple tasks, they performed detailed art historical research; tracked down elusive articles, books, and photographs; secured permissions; and checked thousands of facts. They handled all this with impressive resourcefulness and enthusiasm, and we are greatly indebted to them.

In the Development Department we would like to thank both Judy Wilson and Jim Weidman for their invaluable fund-raising efforts. Judy Wilson went beyond the call of duty, preparing an impressive number of extensive grant applications, and Jim Weidman worked tirelessly to help enlist sponsorship.

Curatorial Administrative Assistants Susan Rowe, Carol Kickham, and Nicola Heim deserve special recognition for the hours of typing, filing, managing numerous details, and for their superb efforts in making all of our exceedingly complicated travel arrangements. Their dependability, organizational skills, and cheerfulness have been greatly appreciated at all steps along the way.

In the Department of Information Services, Cathryn Goodwin's customary outstanding ability to centralize and manage all the documentation and information pertinent to each object has been extremely invaluable and a great source of comfort. This project has been a considerable undertaking for the Registrar's Department. Diane Vandegrift has done an exceptionally professional job of organizing and keeping track of all loan activity, shipments, and couriers, and of pursuing the myriad details that accompany such a large exhibition. We would also like to thank Bonnie Walker for scheduling the movement of artwork and props for in-house photography.

In the Conservation Department we thank Suzanne Hargrove, Objects Conservator, and Zoe Perkins, Textile Conservator, for their professional advice and for leading us to their colleague Gerry Barton, who is mentioned above. Zoe was also extremely adept and patient in preparing the Museum's Caribbean masks and costumes for new photography.

The Museum's Library has also been extremely helpful. We recognize Stephanie Sigala and her staff for their prompt assistance with our numerous requests for ordering new books, tracking down interlibrary loans, and for allowing us to keep all the Museum's mask-related books in our offices the past few years. In the Museum's Education Department we would like to thank Kate Guerra for keeping us supplied with film and for her camera copy work.

In the Museum's Buildings Operations Department both Dan Esarey and Jeff Wamhoff deserve to be singled out. Their great expertise in exhibition production and design has been invaluable, and their collaboration with Alex Castro has both facilitated and enhanced the installation of the exhibition. We thank Larry Herberholt of the Engineering Department for his help with the challenging lighting of this exhibition and Michael Sullivan for his attention to the complicated issues of security.

Quentin Rice of the Museum's security force was the ideal model for photographing the Caribbean masks and costumes. His good-natured patience and stamina under the hot lights and camera was most impressive. When he moved, the costumes danced. We would also like to acknowledge the efforts of Museum art handlers Jonathan Edwards and Michael Lucas for their assistance in preparing works for new photography.

We would also like to greatly thank Nicole Columbus at Harry N. Abrams, Inc., for her terrific editing talents. She miraculously transformed all the disparate manuscripts and captions into a cohesive presentation, for which we are most grateful. We are also especially grateful to authors John Emigh and Lesley K. Ferris for their insight, recommendations, and contributions to this book, as well as to the writers of the extended captions, whose knowledge helped round out our story of masks. All the photographers in the book are credited, but we would like to thank two in particular whose photographic talents, sensitivity, and love of objects were apparent in the many stunning photographs they took specifically for this book: Lynton Gardiner and David Ulmer.

The following experts and colleagues were very generous in sharing their knowledge or advice and patiently fielded questions: Janet Berlo and Alessandro Falassi, for their extremely helpful reviews of our chapters-in-progress; Jackie Lewis-Harris, Director, Center for Human Origins and Cultural Diversity, University of Missouri at St. Louis; Doran Ross, UCLA Fowler Museum of Cultural History, who aside from lending a number of important masks from his institution to this project served as consultant at various points along the way; Luis Luján-Muñoz and Jorge Luján-Muñoz; Douglas E. Bradley, Curator, The Snite Museum of Art, University of Notre Dame; Robert Burawoy, Galerie Robert Burawoy, Paris; Walter J. Karcheski, Jr., Curator, Higgins Armory Museum, Massachusetts; Aarne Anton, American Primitive Gallery, New York; Jehan S. Rajab at the Tareq Rajab Museum, Kuwait; Michel Revelard, Director, Musée International du Carnaval et du Masque de Binche, Belgium, whose museum is a treasure of masks and costumes from around the world. We would also like to thank several of our curatorial colleagues at The Saint Louis Art Museum for their expertise and enthusiastic support: Sidney Goldstein, Steven Owyoung, and Cornelia Homburg.

Various other people whose help we would like to acknowledge are: Peter Marzio, Director, The Museum of Fine Arts, Houston, whose enthusiastic response to sign on as a participating venue was a terrific endorsement; Thomas Alexander III; Didem Atahan; Gerard Besson; Michael Bush; Ingrid Castro; Rebecca Gardiner; Harry Gold at Disney Theatrical; Mr. and Mrs. Richard W. Graham; Manon Herzog; Sheila Hicks; Suzie Jones; Claudia Lango; Kevin Meadowcroft; Carla Panicali and Carlo Battaglia; Lisa Schonemann; Joseph Seubert; Mary Beth Smalley; and Pauline and Stelios Spiliadis.

Lastly, we would like to thank our families, friends, and Museum patrons for understanding our long periods of silence or absence during our preoccupation with this project.

CARA McCARTY   JOHN W. NUNLEY

ACKNOWLEDGMENTS

Introduction

MASKS ARE THE MOST ANCIENT MEANS OF CHANGING IDENTITY and assuming a new persona. From the beginning, putting on a mask has never been a singular activity. In order for masking to have meaning and relevance, it needs an audience, a minimum of one observer. The urge, perhaps even universal human need, to transform ourselves has coexisted with the development of human society.

The origins of the word *mask* are unclear, but it probably comes from the Arabic *maskhara* (*mashara*), which meant "to falsify" or "transform" into animal, monster, or freak. In the Middle Kingdom, Egyptians used the word *msk* to refer to leather or "second skin." This word most likely entered the Arabic language as *msr*, which for Muslims meant "to be Egyptianized," or to wear a mask as did the ancient Egyptians. In Italy the word became *maschera*, and it finally entered English as *mask*. In using this term we are referring to an object placed over the face or covering the entire head so that the face is more or less concealed. We have also employed the word as a verb, "to mask." The expression "masquerade" refers to the ritual performance of maskers as well as theatrical productions with masked and costumed players. As a public event, the social phenomenon of a masquerade might include music, food, drama, narration, a stage, or other performance props.

Masks have appeared in virtually every region of the world. They have been created to satisfy the desires and challenges to which societies must respond in order to survive and prosper, to maintain or reinvent identity. Masks symbolize our ability to change, to transform, to go to other worlds, to appease the spirits. Much has been written about the subject, yet rarely has it been discussed from a global perspective.

This book is about the "journey" of masks from their renderings in prehistoric caves to their use on the moon. In the course of these pages we pursue the origins of masking and five fundamental reasons why humans have made masks and performed masquerades. The strength of each theme is underscored by a selection of masks from a broad geographic range and time period. The diverse cultures within each category can be appreciated in the specifics of the ritual and in the aesthetics of the mask and the materials used. Because of limited space we excluded some masks that are more familiar to us: Halloween masks, wedding veils, Venetian Carnival masks, football helmets. Our respect for issues of repatriation precluded us from representing some of the extraordinary masks created by Native Americans. We also omitted body painting, makeup, tattooing, traditional scarification, and sunglasses. Some of the masks that we did include are used for more than one purpose and could have fit within several of our sections. In so general a survey, it would have been impossible to exhaust our chosen topics, but we hope the power and

Previous pages: Xipe Totec figure, Aztec, 1400-1500, front and rear views. *The Art Institute of Chicago, as a Gift from Mr. and Mrs. Samuel A. Marx.*

beauty of these masks will elucidate some of the common threads and needs that link us humans as a planetary family.

Prehistoric drawings on rocks, cliffs, cave surfaces, and pottery provide some of the earliest records of masks and masquerade. We will never know for certain whether these images actually represent early masqueraders, but similar documented masquerades of cultures today offer convincing evidence that these images do represent some form of masking. Paleolithic hunters and shamans used masks and costumes as decoys, and they performed masquerades before and after the hunt to gain the spirits' blessing and help in assuring a food supply. In these early societies, the men's role in the hunt and its rituals included drumming, blood sacrifice, and mask making; male dominance in the performance and control of masquerades has pretty much continued to this day.

The various stages in the human life cycle are determined primarily by the biological development of the body from birth to death. Rites of passage, including the transition from adolescence into adulthood, the achievement of rank, and the final passage to the spirit world can threaten the stability of a society. These transitional moments must be dealt with cautiously and with a proper respect for the spirits. Masked rituals are performed to bring individuals to the next stage of life. The spirits are often entertained, then solicited through the masquerade, blood sacrifice, and music.

Like the biological life cycle, annual cycles of renewal mark the seasonal changes. New Year celebrations, the planting of new crops, the coming of the rainy season, or preparation for the dry season are occasions for ritual and masking. From the snows of winter to the new life of spring and from the dry to the wet season, masked dancers hope to bring bountiful crops and a renewed food supply. Festivals of the West Indies were originally based on these seasonal changes, and masquerades in Bulgaria, Switzerland, Sardinia, Brazil, China, and Japan are all examples of renewal rites.

Men have dominated masking practices. More often than not, they even play the roles of women in masquerades and theater. Within the masking traditions in many parts of the world, men have tended to categorize women as maidens, mothers, or crones. The maiden is usually portrayed as passive and beautiful, an ideal, unspoiled fantasy in the eyes of men. The mother represents the spirit of fertility. The crone is witchlike; because she is associated with death and the powerful forces of evil, and because she possesses knowledge or wisdom not accessible to men, men perceive her as a threat and believe she must be controlled and appeased through masked performance.

Masquerades are important events in many societies, and most societies have set aside special areas to play out their myths. Theater and movies have grown out of ritual performance whose roots are in mythology and religion. But, unlike masks used in masquerades related to seasons, religious calendars, and the inevitable changes of the life cycle, theatrical masks used in structured performances are recognized more for their entertainment value than for their spiritual or ritual significance. Actors assume specific roles that are usually choreographed and scripted; sometimes their masks are established character types. Narration and language are essential to propelling the story. As part of our human quest to transform ourselves and create a fictional persona, theater masks help transcend some of the limitations of the human condition and play out our deepest images of ourselves.

When we compare a shaman's mask and an astronaut's helmet we find they are not so dissimilar if we understand them both as protective armor. In shamanic societies, the motives and attitudes toward life can be explained by profound beliefs in spirits, sorcerers, shamans, gods, and magical figures. When a community's well-being is threatened by the dangerous forces of nature or powerful spirits, it is up to the shaman to don his or her armor and do battle with the spiritual forces, influencing them through ritual. In our industrial society we, too, wear protective masks to negotiate with competitors or forces that threaten our survival, but ours are of a different type. Military combat, sports competitions, space travel, germ warfare, and terrorist acts are among the challenges facing manufacturers of protective gear in today's technological society.

In addition to disguise and transformation, revealing identity is another reason for masking. Masks empower us to divulge our hidden, true selves or secret thoughts, exposing inhibitions or personality traits that we ordinarily contain or feel unable to express. We even wear masks to become anonymous, enjoying the pleasure of not being recognized. The power of anonymity gives us the protection to behave in ways we otherwise might not, to act aggressively or to break rules.

Masks say much about the people who make them and the cultures that use them. Their materials and iconography provide clues to their meaning and significance: snake forms, shells, and the color red, for example, often symbolize fertility and renewal. The making of a mask frequently requires tremendous amounts of human resources. A community's best artists might be called upon to make the masks, which are sometimes among a society's greatest artistic achievements, although sometimes they are ultimately buried and never intended to be seen by the living.

Masquerade performances entertain, distract, provoke, inspire fear, and instruct audiences as well as participants. Masking also helps reconstruct social memory. In recent years there has been a flourishing revival of masking traditions in Europe and in North America, particularly Carnival. The instability that can come from fragmentation and the redrawing of political borders has prompted a number of societies to revive their heritage, to reassert national and regional or ethnic cultural distinctions. Masking helps us look to the past for guidance and identity, maybe even a new identity.

By now we have seen thousands of masks from all over the world, yet the infinite variety continues to astonish us. A mask consists of only a few features, but the continuing vigor of this art form confirms the richness of the human imagination. The fact that we humans continue to use masks, to reinvent ourselves, means that as mask wearers or passive spectators we still believe in their power to move us.

CARA MCCARTY
The Grace L. Brumbaugh and Richard E. Brumbaugh Curator of Decorative Arts and Design

JOHN W. NUNLEY
The Morton D. May Curator of the Arts of Africa, Oceania, and the Americas

CHAPTER ONE

Prehistory and Origins

JOHN W. NUNLEY

HUMANS HAVE DANCED IN MASQUERADES for at least 30,000 years. Masks have been used throughout the evolution of human society and culture, an indication of how important they are to being human.

I realized the importance of masks and the masquerade while completing research among the Sisala people of northwest Ghana. People from this region had once enjoyed masquerades during lavish funeral celebrations. However, years of migration by young men to the gold fields in the south and to the big cities created a generation gap with respect to sacred knowledge. The young men had not learned from their elders the secrets that would allow them to safely don the masks for life-cycle festivals. Consequently, a few lineages that owned masks never danced with them. Instead, they maintained these objects on ancestral shrines, occasionally offering the blood of sacrificed animals to them and to the individual ancestor spirits, called *dima*.

One hot early morning in February of 1973, I rode my bike, with a chicken hanging from the handlebars, to the village of Bujan twelve miles down the road from my residential compound in Tumu. My field assistant rode in front of me, the back of his T-shirt covered with flies as, I eventually realized, was mine; these insects had learned how to travel from one village to the next on their human shuttles. We met with the head of the compound and negotiated the day's program, which included a discussion about the mask on the shrine, the sacrifice that would be made to it, and the photographs I would take. It was hoped that the blood of the animal would appease the spirits of the ancestors and the mask so that I could photograph it without endangering the local community or myself.

Within the shrine space the headman sacrificed the chicken, then poured its blood on the mask and the ancestral mounds. He plucked the bird and stuck several feathers on the face of the mask. After briefly roasting the animal over an open fire, he then served portions of its flesh to the children in a ritual blessing of the sacrifice. To my astonishment he placed the mask on his face, which was an act involving spiritual danger. Apparently the blood sacrifice had been

Previous pages: **North wall of the rotunda from the Lascaux cave; shaman and bird staff from the shaft of the Lascaux cave, France, c. 15,000 B.C.** *Courtesy Photo Hans Hinz.*

21

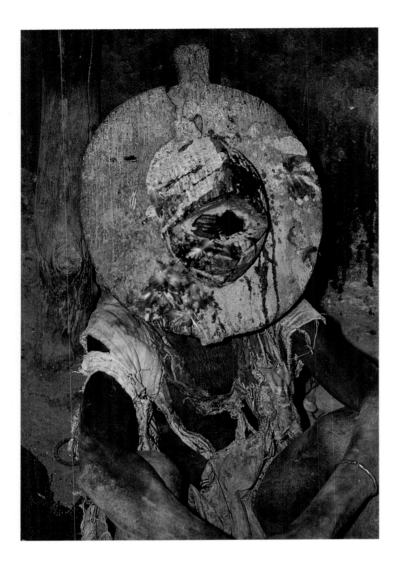

1.1 A Sisala mask used in a blood sacrifice ceremony in Bujan village, Ghana, 1973. *Courtesy John W. Nunley.*

sufficient to safeguard this man as he donned the mask. The compound became extremely quiet. The breeze that began to stir outside the compound on this 127-degree day moved into the compound's central court and found its way to the shrine room. As the cool wind swept over us, the masker went into an ecstatic state, and his body shook with the power of the ancestral spirits (fig. 1.1). We remained quiet until the spell had passed. Although this mask had been retired from public use, its custodian had been able to perform with it inside the compound in order to gain strength through a connection with the spiritual world.

Origins: Early Masks from Around the World
Humans have expressed their individual and social identity through the masquerade over the millennia. In fact, the development of masking has been intricately involved in the development of human society. Ancient sculptures and rock paintings that seem to portray humans in masquerade have been found in Europe, Australia, North and South America, Africa, and Asia.

The earliest evidence of masking comes from the Mousterian site of Hortus in the south of France. There the archaeologist Henry de Lumley found remnants of a leopard skin that was probably worn as a costume more than 40,000 years ago. The wearing of animal skins in masquerades recalls the well-documented depictions of the "sorcerers" at Trois Frères, and ethnographic literature is replete with similar examples from many regions of the world (figs. 1.2a, b, c).[1] Other strong evidence for early masking activities comes from the later Aurignacian period (c. 30,000 B.C.) from the Lonetal Valley in France, where a mammoth-ivory sculpture of a lion-headed man was found in the valley. The sculpture includes two "kill" holes or cuts, which may indicate that a ritual killing of the animal was involved, perhaps in preparation for a hunt. Lions were not hunted for food, however, and thus it is likely that the animal's power was sought to ensure a successful hunt.[2]

The famous cave paintings at Lascaux discovered in 1940 in Dordogne, France, date back to at least 15,000 B.C. These paintings reveal the hunting activities of people who were closely tied to nature and the world of spirits, especially animal spirits. In this region the vast prairies of central Europe provided food for massive herds of horned and hoofed animals, the primary meat source for these hunter-gatherers. Horses, bovines of many kinds, fantastical animals, and a few bears and cats are rendered amid onrushing and penetrating arrows.

Lascaux's caves were difficult to reach because of their lengthy and narrow passageways, thus serving as ideal spaces where rites of renewal and initiation could have been enacted in secret. The cave's images of animals, weapons, and other symbols may have served to teach the initiates about hunting. Rituals of renewal and initiation may also have furthered the process of acquiring, assimilating, and putting into practice cultural behaviors that were coded into the "art information."[3] Because caves are dark and removed from everyday life, the presentation and acquisition of knowledge in the cave was probably secret. This knowledge was kept away from women and from men of other bands who otherwise might thus learn how to develop better hunting and life skills in the competition for survival.

The only scene in the Lascaux cave paintings that includes a human is relatively small,[4] depicting a male figure wearing a birdlike mask, positioned in front of a charging bison whose stomach has been pierced by a spear causing the entrails to spill out (see chapter frontispiece). A bird staff or "wand" and what might be a spear-thrower are shown near the man.

Many interpretations have been offered to explain this "scene," despite rock art specialist Ann Sieveking's warnings that "trying to deduce the meaning of Paleolithic art is fairly unrewarding" and that "it is very probable that we shall never know the meaning of Paleolithic art."[5] The many thousands of rock drawings and paintings throughout the world that illustrate masked men and animals suggest that this food source and the need for its continuation must have preoccupied the minds of early hunters. One hypothesis is that the human subject of this painting is a prostrate shaman who has used the mask and the bird wand to induce a spiritual transformation, in which the shaman's spirit visits the spirit of the animal. By sharing a spiritual state with the charging animal he has negotiated the future return of the dying animal in a new body, thus safeguarding the population of bison for another "harvest" in the next year. Lascaux may be seen as a feminine earthen temple space where the spirits of men and animals played in rites of renewal that most likely included song, dance, and possibly masquerade.

1.2a, b, c. Deer sorcerer, Bison sorcerer, and Antelope sorcerer, drawn from the rock art at Trois Frères, France. *Photograph courtesy Alexander Marshack, after Marshack, Begouen, and Breuil.*

1.3 Masquerader with doll in Tlaxcala, Mexico, 1978. *Courtesy Ruth D. Lechuga.*

William Irwin Thompson further emphasizes the feminine aspect of the scene by asserting that the bison wound is really a representation of the vulva. Because it bleeds each month and then stops, Paleolithic people may have understood the vulva as a magical wound that healed itself;[6] the "male" spear entered the bison, and in the act of penetrating and killing it, new life could be born from the animal's death. Jean-Loup Rousselot, the famous investigator of Eskimo culture, points out that Eskimo hunters view the kill as an erotic venture in which the penetration of weapon into flesh is an act of fertility.[7]

Another extensive record of masquerades comes from the Tassili rock outcroppings of the south-central Sahara. Those paintings originate from approximately 4500 B.C., when the region was fertile and wet, and an abundance of wildlife including elephants, hippopotamuses, antelope, and cattle prospered. Hunting scenes abound here; in one example, from about 3500 B.C., animal-headed hunters dressed as decoys are depicted in pursuit of the game. Another striking depiction of a masquerader from this region comes from Auanrhet and is of the "round-head" style from after 3000 B.C. Here the mask represents a bovine in a highly elongated style, and the masker's body is covered in what seems to be a fiber-net body costume. The costume and mask strongly resemble West African masquerade wear of today, but whether this resemblance represents a continuity in culture or an accident of convergence is unknown. In this painting, an unmasked female dances nearby.

In a rare and almost unique occurrence, two paintings from Tassili showing females in masquerade exemplify a virtuosity of execution on the part of the artists. The first rendering is from

PREHISTORY AND ORIGINS

Sefar and belongs to the "round-head" style. This female wears a waistcloth that covers her front and back and carries a bowl-like object. Her body ornaments include ankle, knee, and arm bands; the mask she wears covers the eyes and nose, leaving the lower part of the face exposed. No supporting materials lend interpretation to this scene; thus the reason for this mask may never be explained. In many cultures bowls, which are often a metaphor for the baby-carrying and nourishment-filled bodies of women, are often shaped like a woman's abdomen. Art historian Natalie Lynn in her discussion of containers has found that this association is nearly universal. Given these associations, the painting may represent a dance of fertility or ritual preparations for the first foods of the harvest. By comparison, bowls are almost never used as props in men's masquerades. In the contemporary Gelede masquerades of Sierra Leone, males dance in fertility rites while a woman carries a bowl with a carved representation of a baby; the men are not allowed to touch the bowl.[8] In the Carnival celebrations of Tlaxcala, Mexico, men wearing masks bounce baby sculptures off a strip of cloth, to provoke the spirits of fertility (fig. 1.3).[9]

1.4 "The White Lady," tracing of petroglyph, Auanrhet, Tassili, southeast Algeria, Mesolithic period (10,000–4000 B.C.). Courtesy Bildarchiv Preussischer Kulturbesitz, Berlin.

1.5 Deceased Led by Isis, Tomb 66 of Nefertari, Valley of the Queens, Egypt, c. 1255 B.C. Photograph by Eliot Porter, 1973. Courtesy Amon Carter Museum.

Cloth can be wrapped as a container to hold small infants.

A second female masquerader from Tassili is the famous "White Lady" or "Horned Goddess" from the same period and located at Auanrhet. Like the female masker discussed above, she is dressed in a waistcloth and decorated with ankle, knee, and arm bands; this particular figure also wears wrist bands (fig. 1.4). She appears to hold two tassels that move through the air as she dances. The face of her mask is visually difficult to read, but the headpiece consists of a cap with cow horns fastened to the sides. Henri Lhote suggests that this figure might be a representation of the Egyptian goddess Isis, who is often pictured in Egyptian art wearing a crown with cow horns (fig. 1.5). Lhote posits that the motif above the horned goddess's head and between the horns represents a field of grain with a shower of kernels falling across the horns.[10]

Southern Africa is a region known for rock paintings that date from about 4000 B.C. The numerous animal-headed human beings include an elephant-headed man and two deer-headed individuals who may well be masqueraders. One of the deer-headed figures carries a bow, which suggests that he may be ritually dressed as a hunting decoy. J. F. Thackeray's recent research on South African rock paintings suggests that

PREHISTORY AND ORIGINS

humans depicted in antelope skins and headdresses at Melikane represent medicine men in masquerade. He believes that the function of this ritual is related to the ability to control wild game and, most interestingly, the control of young males in initiation.[11] From southwest Africa there is a finely rendered bowman whose costume—including arm, chest, and face covering—strongly resembles armor.

One final example from Africa in Zimbabwe is the image of a giant recumbent trancer wearing an antelope headdress. The white dots of latent potency attached to the back of the abdomen and tendril emerging from the penis suggest that this shamanic figure is in trance, contacting the spirits for the regeneration of life (fig. 1.6). Shamanic behavior involving contact with the spiritual world, usually through the agency of flight, is known as the Vision Quest.[12]

1.6 *Opposite, above:* Drawing of a recumbent figure in a trance from rock art in Makoni, Zimbabwe. *Reproduced with permission from Peter Gerlake,* The Hunter's Vision: The Prehistoric Art of Zimbabwe *(Seattle: University of Washington Press), 1995.*

1.7 *Opposite, below:* Winged and horned figures on rock art at Dinwoody Lake in Wyoming, c. 1650-1800. *Courtesy Minneapolis Institute of Arts.*

1.8 **Charles Wimar,** *The Buffalo Dance,* 1860. *The Saint Louis Art Museum, Gift of Mrs. John T. Davis.*

On the other side of the world are the rock paintings of American Plains Indians at the Dinwoody site in Wyoming. Created between about A.D. 1650 and 1800, the rock paintings contain images of three winged creatures and several anthropomorphic figures of various sizes (fig. 1.7). These images may have commemorated the unique experiences of individuals during Vision Quests, shamanistic rituals, or some other spiritually meaningful activities.[13] If, as Evan Maurer suggests, these images portray shamanic activity, then the bird and horned anthropomorphic figures may represent shamans in masquerade. Although evidence for this interpretation is speculative, paintings by Native Americans and illustrations by early Western artists such as Charles Wimar show that people of the Plains did indeed masquerade as buffalo, elk, and deer in the hunt as well as in the ceremonial sun dance, and they continue to do so today (fig. 1.8).

An earlier record of masquerading comes from the American Southwest and the Mimbres peoples. Inhabitants of the Mimbres River valley arrived about 10,000 years ago, although their masking traditions probably did not appear until about A.D. 900.[14] Many petroglyphs portray what appear to be maskers, but the famous Mimbres pottery tradition that flourished between A.D. 1000 and 1170 provides an especially detailed and illuminating look at the Mimbres world of masks. The interior of a bowl usually included a painting that depicted everyday or mytho-

1.9a Man with antler headdress and bat costume, polychrome pottery, New Mexico, Style III, Mimbres period, c. 1000–1170. *Collection of Tony Berlant.*

logical life. The bowl, placed over the head of the deceased, had a "kill" hole at its center, which allowed the spirit of the deceased to pass through to the other world, leaving the "killed" body behind. The bowl thus served as a death mask for this last rite of passage.

Mimbres bowls portray various scenes of masking. In one bowl two hunters and two masqueraders—one disguised as a cat and the other as a bird—seem to be enacting a ceremony to ensure a successful hunt. Another bowl features a man wearing antler horns and a bat costume (fig. 1.9a). Although the meaning is not clear, we know that zoomorphic forms often convey the complicated relationships between humans and animals in the environment. Other examples include a horned serpent headdress worn by a dancer whose costume resembles the Koshare, or clown dancer, in contemporary Pueblo masquerades, and an anthropomorphic bird with a fish catch that may allude to a mythic spirit or a costumed dancer (fig. 1.9b). Mimbres culture fragmented and disappeared in the thirteenth century, and many of its people merged with some of the neighboring cultures of the Casa Grande or Anasazi. The descendants of the Anasazi, including the Hopi, Zuni, and other Pueblo peoples, maintain rich and varied masquerades that have preserved and adapted their cultural identity through changing times.

In western Colorado the Native American culture is represented by numerous trapezoidally shaped men in masquerade (figs. 1.10, 1.11). One striking example features a male who grips a knife with his left hand and wears a headdress that covers his face. A spiral is attached to the hand and the knife by a single line. To the figure's left stands a bird-headed staff with an attached packet of what might represent spiritual medicine and another spiral below. The painting, which dates from A.D. 1000, is striking in its resemblance to the shaman painting in the cave at Lascaux. In the Fremont scene, the spirals may be associated with powers of renew-

1.9b Anthropomorphic bird with fish, polychrome pottery, New Mexico, Classic Mimbres period, c. 1100–1150. *Private collection.*

al and the knife with rites of blood sacrifice. The bird staff may have served as a guide into the invisible world that the shamans at Fremont and Lascaux were seeking to enter.[15]

In Australia, masked rituals have been practiced by the people of the northeast region of the Torres Straits and more recently in male adolescent rites in the northwestern part of the continent. Throughout much of Australia, the initiates' bodies and faces are elaborately painted and decorated with feathers and various vegetal substances, conveying a strong masklike appearance. Although most of the literature on Australian rock painting argues that the hybrid figures represent spirits rather than maskers, images of the ancestor spirits—such as the masklike appearance of Lightning Man from the Calder River in northwest Australia—suggest that masks were associated with spirit and ancestor figures (fig. 1.12). Depictions of warriors there include an element of masquerade: for example, two individuals in the scene who carry spears seem to have their heads covered with some kind of painted crown with streamers.[16] A squatting figure also illustrated by Andreas Lommel shows a person or spirit in striped body paint with lines radiating from the head. We may not know what the artist intended, but some use of masking seems to have had a role in ceremonies practiced during the last 50,000-year habitation by Aboriginal people in Australia. Wandjina spirits depicted in Australian rock paintings also convey a strong masklike appearance.

Mesolithic rock paintings reveal another example of masquerade. In one scene three characters—a bison-horn masker, a figure in a feather headdress, and a figure with a wolf's headdress and claws—are all depicted in a dance. In another scene a figure in feather headdress appears with a bison masker who is holding a stone axe and performing a ritual.[17] From Siberia come many images of masklike petroglyphs and anthropomorphic figures dressed in headdresses and engaged in the hunt. Often the masks display radiating lines on the head, showing remarkable similarity to those found in Australian paintings and examples from North America (fig. 1.13).[18]

1.10 Figure with bird staff on rock art in Colorado, near Fremont, c.1000. *Courtesy Fred Hirschmann.*

1.11 View of Fremont rock art at Cottonwood and Nine Mile Canyons, Utah, c. 1000. *Courtesy Fred Hirschmann.*

1.12 Lightning figures on rock art near the Katherine River in the Northern Territories of Australia, c. 18,000–7000 B.C. *Courtesy Grahame L. Walsh.*

1.13 *Below:* Drawing from Siberian rock art. *Reprinted from Anatoly I. Martynov,* The Art of Northern Asia *(Urbana: University of Illinois Press), 1991.*

1.14 **Robert Davidson, Eyes of the Mind mask, 1996.** *Collection Robert Davidson.*

Masked and masklike images from the early Paleolithic age are strong evidence for the importance of masquerading in human society. Masks have empowered human beings both physically and spiritually as decoys to effect a successful hunt and as invisible spirits made visible through human agency so as to make use of supernatural power in life's most pressing challenges.

Masks: How and Why?

Since the beginnings of *Homo sapiens,* human societies have tended to believe in the existence of a spirit world. The fact that our distant cousins the Neanderthals practiced burial rites by stacking bones, rubbing them with red ocher, and burying them with accompanying objects suggests that they believed in spirits and the idea that invisible forces can empower visible matter. In many traditional societies the practice of rubbing bones with red pigment enables the spirit to become reincarnated. Many Neanderthal graves were strewn with flowers, symbols of new life. This may indicate that early humans understood opposition and paradox—i.e., that new life can evolve out of old life, or death.[19] In understanding opposites, Neanderthals may have appreciated the concept of "I am not myself," a prerequisite construct for masking. Spirits come in many varieties and are manifested in as many ways, as the multiplicity of mask forms testifies. Masks may represent frogs eating their own skin, trolls with hands and feet reversed, water and forest spirits, thunder, butterflies, zoomorphic creatures, and other examples of the animal kingdom, including humans.

Robert Davidson, a Haida artist from British Columbia, affirms the association of mask and spirit: "When I create a new mask or dance or image, I'm a medium to transmit those images from the spirit world" (fig. 1.14).[20] He adds, "Masks are images that shine through us from the spirit world." Masked dances are a means of reenacting the dreams and memories of people and a way of uniting individual and group aspirations.[21]

One way to negotiate with the spirit realm is through the agency of the mask and masquerade. A masquerade turns the world upside down: the invisible spirit becomes visible in the masquerade; the visible person of daily life becomes invisible.

How did humans discover a world of the spirits? The answer may lie in how they perceived their environments. As people began to study the flora and fauna around them, they may have abstracted qualities of those phenomena that seemed wise or foolhardy, strong or weak. Humans probably began to attribute characteristics to particular living and nonliving things in their environments that caught their attention. Without the aid of scientific technologies, the forces and consequences of nature—renewal and decay, viruses, gravity, atmospheric pressure variation, chemical reactions, and the second law of thermodynamics—were all explained by invisible entities, or spirits. The mediation of spirits through masquerades provided humans some way to control their environment. Mask performances could serve to stabilize societies by organizing and assigning activities to specific persons and groups. The assignment of duties for masked festivals, such as food preparation, mask making, and organizing the performance, helped individuals and groups understand their roles in the economy.

Humans invented the act of transformation to make these spirits manifest. An example of an inspiring role model in the animal world is the frog species *Bufo marinus*. Over the centuries this commonly found animal has displayed qualities and attributes that have inspired the human imagination and its ideas about transformation, shape shifting, and masquerading. Among Pre-Columbian peoples of South and Mesoamerica, including the Maya, frogs inspired much in the way of culture, including the arts and symbolism.

One of the primary ways humans have learned how to masquerade is through observing nature. Frogs and reptiles have been major players in traditional mythology, and they strongly convey the masking aspect of nature. Many cultures have focused on *Bufo*, the consummate animal of transformation. The frog begins as an egg, which then hatches into a gill-breathing, vegetarian tadpole. The creature then transforms into a four-legged nocturnal carnivore that can live up to forty years. The animal's longevity must have astonished the short-lived humans of the Paleolithic era. *Bufo* grows rapidly in its early years, and in order to accommodate this growth, a young frog will shed its skin every few weeks. Upon maturity it sheds its skin about four times yearly. Thus Paleolithic peoples aware of the life processes around them could associate *Bufo*'s transforming capabilities with its unbelievable age. In addition, unlike most other skin shedders, the *Bufo* frog actually eats its own horny skin (fig. 1.15). To accomplish this feat it assumes a humped position with its feet drawn up under itself; from that position the toothless animal sucks in the skin starting with its head and ending with the feet.[22]

The frog seemingly eats its old life in order to create a new one. Early humans might have seen an animal's changing exterior to be masking some invisible mystery of regeneration within.

1.15 *Bufo marinus* eating its own skin. *Courtesy Peter T. Furst.*

Human transformation, which is what masquerade is, could be a way to negotiate with the spirit in order to seek longevity and well-being in the group, and to ensure the survival of the next generation. The frog's legendary fertility was also a highly sought-after characteristic that humans tried to attain through ritual performance, especially through masquerades.

One last feature of this remarkable animal is the psychopharmacological nature of the venom contained in its skin glands.[23] Ancient Mesoamerican and South American peoples probably ingested the hallucinogenic

venom to achieve transformation and move into the spiritual realm. The homeopathic magic that carried them into the world of the spirit seemed capable of assuring the continuation of vegetal, animal, and human fertility. Living in the natural world with seen and unseen adversaries (from jaguars to microscopic parasites), humans had to sustain a critical population, otherwise they would be hunted out. Masking can be seen as a statement about and a re-presentation of power. By staging a masked performance and ingesting the *Bufo* toxin, people were able to transform themselves into spirits of nature that could negotiate the power of nature for successful living.

Masks and the masquerade are the domain of men; very few societies entertain masquerades by women. This is probably related to another primarily male activity, hunting. Whereas women often spent more time in gathering food and other resources and developing hearth skills such as food preparation and preservation and sewing, men hunted and made weapons. This gender distinction seems to be part of the evolutionary heritage for hominids from australopithecines of four million years ago to their descendants, *Homo habilis, Homo erectus,* and finally *Homo sapiens.* In the course of this evolution, the division of labor favored bigger, stronger, and faster males for hunting and smaller females. Not surprisingly, males require more food, especially animal protein, than women; this remains true throughout the world today.

The relationship of men to animals of prey is an ambivalent one. Animals are feared for their ability to strike back and kill the hunter, yet they are admired for their remarkable physical and mental abilities. The killing of dangerous animals such as the cassowary bird in Papua New Guinea, the jaguar in the South American rain forest, or the grizzly bear in the North American woodlands helped define a male's identity, giving him the status of a man among men. Yet in most traditional societies the taking of the animal's life was and still is considered a sacred act: the spirit of the animal must be appeased, loved, and respected.

In 1977 and 1978 I studied men's masking societies in the West African city of Freetown in Sierra Leone. Within this urban environment flourished hunting societies, and although men survived by working within the framework of the industrial economy, they occasionally hunted wild game and celebrated the hunt with masquerades. One particular hunting masquerade demonstrated the special relationship of men to animals of prey. A large part of the population of the Foulah Town neighborhood on the west side of the city was packed into a vacant lot where the masquerade was held. The masquerader, disguised as an antelope, wore a headpiece and body costume festooned with bones, empty shotgun casings, herbal medicines, and animal skins. He entered the lot at the call of the *bata* drums, danced briefly, and then disappeared, returned and disappeared. Each time the drummers called the animal masker back to the lot, the intensity of the ever louder, interlocking rhythms of the drums increased. And each time the animal returned, the decibels of the crowd's roar multiplied. Finally, the call of the drums and the crowd encouraged the masquerader to return, this time to remain.

During this phase of the performance the hunter entered the dance area carrying a life-size model gun. The hunter and animal danced together, with the hunter occasionally raising his weapon toward the antelope. Each time the prey eluded the hunter, the rhythm and loudness of the drums grew so intensely that they literally pulsated inside my body. During this phase

the hunter dropped the gun, and within a few seconds the antelope masker picked it up, aimed it at the hunter, and shot him. The animal figure left the lot, and the crowd roared its approval.

This masquerade is one of many that attest to the special and ambivalent relationship men have to animals of prey. It negotiates the ambivalent relationship of men to antelope in a part of West Africa where the wild game has almost been depleted. The performance celebrates the power of the animal symbolically destroying its worst enemy, man; as a result, it assures its own survival and sustains a food supply for humans.

In 1994 I attended a rite of renewal on the day after Christmas at Acoma Pueblo, New Mexico. From atop the mesa I could see the incredible landscape below me punctuated with wildly shaped boulders and escarpments. The cool breeze and late afternoon horizontal beams of light and shadow foretold the coming of a new year. Near the old Catholic church made of adobe in an early Spanish style resembling a fortress, I could hear the chanting coming from the subterranean circular chamber known as a kiva about a hundred yards from me (fig. 1.16). The chanting grew louder when about seventy-five men in deer masquerade emerged and danced in procession to the old church. The heads of the dancers were covered with pine tree boughs and crowned with deer horns. Each of the maskers carried two staffs simulating the front legs of the animal. Announcing each step of the dancers as they slowly processed to the church, the powerful rhythm of the leg rattles echoed against the adobe walls of the pueblo. Finally, the dancers entered the central opening of the church, where they danced from the vestibule to the altar in celebration of deer spirits. The deer dancers were drawing on the powers of their traditional religion as well as the spiritual powers of Catholicism. The dance was part of a rite of renewal for the new year, and it was hoped through the masquerade that the deer would return and prosper for yet another year.

1.16 Deer and buffalo dancers at the San Ildefonso Pueblo, New Mexico, 1940. *Courtesy Western History Collections, University of Oklahoma.*

Animal masquerades generally celebrate the spirits of the various species of animals in order that their physical manifestations continue to prosper. The calling of the deer into the spiritual domain of the pueblo kiva or the Christian church is similar to the painting of animals in the sacred space of caves and rock outcroppings found throughout the inhabited world. The pairing of animal image and sacred space is intended to bring about animal fertility.

Other explanations for the origins of masquerading and its masculine monopoly are related to traditional hunting techniques employed by men in indigenous societies. It is clear that early man hunted in groups. The first weapons consisted of stone, bone, and wood clubs; later, humans used stone blades with chipped and polished edges, and then spears, bows, and arrows. This meant that the kill took place at close range; in Paleolithic days, when such huge animals as woolly mammoths and sloths thrived, it would have required a group of men persistently striking the animal to bring it down. In order to get close enough to the game, the men sometimes disguised themselves as the animal; in other words, they became human decoys masquerading as animals. Such scenes of disguise are found almost everywhere that big game has existed. Western Apache hunters in the American Southwest disguised themselves with deer mask headpieces so they could get within killing distance of their prey.[24] Similarly, the Nupe men in northern Nigeria wear headpieces of the touraco bird and cover their bodies with bushes in order to get within striking range of that large, meaty animal. Similarly, we know from the paintings of Charles Wimar that Plains Indian hunters disguised themselves as buffalo to get close to the wandering herds. In more densely forested areas, men often rely on the local foliage for camouflage rather than on animal costumes.

The Story of Quick-to-See: A Fable of Prehistory
In the time that is now called Paleolithic, a band of skin-clad hunters and gatherers thrived on large herds of bovines that grazed on the rich plains of what is today France. The men of one particular hunting band were known as the People of Lightning. They had received their name years earlier when one of the People had discovered that animal fat could be a good source of light if it was set afire in a concavity of a stone. The light could last an entire night, giving a sense of security in an environment filled with dangerous predators such as bears and large cats. When strangers happened upon their night encampments, lit up by the lamps, these travelers thought the source was lightning.

One day the hunters had ventured far away from the women and children, and they had to camp overnight with their heavy load of meat, which they carried in twine bags made by the women. Two days of rain had made it impossible to light a fire; moreover, one of the hunters had lost the stone lamp in the excitement of the kill. The hunters managed to find protection in a small stone-lined ravine with only one approach. Without any fire, the men ate their meat raw, using stone scrapers to strip it from the animal hide.

The man known as Quick-to-See was playing with a piece of hide and thinking about the hunt earlier that day. It had been a great success, for together the men had managed to bring down a mature male woolly mammoth. The task had taken great effort as they continually pounded with their stone weapons before the animal finally fell. The thunder and lightning that struck that day added drama to the hunt.

During the attack, Quick-to-See had been stationed by the animal's large ribs near its heart. He had actually heard its heart beat when it was stimulated by adrenaline released during the first phase of the kill. The deep sound of the heartbeat left a lasting impression on Quick-to-See. His position, so near the heart of the mammoth during the kill, allowed him the honor of cutting between the ribs and retrieving that organ. Afterward, the men blessed the spirit of the animal and poured some of its blood on nearby rocks and the ground in hopes that Mother Earth would give birth to yet another mammoth. Then they ate the heart.

Quick-to-See was drawn to the animal's insides. He noticed how large and thick the rib cage was and how heavy the skin was that was stretched over the bone cage. While carving its meat he began to strike the interior skin with his weapon. The sound was very loud. He thought about the sound of thunder as he beat the animal and recalled the animal's heartbeat. Quick-to-See tucked the hide into his fiber bag and joined the others who sat huddled next to the stones of the ravine while the sounds of the cats kept everyone awake throughout the night.

Back at the base camp the children came running to meet their fathers and older brothers whose bundles were bulging with fresh mammoth meat. The women prepared hearth fires and began to heat the stones that would be tossed into hide troughs that lined the hollows in the ground. The women filled these "pots" with water. Later, the meat and the hot stones were added to cook the stew. While preparations for the feast continued and the sounds of the hunt were still reverberating in his heart, Quick-to-See took the hide from his bag and began to stretch it between his fists. Then he searched the camp, looking for a tree with a rotted-out core. He cut a section of it with his stone axe, stretched the hide over the hollow cylinder, and tied it off with fresh sinew from the mammoth kill. He discovered that by striking his new creation with the wood handle of his axe he could produce a thumping sound, but it was not as sensational as the sounds of the hunt and the thunder that he loved as much as he feared. He brought it back to the encampment and set it near the fire where some meat was being roasted and, like his fellow hunters, fell asleep. While the women and older daughters continued to prepare the feast, the young boys played "hunt and kill" at the edge of the camp.

By sunset the men woke, roused by the good smells of the food the women were preparing. Quick-to-See also smelled the scalding odor of his new creation, which had been placed too close to the roaring fire. He quickly snatched it up, noticing that the hide had shrunk and tightened a great deal and that the sinew had anchored itself tightly around the perimeter. He struck it once again with his axe handle. This time it made the sound of thunder.

It was nearly midnight when the singing began. The men had eaten much food and were very happy. The *Amanita muscaria* mushroom, which grew in abundance in this region, was already affecting their vision. The songs described the hunt: how strong had been the mammoth, how brave and cunning the hunters. Before too long one of the men appeared by the fire in the bison decoy costume they had used in the hunt. The songs and dancing of the masquerader silhouetted by the tangle of the fire flames was a joyous sight. Then suddenly Quick-to-See began to strike his new drum to the rhythm of the songs and the movements of the masquerader. The People of Lightning were startled—it was the sound of thunder and the kill. It was hypnotic. People roared, children cried. Later, another part of the animal was offered to Mother Earth to encourage its spirit to return once again as a living beast.

1.17 Cajun Carnival
maskers, Iota, Louisiana,
1995. *Courtesy Syndey
Byrd.*

The "lightning" made from the fire and lamps, the thunder from the drums, and the presence of the bison-costumed character were part of an attempt at virtual reality. It was fun, transforming, uniting, risky, inventive, and sincere. It was totally made up, yet alarmingly realistic. For this group of humans, now known as the People of Thunder and Lightning, this new ritual made for good bonding, and it demonstrated to the women and children how important the men were. The People of Thunder and Lightning soon began to play the masquerade at the changing of the seasons and at the deaths of their important men. Masquerading began to spread throughout the region.

A wide-ranging, male-based set of behaviors and perceptions make up the content of this fable. First, in order to hunt, men made stone weapons. Stone is rigid, and when fashioned into hunting tools its phallic association is heightened. Because men monopolized hunting, we can be quite certain that they would have made the weapons themselves. Only by making and experimenting with weapons in the hunt could one assess the success of a particular tool. Making stone weapons involved a constant striking of the arm, the same arm exercise used when killing an animal at close range. The pounding of the drum against the animal's dead skin required the same blows. Indeed, in many cultures, the hide-covered drum is regarded spiritually and metaphorically as an animal; drums are considered to be spirits, and like masks, they are often presented sacrifices intended to ritually feed them. Not surprisingly, the playing of drums is mostly done by men.

The ritual sacrifice at the kill and at the beginning of the feast in the People of Lightning story also represents a practice dominated by men. Males control the production and use of the hard- and sharp-edged tools that are used for cutting animals in bloodletting sacrifices. Many masquerades are accompanied by animal sacrifice executed by males. And one more male detail: in the story, it is a male dressed in deer decoy who masquerades during the feast. Males almost exclusively perform masquerades today. The exceptions include women devil maskers in Bolivian Carnival, the Cajun Carnival female maskers of Iota, Louisiana (fig. 1.17), the female initiations of the Mende people of Sierra Leone—and, of course, occasions such as Halloween (fig. 1.18).

The People of Thunder and Lightning story points to a cultural complex in which drumming, masking, and sacrifice are generally the cultural properties of men. Underlying this monopoly is the apparent male need to symbolically and culturally control fertility for the group and society, even though it is the female who has the responsibility of carrying, bearing, and nourishing the child to adolescence.

Negotiating with the spirits of animals or getting within killing distance are important reasons for masquerade. There are certainly other explanations that are unrecorded in the early development of human society. One intriguing possibility is related to the cognitive development of human beings and the emergence of our concept of self.

What is so extraordinary about humans is our capacity for deception. We have the ability to act one way and feel a different way. Without this capacity masks would never have been created. Someone who answers "Great!" to the query "How are you?" may actually be feeling terrible. The answering smile, tone of voice, and accompanying body language mask the true feelings of the person. Someone who is feeling rotten may have masked her or his identity in order to negotiate the day.

1.18 Children in costumes on Halloween, 1992. *Courtesy Stock, Boston.*

Pretending to be not oneself is most fully developed in human beings and most spectacularly so in the masquerade. Other higher mammals and primates have this capacity, but to a large degree it is only expressed in play. Chimps may act aggressively in rough-and-tumble play, but they do not bite; they pretend to fight and have a good time. Cats may put bottle caps under a rug and then position themselves on the opposite side of the room to stalk and pounce on the bottle cap prey, as if pretending to kill it. Thus, pretending, assigning certain characteristics of something else to self or projecting such characteristics onto other things, is not uniquely human. Yet above all other animals, humans have developed this faculty.

Humans have been so successful, in fact, that they have developed the capacity for self-deception and attribution to the extreme. In our bid for survival, our capabilities for duplicity have allowed us to become the most manipulative creatures on the planet. Yet abstracting ourselves out of nature in order to control it also results in a sense of separation from nature. Many cultural mythologies refer to a time when there was no death, when humans lived within nature as participants in an equilibrium. Through language, art, music, and poetry, the very things that seem to distinguish us from other animals, humans seek to return to that natural order, if only for the duration of festivity and ritual. Often the assembly of music, poetry, and feasting have been highlighted by masquerades. Masking, which incorporates elements of music, art, language, and poetry, indulges the need to not be oneself, even not to be human, in order to reunify ourselves and reconnect with nature. For the period of the masquerade we can contradict our ability to abstractly define and give attribution to things in the world around us.

While these examples and theories about masking are general and far-ranging, the fact that masks are so universal in time and place argues that the role they have played in human development has been profound. Controversies about the spiritual properties of masks abound. Do the performers of masquerades really transform into a spirit, or are masks made merely to represent spirits? Do audiences really believe that masqueraders are in fact spirits? Moreover, how do the kinesthetic joys and ludic pleasures of masking relate to its ritual and symbolic content? How and why did the various components of the masquerade, including music and sacrifice, develop and merge?

As the record on rock seems to indicate, it is likely that various groups of peoples from Paleolithic times began to produce many arts and artifacts that focused on masking behaviors. By taking the sounds and sights of a natural world animated by the world of the spirit and reproducing it in a controlled environment, human beings (and men in particular) felt empowered. Such empowerment provided the necessary confidence to invent culture and to assign meaning in a world that was, and is, always verging on chaos, danger, and death. The mask provided security in an unpredictable world. It allowed for human emotion to be displayed and negotiated in times of joy and stress. Its strength has been renewal itself.

From Paleolithic times to the beginning of industrialization, the natural world predominated. Beyond the base camp was the wilderness. People who lived in and directly reacted to nature with minimal cultural mediation probably had a different perception of self and personhood than we know today. Mythological stories abound with cultural heroes who assume many animal and zoomorphic forms. Behind this lies a less rigid sense of a prescribed social self: one can let go and become something else. Shifting shape was and is simply a way for humans to express and mediate their relationship to the world. Anthony Shelton affirms this view of personality in his study of the Aztecs of Mesoamerica:

> . . . [T]he use of mouth masks, and the greater popularity of headdresses and face paint, suggest they were meant to allude to the coexistence of multiple human, natural, and supernatural qualities within the same body.[25]

Masking allows the individual to act on the wish or need to express "I am not myself," and by the communal endorsement of the larger deception that "we are not ourselves," humans could bridge the gap with nature. This gap has been widening ever since humans began to attribute characteristics to everything in their habitats. Cultural mapping, indeed, contributed to survival, but beyond that, it was and is fun to play, to take a time out of humanly constructed time in order to wander in and around self, society, and nature. Play allows for the improvisational, the unexpected, leaving the spirits of people open to new and sometimes very useful discoveries. Through the deception of the masquerade, people could act without being emotionally driven by the direct and sometimes terrifying experience of nature. Establishing a second nature—a virtual reality—allowed people to confront culture/nature and reinvent identity as mutable nature, and masked humanity continued to dance.

rites of passage

MASKS 1 TO 24

MASK 1

MASK 2

MASK 3

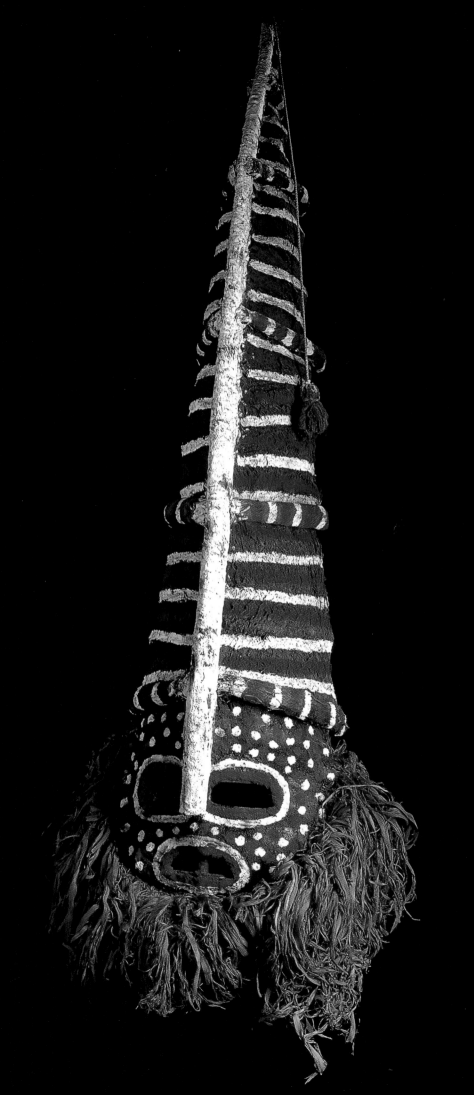

MASK 5

MASK 7

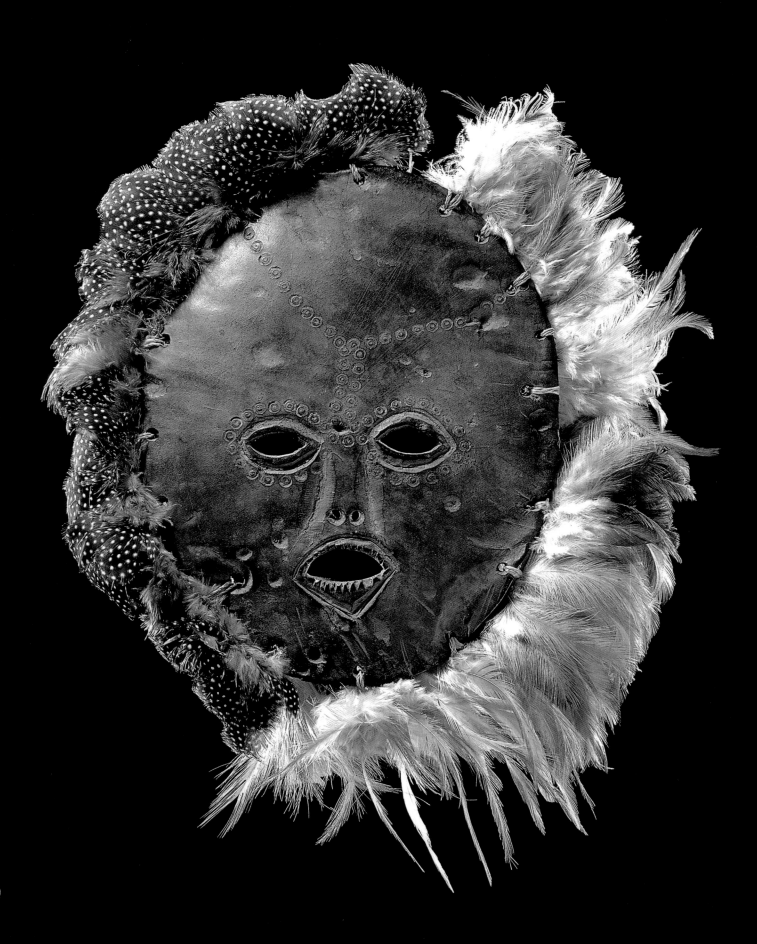

MASK 11

MASK 14

MASK 15

MASK 17

MASK 21

MASK 23

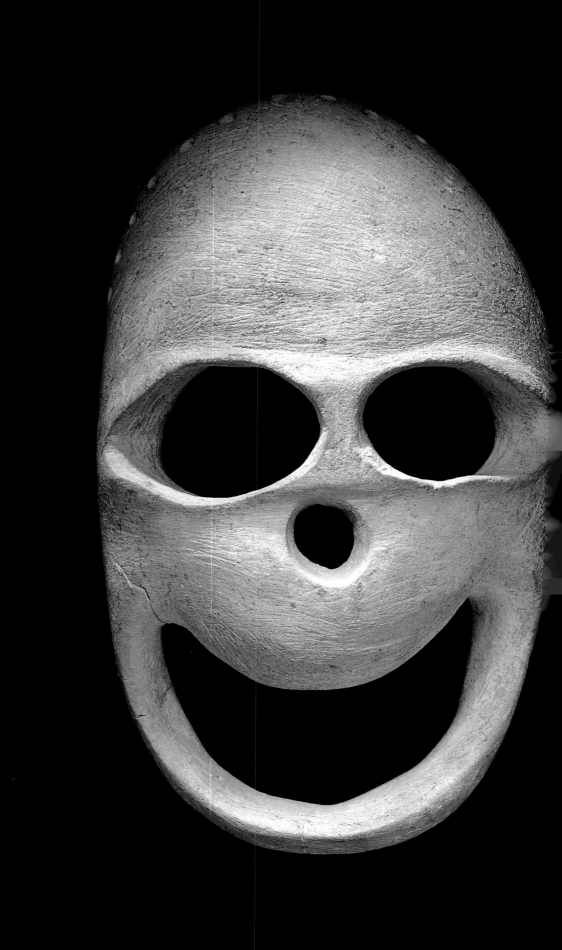

Rites of Passage

JOHN W. NUNLEY

O NE EVENING IN NORTHERN GHANA, in 1973, a Sisala friend invited me to the burial rites of an important elder. In the low-ceilinged room of the deceased, lit by several torches, three people were rubbing the corpse with lavender oil to keep it from stiffening.

Outside of the room, many women were keening on the old man. Several men carried the corpse through the door on a cowhide and proceeded with it to a nearby baobab tree, where old men sit during the long hot days of the dry season. There the wild dirge was replaced with the high, optimistic energy of praise songs. It was the beginning of the journey of the man's spirit (*dima*) to the land of the ancestors (*lelejang*). Several songs later, the hide and corpse were raised again and carried to the opening of a subterranean tomb that lay beneath the compound courtyard. A ritual argument ensued between the relatives of the deceased and those who were to place the body in the tomb. After the disagreement was settled, a group of men raised the hide and tilted it toward the opening, where the body slid quickly and dramatically into the earth. Weeklong funerary rites to mark the passing of this man's spirit to *lelejang* would occur during the dry season a year or so after his death as well (fig. 2.1).

The comparison of this ritual exit of a loved one, with so much social and cultural action, to that of most Western rituals is striking. Elaborate rituals and festivities involving masquerades in rites of passage occur most dramatically and most often in societies where agriculture, hunting, fertility, and oral traditions matter greatly.

As the pioneering anthropologist Arnold Van Gennep realized early in the twentieth century, rites of passage are in reality the recognition of the biological transitions that happen at birth, onset of adolescence, and death.[1] These points of transition are especially critical in traditional societies, where a death may threaten the survival of a group; it must be countered by birth, and birth is dangerous for both mother and newborn.

The youthful and often uncontrolled energy of adolescents, particularly of males, must be harnessed and channeled for the benefit of society in a relatively short period of time. As the anthropologist Victor Turner has explained, such persons are in a state of "liminality": at adolescence one is neither child nor adult, but instead is betwixt and between. The disorder brought about by the inchoate nature of this transition must be institutionalized for the welfare of society.

The crisis posed by these transitions generates the energy required to stage rites of passage. During these dangerous and precarious times the world of spirits is as unsettled as the world of humans. Rites of passage provide a way to deal with the challenges of biological changes by placing them within a cultural context. Culture is called upon to frame these transitions, to provide meaning where there may be none. This cultural response is frequently offered through the agency of the masquerade. Life transitions are destabilizing, for both the person and society are faced with a situation in which the past has lost its grip on the present and the future is uncertain. At this juncture, the masquerade serves as a guide through the passage of life. Its face, dance, and narrative create the certainty, and the masquerade creates order so that life and social living continue in a meaningful and purposeful way. Rituals provide fixed markers against the lack of fixation. The unchanging face of the mask provides a further sense of permanence during unsettling times of transition. The transformation of man to masked dancer symbolizes the states of transformation people experience in life cycles.

2.1 Sisala men dancing at a funeral in Ghana, 1973. *Courtesy John W. Nunley.*

Ever since humans first made analogous propositions through the construction of symbols and metaphors, social and biological life have existed in a cultural poetry. In many cultures, for example, the phases of the moon are seen to symbolize the phases of the female life cycle. The new, full, and fading phases of the moon are analogous to maiden, mother, and crone. In the transitions between these phases, the individual is betwixt and between: at birth one is transformed from fetus into babe, at adolescence one is neither child nor adult, and at the stage of natural death one is no longer an elder nor quite yet ancestor.

Birth

Societies have rarely held masquerades at the birth of individuals. Jan Vancina does cite the use of masks at the birth of twins among Bantu-speaking peoples of central Africa.[2] But twins raise concerns about their spiritual association: do they have one or two spirits? Moreover, the community must consider how two individuals can occupy one social space in societies where gender and birth order lay great claim to one's later social standing. In short, for the Bantu people, twins are trouble, and their appearance may require a cultural intervention that could include masking.[3] Other evidence for masked ritual at a birth comes from a wall relief at the Temple of

Hatshepsut at Deir al-Bahri, depicting priests and priestesses dressed in masks and costumes. However, this is no ordinary birth that they attend—it is the birth of a future pharaoh.[4]

In societies where the infant mortality rate might be 50 percent or higher for children under the age of five, it does not make sense to invest the many resources required by a masquerade at birth. In some societies, the naming becomes the dramatic event. In this practice, a child is given a name when he or she is about two years old; at this age the mortality rate is much lower. The naming transforms the child into a social human being; the name in a sense constitutes the cultural mask.

In many societies, from ancient times to the present, from Papua New Guinea to Africa to the Americas, elaborate rituals are held at birth, but masks are not part of these events. Victor Turner's comments on male Mukanda initiations in East Africa are revealing in this regard:

> It is interesting that the main theme of Mukanda (the boys' initiation ceremony in which masquerades are performed) should be productive activity (i.e. hunting), while that of Nkng'a (girls' initiation ceremony) should be reproductive activity, which is, when all is said and done, essential to the existence of the community, is hardly ritualized at all, while that of men is steeped with ritual.[5]

2.2 Childbirth images on a Mimbres bowl from the Swarts Ruin, mid-Mimbres Valley, c. 1000–1150. *Courtesy Peabody Museum of Archaeology and Ethnology, Harvard University.*

Indeed, a survey of the art from every known society reveals that depictions of childbirth *itself* are very infrequent. Childbirth is rarely enshrined by material culture at all. Some notable exceptions include the Chokwe peoples of Angola, some Sepik River groups in Papua New Guinea, and a few Pre-Columbian cultures such as the Mimbres of the American Southwest (fig. 2.2) and the Moche of Peru. The Chokwe depictions of birth appear on elaborately carved chairs, while figural sculpture and pottery represent this biological event in New Guinea and Pre-Columbian cultures. According to the findings of artist Phyllis Plattner, who has researched birthing art and how it relates to issues of gender in society, birthing scenes have purposely been kept out of the official art of most cultures—an official art generally controlled by men. She explains that heroic male exploits include hunting, killing, and building cities and complexes; birth has no place in this set of heroic feats. Thus it comes as little surprise that masks, usually constructed by men, are hardly ever associated with the event of birth. Masks are used at points within the life cycle to facilitate male bonding. This occurs most dramatically during adolescent initiation ceremonies.[6]

Adolescent Initiation

The incidence and particulars of adolescent initiation reveal much about the social organization of a community. In hunting and gathering societies where populations are small, female initiation plays a strong role, at the expense of male initiation. Because females are in short supply, their fertility is highly valued for the group's survival, and ritual initiation is believed to guarantee fertility.[7] In other societies where women produce a high percentage of food, giving rise to larger populations, both male and female initiations occur. The relationship of female sexuality and the hunting of animals is of particular interest in the research of Schlegel and Barry, who noted that there is a widespread belief that menstrual blood is dangerous and counterproductive to the hunt, and thus males refrain from sex prior to such forays. The authors speculate that the fear of female blood comes from hunters' belief that the smell of blood scares off herbivores, for they recognize that such a smell attracts enemy carnivores. Hunters carrying the smell of female blood would likewise scatter the game, while attracting competing carnivores. Thus the advent of menstruation in a young woman is an event of mixed meaning: even as it provides the possibility of a next generation, it also endangers activities through blood pollution. Initiations of female adolescents are held in order to celebrate the potential promise and ward off the potential danger.

Few female initiation rites use masks. Some female initiations are celebrated by male maskers, as in the case of the Apache Gaan masquerades (fig. 2.3). Only among the Mende and related peoples of Sierra Leone and Liberia in West Africa is the masking done by females at adolescent initiation ceremonies.

Early written accounts by Portuguese explorers describe a women's secret society called Bondo (also known as Bundu and Sande). Bondo is a society shared by a number of groups including the Mende, Vai, Kono, Temne, Basa, Gola, and Koranko, among others.[8] The purpose of the society is to instruct young women in agriculture, traditional medicine, politics, marketing, child rearing, and pleasing a husband. Until the mid-twentieth century, the girls were taken to the forest for several months to receive instructions. However, with the establishment of public school systems based on European models, time spent in the bush has been greatly reduced. In some instances, the young women experience only a few weeks of initiation.

The greatest single act of female initiation in Bondo is the clitoridectomy. The practice is based on the underlying belief that this operation civilizes the young women and teaches them how to fulfill their social and female obligations to society. Much controversy surrounds this operation, and many young women, particularly those with a modern education, refuse to

2.3 Apache Gaan "Mountain Spirit" dancers, July 1935. *Photograph by Morris Opler. Courtesy Mrs. Lucille Opler.*

undergo it. Yet despite opposition, the men prefer wives who have been through initiation, and thus the practice remains widespread.

MASK 2 The female masker, known as Nowo or Sowei (literally, "the mask play person"), appears in the village at sunrise to inform the inhabitants that initiation is in progress. Nowo also appears at the time of the genital incision and is said to mesmerize the young girls, thereby relieving the pain of the operation (fig. 2.4). Nowo stands as a menacing spirit, and as judge of infractions of Bondo law she metes out the appropriate punishments. When the girls leave the sacred bush and river where they have been ritually purified, they return to the village or town led by masqueraders.[9] Nowo also occasionally performs at the funerals of Bondo members. During these events many maskers may appear, and other unmasked members will fan the dancers to keep them cool and pick up costume fragments to avoid dangers of contamination.[10]

The Nowo mask included here exemplifies the symbolic and formal treatment of its type. The complete costume would include strands of dyed black raffia suspended from the base of the helmet and extending to about the knees, thus concealing the body of the dancer. Dark cloth is used to cover the hands, feet, and legs. The color black symbolizes the physical world of nature and its regenerating properties.

The mask itself is conceptually and formally divided into four zones: the "neck rings" at the base of the sculpture; the face; the coiffure; and the crest or head ornamentation. The neck ring of this Nowo mask most likely represents the chrysalis of the moth or butterfly. From this biological creature, with necklike rings at the base and labia-shaped upper portion, the butterfly or moth emerges. The chicken appearing behind the mask and placed on top of the ring represents motherhood. The hen is often symbolic of good mothering. The bird's wings may serve as a visual pun for female labia as well. The ring also stands for water and the serpent, both of which are associated with fertility.

2.4 Bondo ritual masker with officials at a ceremony of the Temne people in Sierra Leone, 1976. *Courtesy Frederick Lamp.*

From this section of the mask the face, symbolizing the young initiate, emerges. The high black and shiny forehead is a sign of female beauty as are the small, well-composed nose and eyes. From the top of the forehead spreads the coiffure; the plaited hair is an allusion to the cultivated gardens that women tend; it also represents cultural refinement and adult maternal status. The replicated rows of the small horns of the blue duiker antelope and the square Islamic amulets on the top of the coiffure refer to spiritual power: the horns stuffed with medicine represent traditional healing, while the carved amulets represent the power of Islam, an outside religion that has been incorporated into the traditional religion of the Mende and their neighbors. Thus, spiritual power from two sources guarantees the fertility of the garden and, by extension, female initiates. The three lobes of braided hair at the top of the mask represent sprouting foliage, which is the result of good gardening. The object on the top of the central lobe recalls large Islamic amulets worn as pendants.[11]

The initiation of Bondo females is meant to ensure their metamorphosis from girls to mature women who are prepared for the responsibilities of adulthood. Like all rites of passage, the Bondo initiation and masquerade provide stability for persons who find themselves betwixt and between. It inspires confidence in the young women whose pasts are no longer relevant to their present existence and whose futures are not yet a certainty. Lamp concludes:

> The presiding spirit of Bondo is most certainly also the reincarnation of a primordial ancestor, the original black woman responsible for the maturing, the ritual metamorphosis, of the young. The Temne recognize that from the spirit of the dead, new life is germinated. Nowo is that chrysalis shell of the noble deceased from which new life will spring in the cultivating milieu of the village through the mediating force of women.[12]

Thus from the fertile spirit of the deceased new life emerges.

Masquerades are far more common in male initiation rituals, especially in communities where same-sex bonding occurs, and labor-intensive agricultural practices and hunting are the basis of subsistence. Physical and role differences between the sexes also help explain why male initiation is far more elaborate.

The most elaborate and numerous adolescent rites of passage occur in societies where same-sex bonding is most important. In such groups, chores are divided according to gender. Adult males leave their infant sons in the care of the mother and other females of the extended kin to be raised until the onset of puberty. At this time the fathers and elders remove the young males from the maternal environment. In such societies the men say that through initiation they are "giving birth" to the "social" man. The Chewa peoples of East Africa, for instance, explain that because women give birth in secret, the men give "social" birth, or manhood, in secret as well.[13]

In order to give birth to the social man, an initiate in many societies has to endure body modification such as circumcision, scarification, or tooth filing. Such physical alterations symbolize the rebirth of an individual in his new status within the fraternal order of men, in which he learns the secrets of the male realm of society and the way of the ancestors. A primary task of the initiate is to learn how to perform the funerary rites for the deceased members so that they may become proper ancestors. The ancestors, remembered and vitalized by ritual, provide protection and stability to the town or village. In many cases, the ancestors are thought to be reincarnated as new offspring, thus reaffirming the cyclical nature of life and supporting the quest for immortality.

Masks frequently appear at the beginning of the initiation when the boys are sequestered at a secret location, and they commonly reappear at the end of the experience when the young men are reintroduced into village life. In many initiations masked characters act out plays that teach lessons about morality, ethics, and attitudes that facilitate and define a successful life. During this experience the young men internalize the local mores and social rules, in this manner "buying in" to the system. In their liminal state, they bond and establish alliances that will bind society as the future generation takes control.

Masquerades are also a prominent feature in the male initiation rites of the Chokwe, who belong to the Bantu-speaking peoples. Until the end of the first millennium, they were part of a migration pattern that brought settlers from the north into the present-day Democratic Republic of Congo (formerly Zaire) and northern Angola. Like all Bantu groups, the Chokwe believe in a "natural" world of animals and people, and a super- natural world where spirits reside. The ancestors, in spirit form, are the necessary mediators for transac- tions between humans and the supernatural sphere, and it is through their goodwill and power that intangible forces are held in check or moved to benefit society.

Among the Chokwe, the ancestors are known as the *akishi*, and along with other abstract beings and natural forces, these entities determine the fate of the living. Chokwe art is a system of symbols that conveys concepts of power and authority, and it is used to establish hierarchy in a chieftaincy form of social organization. The institutions of secret soci- eties are thus very important, as they give social cohesion and stability, particularly in times of crisis. One such moment occurs when the young boys in a village enter adolescence: in a short period of time they must turn from their protective and nourishing mothers and quickly enter manhood. These younger males who are in transition are poised to test or challenge authority, and they are thus dangerous to society. To alleviate the danger the boys enter a bush school known as the Mukanda. Until recently this school taught young men the arts of hunting, farm- ing, and the cultural traditions of society. Today the initiation period has been much reduced. Each young man learns the secrets of the Mukanda and is circumcised. In the world of the Mukanda, the spirits are called upon to help educate the boys and conduct the rituals of the secret societies. Women are not allowed to see most masks.

2.5 Dancing maskers wearing *akishi* masks, with Cikunza at right, in the Democratic Republic of Congo, c. 1935. *Photograph by E. Steppe, Courtesy Royal Museum for Central Africa, Tervuren, Belgium.*

MASK 5   The masked spirit Cikunza is one of the important tutelary spirits responsible for the suc- cess of this rite of passage (fig. 2.5). Made of black resin, the mask is characterized by a tall con- ical headdress, which represents the horn of the antelope. The costume is completed by a large fringe that extends from the neck to cover the shoulders and an equally large fringe that encir- cles the waist. In profile, the masquerader resembles a grasshopper, an animal noted for its fer- tility, which the Chokwe also call *cikunza*.[14]

As in many other societies, the masquerader usually conveys many metaphorical associa- tions; in the case of this mask and costume, the antelope and insect are most important. The antelope is a large and powerfully built animal that is difficult to track down and kill. Therefore, the spirit of the animal must be appeased through the masquerade if the young men are to become successful hunters. The young men must not only provide meat for the table, but they must also be fertile, like the grasshopper, so that the next generation, which will take care of the present initiates when they become elders, is guaranteed. The next generation will also preside over the funerals of their elders, conveying them into ancestorhood.

The grasshopper costume is also appropriate for initiation ceremonies because of the nature of the insect's growth and development. Grasshoppers experience an incomplete metamorphosis, not undergoing a larval state. Instead each animal goes through many "nymph" phases in which each stage leads to the shedding of the skin and the emergence of a slightly altered and more mature form. The growth of the grasshopper resembles the development of humans who must go through several stages or rites of passage in their progression to the status of an important elder. Like the grasshopper, humans who wish to become an ancestor must go through a predictable and steady process of development.

At the appropriate time, the Cikunza enters the village with a sword in his right hand and a spreading branch, *citete*, in the other. His appearance signals the beginning of the initiation and the circumcision. Other maskers escort the boys to the place of circumcision and, after the Mukanda is disbanded, they escort them home. Other maskers of lesser stature appear in the villages to beg for food when supplies dwindle in the bush. One such character has a huge body costume in which two shelves are constructed in order to hold cooking pots full of food given by the women to feed the initiates and their male attendants.[15] The final event of the initiation is the stunning revelation that the *akishi* are really human beings who have given the initiates their own lives. The newly initiated are told not to reveal this astonishing revelation to the uninitiated on pain of a curse.

After returning from the bush, the young males are prepared to assume the responsibilities of adulthood and become productive members of the community. Their generation eventually assumes the leadership in the community.

MASK 40 The need for rites of passage persists in other parts of the world, including Europe. The Souvrakari masquerades of Slavic origin in Bulgaria today, for example, serve to mark the transition of young males to adulthood. These masquerades occur especially in the western regions of the country. Prior to the masquerades, which are held on January 1 and 14, the young men hunt small animals and birds, which they will use in the construction of their costumes. The more elaborate the costumes, which means the more animal parts, the more successful the hunter. When hunting was a primary occupation of men, such elaboration might have been highly attractive to females. During the masquerades, the young men travel from house to house and perform in exchange for food and drink. Their mummery brings good luck for the new year to the families they visit. The masquerade entourage includes animal masks, a bride and groom pair of maskers, and an orthodox priest character. Mock weddings and the general mood of satire and buffoonery in this masquerade are reminiscent of the young male charivari maskers common in Europe from medieval times. After the Souvrakari players complete their tours they return home. The young men then remove their headpieces at which time their girl-

2.6 Maskers known locally as *babuguri,* celebrating the new year in the Bulgarian village of Bonsko, 1970s. *Courtesy Dimitar Bistrini.*

friends encircle them, indicating that each couple will someday be married. Through this masquerade the young males have completed a rite of passage, thus marking their maturation into men who will assume adult responsibilities, including marriage (fig. 2.6).

While gender divisions and initiation associations decline as societies become increasingly more industrial, the need for such rites of passage remains. Western societies have retained some forms of initiation and have created other new ones. Many religions have coming-of-age ceremonies, such as the bar or bat mitzvah in Judaism, and confirmation in Christianity. Both events take place in adolescence, and at that time the "initiates" are presented to the congregation as responsible adults, who now fully understand the mores and expectations of the religious community. They are now ready to participate and, in the future, lead, thus guaranteeing

RITES OF PASSAGE

the continuation of the community into the next generation. Countless examples of rites of passage exist in our society—the only difference, perhaps, is that they do not involve the use of masks.

New rites of passage have evolved with medical technology. A plastic surgeon has suggested that plastic surgery might be a modern rite of passage for young women disappointed in the physical outcome of their adolescence. During the transition from childhood to womanhood their bodies have not acquired the desired size and shape, leading some to choose plastic surgery. The first step in this medical procedure is for the female to select the appropriate doctor and then attend an orientation where photographs of her body are taken. On the next visit the patient brings several photos of women whom she might want to resemble; most often the young woman will bring magazines such as *Playboy* and *Penthouse*. The models in these publications have themselves usually been shaped by the surgeon's knife, and thus the patient builds her own image upon an artificial one, artifice on artifice.

At this point the patient (initiate) is ready for surgery. The surgeon scrubs down, and afterward a nurse places a complete face mask on the doctor's face. The patient is strapped down on a table in the surgical theater, anesthesia is given, and the operation begins. With knives in hand the surgical team begins to remake the person. One is reminded of the circumcision and clitoridectomy performed by medicine practitioners in many societies already described. Here, too, it seems that humans are not content with the work of nature as they disfigure in order to create the desired appearance. In these transitions bodily mutilation adds cultural meaning to the adolescent transition to adulthood.

After several hours of surgery the patient is placed in a recovery room and observed in order to diagnose any complications. She recuperates at home, moving slowly and carefully to avoid pain. Painkillers are prescribed to make the rite of passage more comfortable. In a few weeks the patient returns to the doctor's office and is examined and again photographed. Comparisons with the initial pictures are made, and if satisfaction is obtained, she leaves a new woman.

Whereas rites of passage in most societies have a built-in sense of the future with the arrow of time pointing forward, this surgical rite points to the past. The young woman, obviously disappointed with her first adolescence, returns via surgery to make amends for natural shortcomings. In this rite, modern medicine is called upon to rectify the failure of nature. Later in life a woman may return for another surgical experience in order to look like a younger female rather than a woman in late middle age.

High school graduation is another modern rite of passage. In cap and gown, the initiates march into the gym, stadium, or football field and take their chairs in front of their parents and elders. Speeches by faculty and students follow, songs are sung, and finally, caps are thrown into the air to conclude the event. The new graduates mingle with friends and relatives while pictures are taken. Later the graduates attend all-night parties. Other coming-of-age ceremonies in Western culture include the Outward Bound programs, wilderness hiking and camping trips for young men and women, and the fraternity and sorority initiation rites of college freshmen.

Age, Grade, and Rank

Among Native Americans of the Northwest Coast, the peoples of the Sepik River area in Papua New Guinea, and various groups in western and central Africa, masked festivals and rituals mark the advancement of men from less to more prestigious ranks and titles. The Aztec, Pre-Columbian, Maya, Inca, Moché, and Nazca cultures also used masks to demonstrate power and prestige. These cultures performed masquerades to honor men and women of prestige with lavish displays of food and numerous dramatic rituals. Masquerades that function in the context of a change in social status honor those who have ascended in rank, taken new titles, and become "big men." Societies that offer such positions are in the strictest sense nonegalitarian. In contrast, completely egalitarian societies, including the San of southwest Africa and the Pygmies of the central African Ituri rain forest, have no such social ranking and thus find no need for masks. Communities with differences in status, rank, and prestige have a sociopolitical system that divides labor into special categories for the gathering and processing of resources and then distributes them unequally. Within these societies individualism is encouraged from birth. The young admire the head of the clan, they are told about the heroic exploits of past kings and chiefs, and they stand in awe of the secret meetings of elders held in the secret society house.

In some societies a man accumulates wealth through the growing of staple crops such as corn, wheat, millet, or yams. He may hold lavish festivals to demonstrate his economic worth, and in turn use that power in men's political meetings to make decisions for the benefit of himself, his close relatives, or his friends. By bestowing fishing or water rights to an up-and-coming individual, he receives both personal economic gain and ever-widening support from those that benefit from his success.

Further up the ladder are kings and chiefs, who receive investiture upon obtaining office. The power of these individuals is often predicated on spiritual association. The blood of previous officeholders or of sacrificial victims is sometimes consumed by the newly appointed head. The spiritual power flowing in the fluid of previous rulers by consumption empowers the new king. Thus applies the familiar exclamation, "The king is dead! Long live the king!" Such leaders are the embodiment of the state, and through their communication with royal ancestor spirits they secure successful crops, triumphal warfare, expanding trade, and the good life for their constituencies.

To confirm and sanctify the leaders in their new positions, masquerades are often held. These masks often represent the spirits of power. The transformation of dancers into spiritual entities echoes the transformation of an appointed person to a new and frequently spiritual position. The dramatic performance of the masquerade, the taking of oaths, the musical performance, and the consumption of festive foods seal the bond between the ruler and his people. The masks have legitimized this important act of transformation. MASKS 8, 9, 11

Other widespread uses of masks in connection with status occur in societies which are less stratified. In these groups the secret society prevails. One such example is the Bwami association of the Lega people of the Democratic Republic of Congo. This public association provides a strong structure for uniting a network of small villages or smaller social groupings. Organizations such as Bwami take the place of centralized political organizations, making major decisions about warfare, taxes, distribution of resources, and other matters that affect the general welfare. Its members pass from one grade to the next, spending much wealth on masks and figure carvings to indicate their status. The highest grade, known as *Kinbi,* is often honored by masks and other objects.[16]

Funerary Rites

Since the Neanderthal age, humans have called upon spirits, especially the spirits of the dead. In Freetown, Sierra Leone, the ancestors are referred to as the living dead; thus, they too must reside in a designated space.

When the population living in bands, tribes, and village settlements is small in number, the death of an important elder creates a crisis (fig. 2.7). The knowledge, wisdom, resources, and decision-making capabilities associated with that person are lost, and for the survivors, the

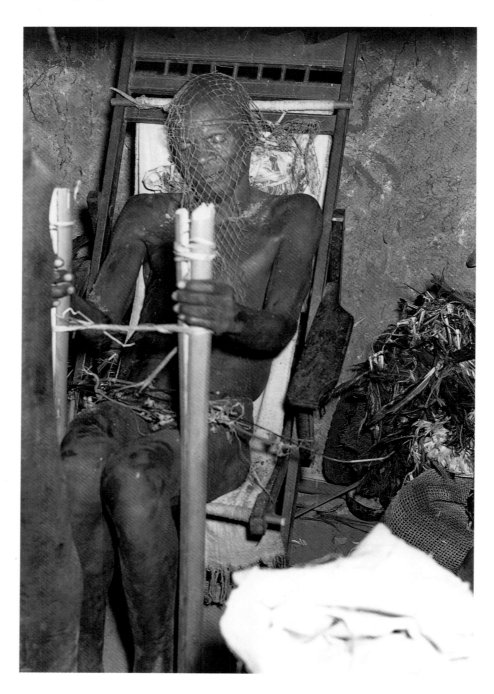

2.7 The corpse of a leader awaits burial by the Mambilla people in Nigeria, May 13, 1947. *Courtesy Evan Schneider.*

2.8 Ram masker at a funeral among the Bobo people of the Sanu village in Burkina Faso, April 1984. *Photograph by Christopher D. Roy.*

future becomes uncertain. A replacement for the village elder or king must be decided, and such replacement causes additional social tension, particularly in strongly patriarchal societies. Moreover, there may be a feeling of ambivalence held by society toward the newly deceased spirit. A strong father or leader would be embraced and loved for the security and protection he provided, yet feared and despised for the physical or political abuses of power he may have indulged in. This love-hate relationship would be projected onto the spirit of the deceased[17] who is missed and loved, but also feared. The spirit must be appeased and brought to a metaphysical realm where he cannot endanger the living. The masquerade is often called upon to move the spirit into a safe realm. The mask and funerary rites open the doorway for this final rite of passage to the living dead. Just as hunters have worn masks to revive the spirits and bodies of killed animals, men have masqueraded at funerals for the safe journey of the deceased to a place where he or she may contribute in a positive way to society in times of crisis (fig. 2.8).

In ancient Egypt the spirits of important people were thought to return and live in their tombs, inhabiting the mummies. During the seventy days of embalming procedures, the priests wore the mask of Anubis, the god of mummification (fig. 2.9). The masks may have had two functions: by calling on the powers of Anubis through masquerade, the priests could successfully prepare the spirit of the deceased for eternity; secondly, the long-snouted mask may have protected the embalmers from foul odors and the dust of the natron powder used in the mummification process.[18] A death mask was placed on the face of the mummy, ensuring his

77

2.9 Carved relief on a temple wall at Kom Ombo, Egypt, shows a coronation scene in which priests wear ceremonial animal masks, c. 30 B.C. *Courtesy Arlene Wolinski.*

spirit an everlasting life. The spirit of the deceased was probably transported to the spiritual world through the mask.

Pre-Columbian cultures of the Americas included many traditions involving death masks. Although none of the spectacular masks from the ancient city of Teotihuacan, near present-day Mexico City, have been found in burial sites, it is believed that they were associated with the funerals of important statesmen.[19] A ceramic sculpture from Teotihuacan may further support the association of these masks with death. It represents a face mask attached to what appears to be a funerary bundle. Teotihuacanos buried their dead in seated positions, wrapped in mats or cloth, and some may have had masks attached.[20]

The neighbors to the south of Teotihuacan, the Maya, also used stone masks in their royal burials. One sensational discovery in 1952, by the famous Mexican archaeologist Alberto Ruz, was of the crypt and sarcophagus of a mighty Maya king of Palenque, known as Pacal. This royal figure was said to be eighty years of age at his death, and through his rule Palenque reached the height of its power and extravagance.[21] Inside the sarcophagus lay the bones of Pacal and a jade mosaic mask representing a young king (fig. 2.10). A T-shaped symbol associated with the rain god was placed in the mouth and served as an amulet for the king's survival as he descended into the realm of the underworld known as Xibalba. A relief sculpture on the stone slab that covered the sarcophagus shows Pacal's descent (fig. 2.11). He enters through the

MASK 22

MASK 20

78

2.10 Maya king Pacal's jade funerary mask Chiapas, Mexico, c. 683. *Courtesy Museo Nacional de Antropología, Mexico City.*

2.11 Sarcophagus lid in the tomb of Pacal, Chiapas, Mexico, c. 683. *Courtesy Merle Greene Robertson.*

RITES OF PASSAGE

2.12 Mummy bundle, Chuquitanta, Peru. *Staatliche Museen zu Berlin, Preussicher Kulturbesitz, Museum für Völkerkunde.*

monster mask of the underworld sun. The top half of the mask is fleshed out, whereas below the eyes, the face turns skeletal to symbolize a gradual death by descent. As Pacal falls, his decaying body turns into a ceiba tree. The blood of the sacrificial victims and the blood-filled bowls on the relief symbolically empowered the king to overcome the trickery and treachery of the underworld gods so that he might ascend to a place by the North Star; there he would become an immortal being who could guarantee successful crops and the fertility of his people.[22] His successor would perform rituals on top of the temple in order to visit the divine Pacal and solicit his powers for the living. It was a Maya belief that the creator gods made human blood and flesh from water and corn, but in return, in order to energize the gods, humans had to sacrifice blood and flesh to the gods.

Another culture from the Americas, the Mississippian peoples of North America, produced stone and shell masks that also may have been associated with the burials of rulers. Similar uses were made of stone masks in the Olmec civilization. In numerous Peruvian Pre-Columbian

MASKS 18, 19, 23 societies, the bodies of men, women, and children were mummified in bundles on which masks were placed near the face (fig. 2.12).

2.13 William Woolett, after a drawing by William Hodges, "A toupapow with a corpse on it," from Captain James Cook, *A Voyage towards the South Pole and Round the World, 1777*, vol. 1. *Courtesy The British Museum.*

2.14 A Simmalungen Batak mask dancer in *huda-huda* funerary rites at Pematang Raya in northern Sumatra, Indonesia, 1938. *Photo by Claire Holt, Courtesy New York Public Library Center for the Performing Arts, Dance Collection.*

MASK 13

Anthropological accounts from the end of the nineteenth century detail funerary masquerades in societies throughout the world at that time. In these examples as well, the masquerades assisted the spirit of the deceased on his or her journey to the place of the ancestors and helped ensure the general welfare of the survivors. In traditional cultures of the Pacific, funerary masks are used in performance among the Batak, Tahitians, Asmat, and many cultures of Melanesia, including peoples of the Sepik River, New Ireland, and New Caledonia. Western and central African societies have also used masks in funerary rites (fig. 2.13).

The funerary rites of the Batak peoples of Indonesia demonstrate the ambivalent attitudes that the living harbor toward the dead. The Batak believe that if the spirits of important deceased men are not honored by a ceremony that includes offerings, dancing, eating, the distribution of a ritually slaughtered cow, and masquerades, the spirit of the deceased will become furious and cause havoc among the survivors (fig. 2.14). Maskers in this ceremony include a horse character and another masker who represents a man. The masqueraders follow the coffin from the house to the grave, and after the burial the masks are deposited on the grave or hung on the grave post. Again, the

masquerade assures the deceased that his descendants will care for him, and he, in turn, will protect them.[23]

The masks of the Kanak people of New Caledonia are associated with chieftaincy. They are famous for their bold plasticity, especially those masks that come from the northern region. The first description of a New Caledonian masquerade was recorded in 1843 by French explorers, who condemned the ritual for its hideous, depraved nature and reported that the chief played a central role in regulating the masked dancers.[24] Although the masks are no longer used, accounts by missionaries and explorers suggest that they were associated with the funerary rites of chiefs and other important persons. In the north the masquerade consisted of two maskers, one signifying the chief and the other representing his subjects, in a duality expressing the political reality that once existed in this region (fig. 2.15). The costume has three parts. The mask itself is carved from a local tree known as *houp;* this wood is also used to carve the finial for the chief's

2.15 Chief and subject masqueraders with Kanak war masks in New Caledonia, c. 1900. *Photoypie by A. Bergeret & Cie., Courtesy Anthony JP Meyer Archives, Paris.*

house. The coiffure is made of a vegetal material to which is attached bark cloth as well as human hair from mourners of previous funerary rites. The frock or mantle, which hangs to the waist, is made of fishnet decorated with feathers and other materials.

The masks provide for a transition of power at the death of a chief. The authority of the deceased chief, which must be transferred to a new leader, is transmitted through a connection between the chief and the underwater world of the ancestors and other spiritual forces. The large curving noses that point to the mouth are said to symbolize the sacred serpents that provide food and nourishment to the ancestors.[25] The fishnet foundation of the mantle makes it possible to capture the spirits of the dead. In the natural world the fishnet catches fish; when it is ritually used in the masquerade, it catches the spirits of the ancestors who reside in the same world as the fish. The strong association of masquerade with chiefs suggests that such personages had the exclusive ability to contact and even control the ancestors, a spiritual power which in turn sanctified their earthly powers.

These New Caledonian masquerades provided continuity and stability in a time of crisis, yet they also point to a common theme in the funerary masked rituals of many societies. Masking rituals provide the means by which the deceased may make a safe journey to the place of the

2.16 This basketry masquerade of the Chewa people of Zambia portrays large animals, 1985. This type of Kasiya Maliro mask is believed to capture the spirit of the deceased. *Courtesy Kenji Yoshida.*

spirits, a place at once distant enough from the living so that its power may not accidentally incur misfortune, yet close enough to be contacted in times of crisis.

Rites of passage help sustain the social order. They appear at times when biology rules. Culture, through the agency of masquerades, attempts to frame and to some extent control those biological experiences. By framing the transition through ritual means, individuals as well as the entire social group derive moral and ethical meaning from the biological crisis. Society can redefine the individual, be it at birth, child naming, adolescent initiation, aging, or death. In turn, the individual moves from a past stage, through a liminal one, and into the next stage: the person moves from the biological stage of being betwixt and between to something culturally concrete.

Masks are crucial props in rites of passage. As these rites seek to stabilize and provide continuity over the generations, the fixed gaze of the mask becomes a metaphor for that continuity. Among the Chewa people of east central Africa the newly initiated young men eat the ashes of certain ancestral masks. It is said that upon consuming the ash the initiated ones become immune to the heat of the deceased's spirit (fig. 2.16). The ritual allows the newly deceased to be placed into a cultural space as the young men establish themselves in their cultural place. After the ceremony, the parents say to their sons:

Today, you have grown up. From now on, you should not step into the bedroom of your parents. You should build your own house and live there on your own. Also, you should never touch cooking pots. That is the business of women. Watch your manners. You have grown up. From now on, you can take part in the funerary rituals as a full-grown man.[26]

RITES OF PASSAGE

festivals of renewal

MASKS 25 TO 65

MASK 27

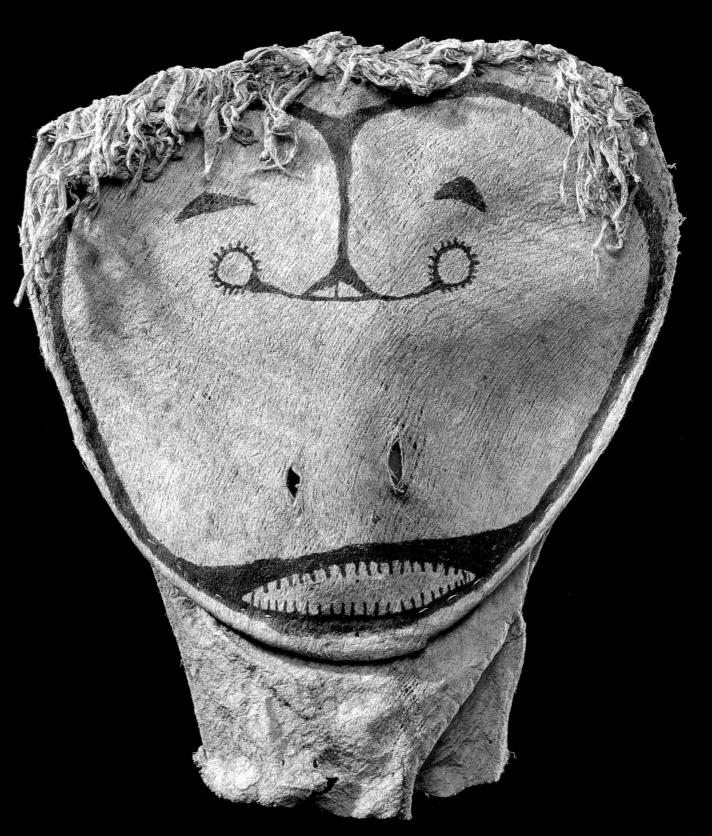

MASK 29

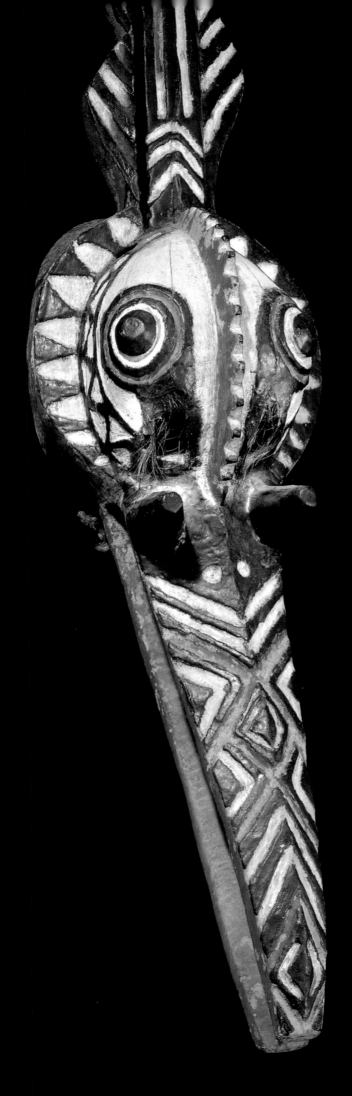

MASK 31

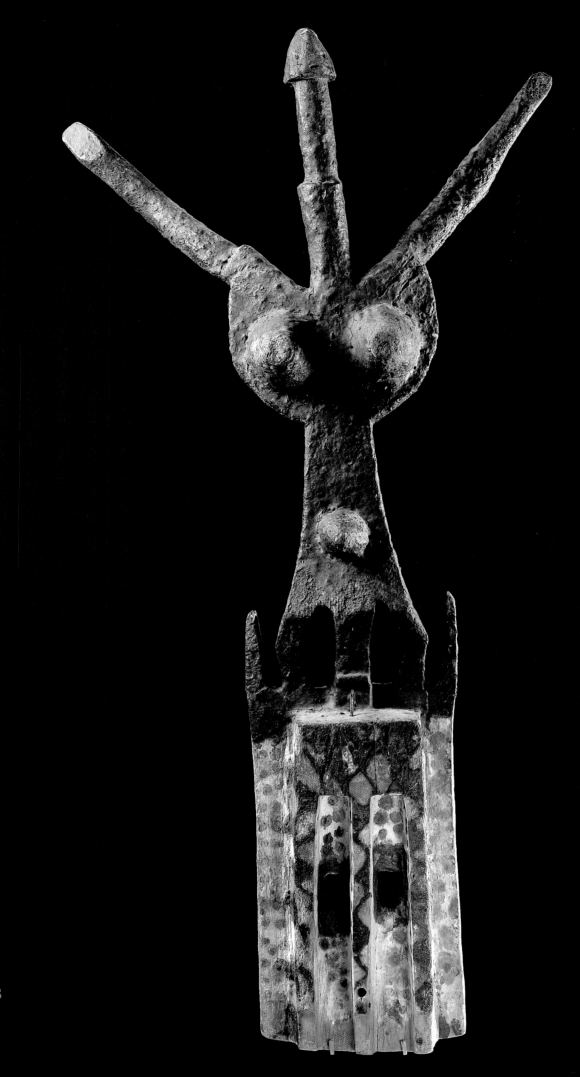

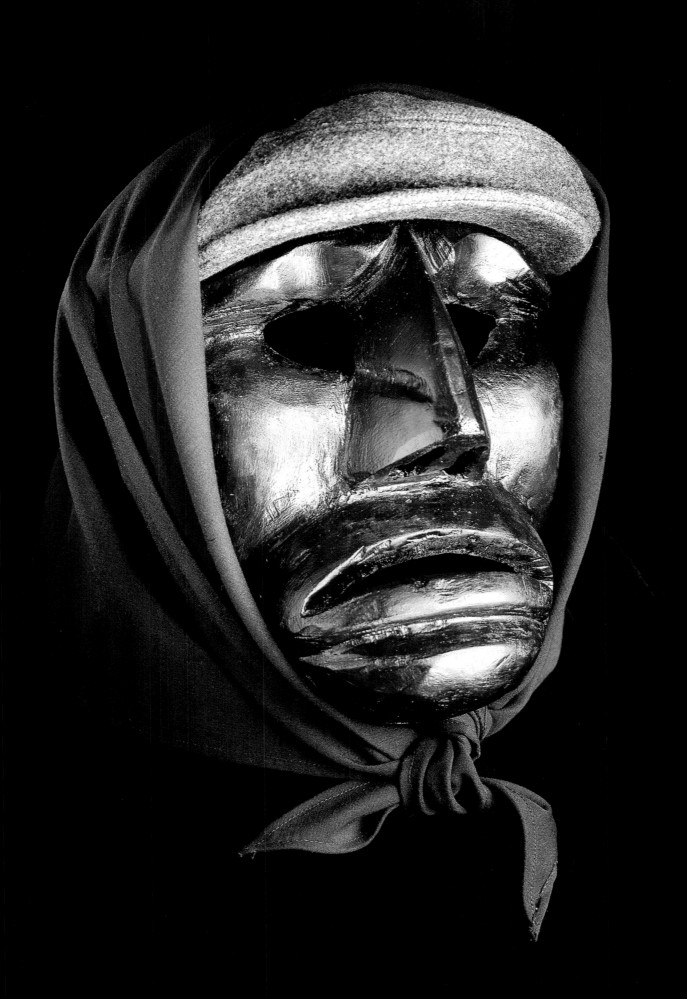

MASK 37

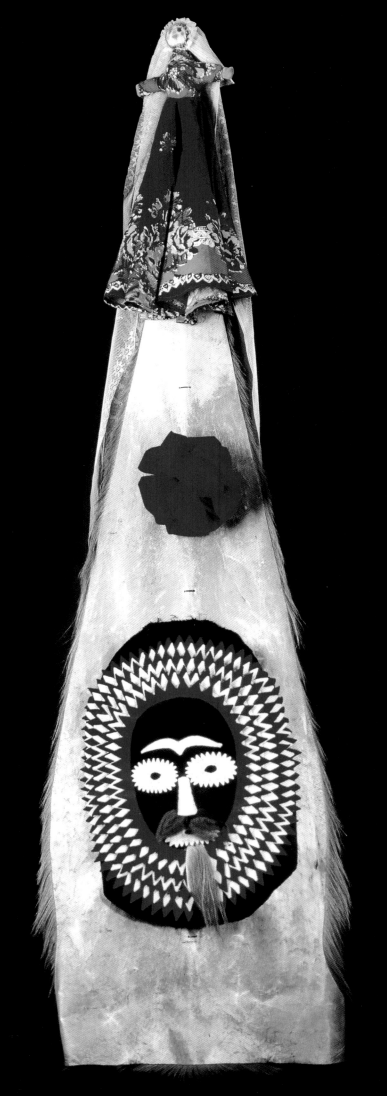

MASK 39

MASK 42

MASK 47

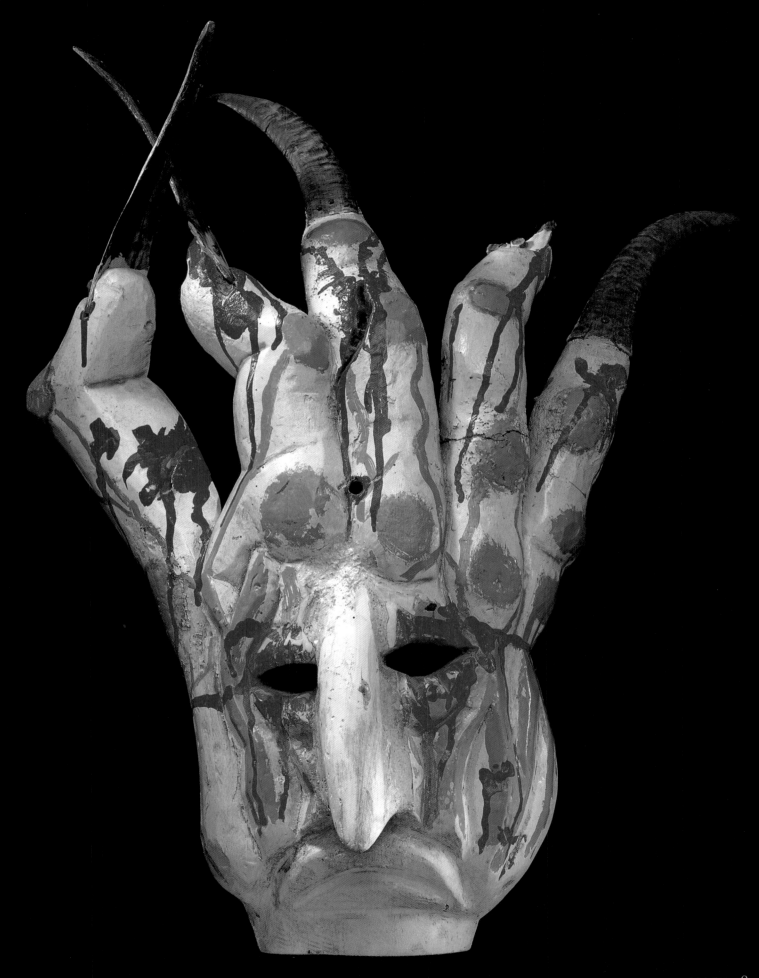

MASK 49

MASK 51

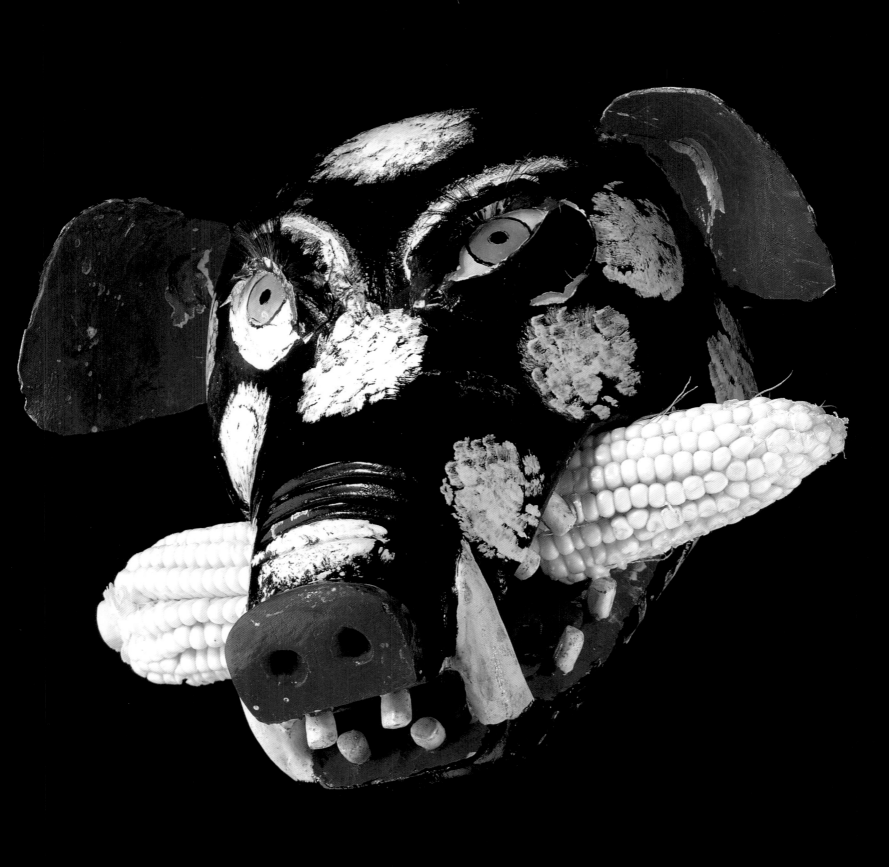

MASK 53

MASK 55

MASKS 57, 58

MASK 62

Festivals of Renewal

JOHN W. NUNLEY

ONE OF THE MOST STRIKING MASQUERADES of renewal belongs to the Ait Mizane peoples of Morocco. The masquerade promises a successful harvest, fertility, and prosperity for the new year. The rite, known as Bilmawn, occurs during the last month of the Muslim lunar calender, Dhu'l-Hijja, which marks the transition from the old to the new year. Several billy goats are sacrificed in preparation for the feasts that follow. The skins of the goats are saved in order to make costumes for the masquerade performers.

The main character is called by many names, but Bilmawn is the most common. His body is covered by four skins, one around each leg and one each on the front and back. A goat head and burlap cloth cover the masker's head. This costume recalls the 40,000- to 60,000-year-old Mousterian remnants discovered by de Lumley discussed in chapter 1.

In one scene in this complex ritual, Bilmawn lies on the ground belly up, while a character dressed as a holy man sits on the masker's chest with his back toward Bilmawn's face. The holy man then raises and lowers the masker's legs in quick succession, imitating a bellows whose resulting fire will heat the plowshare so that it can be sharpened for the ritual plowing. Another participant places the plowshare near the top of Bilmawn's phallus (which serves as a symbolic anvil) and strikes the iron. While striking the object several times, he speaks to the phallus in these words: "May you grow and prosper!"[1] Several of the masqueraders then take out their penises and urinate on Bilmawn, who afterward is harnessed to the plow and transforms into a cow. After a ritual tilling of the fields, a harvest is ceremonially performed. During this scene Bilmawn is transformed into the holy man's wife, who symbolically prepares all the foods for the field hands. In her husband's absence she sleeps with all the hired help as well as the slaves and, much to the amusement of the villagers watching this masquerade, she feigns frenetic copulation. Each male takes his place on top of her in succession. In every exchange the newcomer and the former lover engage in a mock fight. These erotic acts ensure renewal of all the local vital resources.

3.1 Log fires in a replica state capitol on New Year's Eve, Louisiana, 1989. *Courtesy Syndey Byrd.*

The fertility magic in this remarkable masquerade is initially supplied by the blood sacrifice of the goats. In the masquerade itself the character of Bilmawn undergoes three transformations, from goat to cow to woman. In this progression the character starts as a highly sexed male animal, and then turns into a domesticated milk-giving cow, and finally becomes a woman whose appetite for sex is demonstrated in the masquerade. Thus the main character brings together strong male and female valences to insure the fertility of the crops and the renewal of the next generation. Renewal in an extremely harsh environment is guaranteed by the masquerade.

Rites of renewal are concerned with the new year, the waning winter sun, or the onset of the wet season. These events are caused by the axis of the earth in relationship to the sun, phases of the moon, monsoons, and seasonal winds—great forces independent of society and external to it. However, such events determine seasonal cycles that impact economies and social moods. Cosmic changes are much larger than issues of social life, and to meet their challenge renewal rites frequently start with a big bang. They may begin with prodigious eating and drinking, fireworks, dramatic public masquerades, and the raising of monumental objects like giant papier-mâché figures, towering log fires, or large and complex floats (fig. 3.1).

Throughout human societies, among hunter-gatherers and in sprawling state systems, people have long celebrated rites of renewal that inspire hope and prospects for the good life. As in life-cycle rituals, renewal festivals are frequently accompanied by masking. Whereas life cycles cause social tension and anxiety in reaction to the biological changes of birth, adolescence and adulthood, status change, and death, renewal rites respond to changes in natural forces outside of society. However, agricultural rituals often relate fertility of the land with human fertility.

Many rituals of renewal are driven by the need to predict and control agriculture. During the sixteen-day Powamu ceremony of the Hopi, for example, masked dances accompany the planting of beans in the warm sands of the underground circular kivas. The beans sprout in the cold of winter, symbolizing the harvest to come and assuring that it will be a plentiful one.[2] The ancient Egyptian celebration of Opet occurred at the highest point of the Nile's inundation, a time when the flood waters reached the greatest number of fields, which promised the season of "Forthcoming."[3] In the ancient Greek ritual of Thesmaphoria, the rotted flesh of last year's pigs was placed on altars and mixed with seed corn to determine the successful sowing of new crops.[4] Today in Laza, Spain, villagers celebrate Carnival in the cold of the high mountain air with highly erotic masquerade presentations. Like the Greeks, they reserve smoked pig's heads as the sacred meal that guarantees new wine and crops in the next harvest.[5]

During the O-kee-pa renewal rites of the Mandan people of the Upper Missouri River, men masqueraded as buffalo to insure the animals' return for the hunting season (fig. 3.2). Initiates of the O-kee-pa performed self-sacrifices which included bloodletting. Renewal rites of the ancient Maya, Teotihuacanos, and the Aztecs—which also involved bloodletting, masking, and human sacrifice—were believed necessary to guarantee a successful harvest of corn and other staples. And not until well into the nineteenth century was the practice of executing a criminal at the climactic closing of the Roman Carnival outlawed.[6]

MASK 25

Blood plays an integral role in rites of renewal, and although there are exceptions, the occurrence of blood rituals must be considered. Why is there such a need to pour blood during

3.2 George Catlin, *O-kee-pa of the Mandan,* from the Catlin *O-kee-pa* manuscript in The British Museum. *Courtesy The British Museum.*

these events? Our search for an answer takes us back to the tale of the People of Thunder and Lightning who invented the masquerade (see chapter 1). We saw that the men who created and directed this ritual beat drums, let blood, and masqueraded. While the males constructed this virtual reality, the women prepared the foods for the feast. The men's interests were directed toward the "encouragement" or *provocation* of fertility (by assuring the supply of game), whereas the women's interests were more concerned with the "benefits" of the harvest, by *processing* the bounty. The release of blood by men in renewal rituals mirrors the women's menses that dramatically represents human fertility. By abstracting the female blood cycle and incorporating it symbolically and metaphorically into a yearly blood cycle within rites of renewal, men become the cultural agents who seek control over the entire fertility cycle of flora, fauna, climate, and human reproduction. In the wake of that responsibility, men endeavor to control the resources of society upon which hierarchy is established and from which masquerades are made possible.

In American culture, professional sports might be seen as a renewal ritual. Athletic events have long accompanied rituals and festivals—for example, the ball game of the Maya, or athletic competitions in ancient Greece and Rome. The sports spectacle also provides a ritual of national renewal, as regional teams from the same country compete to prove who is the fastest and strongest. Baseball, for example, starts in the spring, coinciding with the planting of crops, and ends with the World Series during the fall harvest. Football begins in the fall and ends in the cold days of January. This game is played in successive weeks as the sun sinks farther to the south, causing the days to grow shorter and the shadows to extend over the playing field in the fourth quarter, reminding the onlookers that the year is ending. The final championship college games are played in bowls of plenty such as the Orange Bowl, Cotton Bowl, Sugar Bowl, Rose Bowl, and Citrus Bowl. Each of these larger-than-life bowls, symbolically filled with the crops of the region, gives promise to a bright new year and a successful harvest. Each team and its fans are driven to spirited enthusiasm by mascot masqueraders, which include lions, wolverines, huskies, bears, and alligators, to name a few. The professional championship football game, the Super Bowl, is the climax of these new-year rites, featuring half-time shows that include bands, parades, and fireworks.

The largest festival of renewal that involves masquerading is the New Orleans Mardi Gras. Masked balls honor the Kings and Queens of the various Carnival clubs, known as "krewes." During the Monday and Tuesday before Ash Wednesday organized parades featuring the krewes and their floats parade down Canal Street before hundreds of thousands of people. Informal groups masquerade as political and media personalities, while others cross-dress or wear erotic costumes that celebrate fertility. Music from every quarter and festival foods and drinks highlight this dramatic event. Through Mardi Gras the city of New Orleans is cleansed and renewed for yet another year.

West African Renewal

The sub-Saharan regions of West Africa are characterized by two seasons: the wet and the dry. During the dry period, agriculture is at a standstill and economic productivity gives way to cultural enactments that include rites of passage and festivals of renewal. The temperature during this time may exceed 120 degrees; the earth is baked hard and dust fills the air. Old men sit nearly motionless sipping millet beer under massive baobab trees. People begin to wonder if the rains will return and if life will continue, for drought is certain to bring death (fig. 3.3).

For the last 300 years, the Dogon people of Mali have responded to this time of dryness with rites of renewal known as the Dama and the Sigi. The Dama is for the fertility of the crops, initiations, and farewells to the deceased, while the Sigi is for the fertility of the next generation of Dogon. The most public and dramatic events during these renewals are the masquerades.

According to tradition, the power of masks is derived from the bush spirits, *yeneu,* who gave the masks to the black ants, *kei.* The black ants were the first to dance with the masks, but soon a bird stole the masks and dropped them at a place called Yougo, where a woman named Sadimbe found them.[7] Gaining power by dancing with one of the masks, Sadimbe terrorized the men of her village. The men banded together and managed to wrest the masks from her. However, once the masks were introduced into the community, the Dogon ideal state of existence collapsed, and death, disease, and other hardships became part of everyday life.

In order to overcome these hardships, men invented masquerade

MASKS 32, 33, 35

performances of renewal. The masked characters of these performances included antelope, monkeys, birds of prey, beautiful nomadic women called the Fulani, and the woman who first terrorized the men with masks, Sadimbe. Two abstract masks—one known as Kanaga and one known as "big house or trees," which features fifteen-foot superstructures projecting from the face of the mask— became part of the performance (fig. 3.4).[8]

The most important parts of the masquerade costumes are the bundles of dyed hibiscus fiber that are attached at the waist of the dancers to form skirts; the red skirts symbolize menstrual blood. The men thus marginalize women by transforming themselves into feminized beings who control procreation and the fertilization of crops.[9]

The Dama is held about every thirteen years, depending on the number of initiates and the decision of the elders as to the urgency of the event and the available resources to sponsor it. The young men who perform this ritual for the first time remove themselves to the bush, where they collect and plant hibiscus fiber for the costumes; the dancers usually carve their own masks as well. At night the men

3.3 Snake mask danced in the Bwa village of Pâ, Burkina Faso. *Courtesy Christopher D. Roy.*

3.4 Dogon Kanaga maskers in the Sangha region of Mali, 1959. *Photograph by Eliot Elisofon. Courtesy Eliot Elisofon Photographic Archives, National Museum of African Art, Smithsonian Institution.*

practice dancing at the edge of the village, safely removed from women and children who would be punished if they came too close to the dancers. Large quantities of beer and an abundance of other foods are prepared.

In the village of Amani the Dama lasts four days. In preparation for this event a pole, called a *dani*, and an altar are placed at the heart of the dance area known as Bugura. On the first day, a group of maskers descend from the cliff above the village and are announced by drums, which warn women and children to keep away.[10]

As the drums beckon the maskers, the *bedye* masked dancers appear first; they are followed by antelope maskers, who maintain control of the performance, making certain that the maskers do not lose control and step out of the prescribed masking space. A group of stilt maskers, known as Tingetange, dramatically make their entry, followed by Sadimbe, and then a large group of Kanaga maskers and a cluster of men wearing tall masks known as Tiú. During the second day, a mask dance contest is held, much to the excitement of the young performers and guests from other villages (fig. 3.5).[11] Toward the end of that day the elders perform farewell rites for those who have died since the last dance. Each elder, in descending order of age, shatters with one powerful blow a special stool belonging to a deceased ancestor, and a chicken is then sacrificed on the altar.

On the third day male relatives of the deceased drink a final round of beer, which they share with the deceased by pouring some on the ground. This assures peace to the ancestors. On the fourth day the masks draw the largest crowds. Thousands of well-dressed people watch the dancers move into the square. When the dancers have finished, an elder thanks them and bids them farewell. The fertile power of the bush where the masks are made, the men's masquerade, and the ritual bloodletting when the throats of domesticated animals are slit, combine to guarantee the renewal of crops and human fertility for years to come.

MASK 34

3.5 Dogon stilt masquerader's costume, Mali. *Musée de la Civilisation, Quebec.*

Carnival in Europe

Multiple versions of Carnival from around the world share many features, and some of the similarities are based on historical connections. Yet it is very difficult to trace these histories and diffusions over several millennia. One reason for this difficulty concerns the nature of these festivals that in many ways reside outside of—and are sometimes at odds with—the legal codes of their political systems. For this reason Carnival festivals usually remain outside the officially recorded history, i.e., the history of the state and its political, military, and economic accomplishments. Making connections among renewal festivals such as Carnival across time and space is at best speculative. However, based on the work of scholars who have studied archival materials, oral traditions, and contemporary festivals it is clear that in a socially complex society these festivals are driven by the mixing of a variety of cultures. This mixing is known as creolization.[12] The origins of Carnival lie in the festivals of ancient Rome, and successors are found in Bulgaria, the West Indies, and Mexico, to name only a few examples.

The ancient Romans celebrated renewal with the festivals Lupercalia and Saturnalia. Occurring in the winter months, these festivals included masking. Lupercalia, celebrated in February, featured purification and fertility rituals. This holiday may have originated as a shepherd festival for a pastoral god, intended to ensure the fertility of fields and flocks. It was later associated with the god Faunus, who resembled a goat, an animal thought of as the embodiment of sexuality. The Lupercalia festivities began in a cave, where priests called *luperci* sacrificed goats, smearing two noble youths with the sacrificial blood, then cleansing them with milk. The *luperci* then clothed themselves with the goatskins and ran through the streets of Rome, lashing everyone they met with goatskin strips to make them fertile. Plutarch wrote, "Young wives do not try to avoid them, because they think it will promote conception and easy childbirth."[13] No doubt the Romans celebrated these festivals in their colonies, while the Gauls, Goths, Visigoths, Franks, and Bulgarians would look on; the colonized had their own ritual masquerades.

Saturnalia, which occurred in December, was a winter solstice festival honoring Saturn, the god of seed sowing. Slaves were relieved of their duties and would dress as their masters, who in turn would dress as slaves and serve. Houses were festooned with greenery in anticipation of a bountiful harvest. By turning the social world upside down during this limited period, it was promised that the proper social order would be maintained the rest of the year. In this manner the new year was greeted and good luck guaranteed.

Throughout Europe men masked as women, wolves, sheep, and other animals, much to the horror of the Church. The Spanish historian E. A. Thompson wrote this about the Church's attitude in the seventh century:

> The 1st of January was celebrated among pagans with mimes and feasts. Even Christians would sometimes join them in dressing up in the skins of wild animals or in women's clothing. They consulted augurs. They danced. They sang in mixed choirs of men and women (the worst offence of all, according to St. Isidore), and they got drunk. But the Twelfth Council considered other matters than augury, magic, or New Year celebrations. The worshippers of idols, those who venerated stones or lit torches and worshipped sacred trees or fountains, were to be hunted out by the local bishop and judge—ever since 589 the two had been obliged to combine in exterminating paganism—and their idolatries stopped.[14]

3.6 Pieter Bruegel the Elder, *The Combat of Carnival and Lent, 1559. Courtesy Kunsthistorisches Museum, Vienna.*

The writings of the church fathers describe such events and the laws they created to proscribe such pagan practices. Lupercalia, however, was so popular that in 494 Pope Gelasius I institutionalized the day as a Christian holiday, designating the fifteenth of February the Festival of the Purification of the Virgin Mary.[15] The ritual of role reversals in Saturnalia was reinterpreted in the medieval Christian Feast of Fools, which was based on a number of pagan rituals. On this day, low-ranking clergymen parodied the rites of the Church. Church officials fearful of the pagan and subversive element of these rituals eventually put an end the Feast of Fools. The tradition, however, was kept alive in the English Renaissance courts, in the forms of the Master of Revels and the court jester.

The festivals finally became fixed as a period of pre-Lenten festivities, generally referred to as Carnival—a time of jubilant, anything-goes fun, before the fasting and sacrifice for the forty days before Easter (fig. 3.6). Carnival in medieval Europe was developed by the upper classes, and by the time it reached the rural peasant regions, it had merged with local pre-Christian beliefs about fertility and the world of spirits.

In Bulgaria, Carnival is known as Kukeri. Local opinion traces its roots to Greek and Thracian Dionysian cults of renewal in which the god of wine was sacrificed during an annual festival in order to bring new life. The first known occupants of the area that is now Bulgaria were the Thracians, who migrated to this region during the second millennium B.C. Like the Greeks, they worshiped the god of wine, Dionysus. Much later, in the sixth century A.D., Thrace and Moesia were settled by Slavic tribes, tillers and stockbreeders who embraced an agricultural cult around a supreme deity known as Perun; aspects of Kukeri may thus have Slavic origins as well. In 679–80 Bulgar tribes from the banks of the Volga subjugated the Slavs and formed the first Bulgarian empire in 681, although the language and culture remained Slavic. Bulgaria was later conquered first by the Byzantine empire and then by the Ottoman empire.[16] The Russo-Turkish wars of the 1870s succeeded in liberating Bulgaria. In the 1940s the Communist party gained control in Bulgaria, which became a satellite state of the Soviet Union. With the collapse of the Soviet Union in 1989, the country once again regained its freedom.

MASKS 38, 39, 41

Kukeri has thus survived much cultural and political change, which is reflected in the masquerades. Although different versions of the festival are found in Bulgaria, they share many features. The festival has three major components: a masquerade, a mummery, and a feast. The masked characters include a king, a bride and bridegroom, gypsies, a doctor, a Greek Orthodox priest, sheep, goats, deer, a tax collector, and old men and women. The characters are all played by males.

Early on Sunday or Monday morning the processions of the kukors begins. The masqueraders cluster around a king who wears a mask, a white beard made of yarn, and a costume of white linen. He often wears great displays of medals on his chest, and his crown resembles a turban. During the house-to-house procession, the masqueraders perform and eat or collect food and drink for the evening celebration. Along the way the priest/masker reenacts a wedding of the bride and groom, which is conducted with suggestive erotic behavior and much laughter. Meanwhile an old woman masker carries a doll as a symbol of human reproduction, and at Pavel Banja maskers have dolls surmounting their headpieces (fig. 3.7). Ram and goat masqueraders also signify the fertility of animals. The long red noses of the kukors and the carved wood red beans carried by some of the dancers represent and celebrate the male sex. The presence of a masked tax collector with a ledger refers back to the Turkish taxation of the locals.

3.7 Kukeri masqueraders in the Bulgarian village of Pavel Banja, 1998. *Courtesy John W. Nunley.*

3.8 Masqueraders enacting the struggle of the *boes* and *merdules*, Sardinia, c. 1970s. *Courtesy Istituto Superiore Regionale Etnografico.*

Later the masqueraders and townspeople, inspired by the music of bagpipes and bells suspended from the costumes, proceed to the village square, carrying the king in a wooden cart. At the square the maskers stomp the ground and swing their ceremonial hoes and swords in order to arouse Mother Earth for yet another fertile growing season. The king, accompanied by an entourage, is lifted from the cart and placed on the ground. While he raises a glass to propose a toast, one of the kukors places a rope, attached to a wooden plow, around his waist. As the king attempts to swallow his drink someone pulls the rope, causing him to fall. The bowl with kernels of grain, which he is carrying in his other hand, falls and scatters on the ground. The king repeatedly comes to his feet to pull the plow, but each time he is knocked down. When the ceremonial plowing is completed, the maskers return to the king's house for prodigious feasting.

The ambivalent attitude of the maskers to the king is noteworthy; the medals on his chest make reference to the Russian tsars and the turban crown suggests the Turkish sultans, both feared and dreaded symbols of past authority. With the addition of the gypsy maskers, as well as reference to both Islam and Greek Orthodoxy, the social past and present is played out within a Carnival celebration that focuses on renewal.

Sardinians of the town of Ottana have been celebrating Carnival for many years. One of the principal masquerades includes several characters representing oxen, or *boes,* and the cowherders known as *merdules.* In the masquerade the herders goad and beat the *boes,* who are often tied to ropes. The cowherders gather strength for yet another year of toil by humorously mocking their own situation (fig. 3.8).

MASK 37

FESTIVALS OF RENEWAL

Festivals in the Caribbean

Caribbean festivals of renewal, including Carnival, represent the convergence of another variety of cyclical festivals, from Africa, Europe, Native America, and India from as early as the sixteenth century. The immigrants, who came as slaves, indentured servants, free men and women, and government and church officials, introduced their traditional festivals from the native cultures they came from. Those festivals were adapted in the Caribbean as well as in other parts of Latin America, where together they helped to build social stability under conditions of extreme cultural diversity and ethnic rivalry.

In the twentieth century, such festivals have helped shape the national identities of the various Caribbean states. The two major festivals of the Caribbean are the masquerade known as Jonkonnu and the pre-Lenten celebration of Carnival. Today, offspring of these festivals appear in many cities of North America and Great Britain where large West Indian populations have migrated.

Jonkonnu masquerades have been celebrated during Jamaica's Christmas season since the beginning of the eighteenth century. The participants, all of whom are male, parade in a variety of costumes and wire-screen masks and perform established dance routines, accompanied by small musical ensembles. Jonkonnu groups are called either "Roots" bands or "Fancy Dress" bands (fig. 3.9). Roots bands feature costumes of animal characters derived from African masquerade and those inspired by American Indian dress (figs. 3.10, 3.12); Fancy Dress bands generally show a strong preference for costumes based on the European dress of a courtly entourage. The costumes utilize striking contrasts of color, pattern, and texture.

In the eighteenth and nineteenth centuries, Jonkonnu bands performed for the owners of great houses on sugar plantations. In Jamaica today, the former colonial plantocracy has been replaced by indigenous Jamaican plantation owners. Although the performance of Jonkonnu on plantations is a tradition of the past, it still occurs in the Parish of St. Elizabeth, where its affiliation with renewal and the ancestors

3.9 An all-male Jonkonnu band with Belly Woman performing at Duheny Pen in Jamaica, 1976. *Courtesy Judith Bettelheim.*

3.10 Horsehead and Mother Lundy performing at Jonkonnu in Jamaica. *Courtesy National Library of Jamaica.*

3.11 Frog masquerade at Jonkonnu in the Bahamas. *Courtesy John W. Nunley.*

MASK 59

remains strong.[17] A stylized version of Jonkonnu is often performed on local stages. Other variants of Jonkonnu that are celebrated during the Christmas and New Year holidays include the "masquerade" of Saint Kitts–Nevis, the Jonkonnu of the Bahamas, the celebrations of the Garifuna masquerades of Belize, the Gombey masquerades of Bermuda, the Cuban Ireme masqueraders from the Abakuan Self-help societies, and the stilt maskers of the U.S. Virgin Islands (figs. 3.11, 3.13, 3.14, 3.15, 3.17).[18]

MASKS 55, 60, 61, 64

Carnival celebrations in the Caribbean began on the plantations. Beginning in the early nineteenth century, enslaved Africans created their own version of the festival, performing for themselves and the white aristocracy. Following the emancipation of the slaves in 1838, Trinidad's Carnival took to the streets in the capital city of Port of Spain and was dominated by former slaves as well as free black indentured workers. In time the festival became a major political force, featuring satirical musical lyrics and masqueraders who mimicked and chided politicians (fig. 3.16). Today, Carnival is a street festival celebrated on the two days preceding Ash Wednesday. Prior to the two-day parade of the bands is the opening event called Jouvay (from the French words *jour ouvert*, meaning "opening the day"). As early as two o'clock on Monday morning, people begin to celebrate the birth and renewal of Carnival by moving as a group through the streets to Independence Square. Between 50,000 and 100,000 people participate in this event.

MASK 62

I have played Jouvay many times. Its music, performance, and people have always prepared me for the liberating force of Carnival. Well smeared with mud and a clay slip over my entire body, I have moved with my Jouvay band from the outskirts of the city to its core. At first we see only a few other groups and hear the distant sound of other musical bands. Near the center of town the density of Jouvay players increases dramatically. Improvised bands using spoons, bottles, brake drums, and industrial-size plastic mayonnaise containers compete with the rhythms of the larger steel bands, calypsonians, and soca ensembles. As we all move to Independence Square, the sun begins its climb from the horizon to the top of Leventile Hill. By this time 20,000 people have filled the square, moving back to back, front to front. As the sun rises over the hill, arms rise to the sky while the music plays. Liberation has come, another year passes, and the new songs sing of a new spirit; Carnival has begun. Jouvay sets the pace for the masking and feasting of the next two days until Carnival abruptly ends with the arrival of Ash Wednesday.

Unlike Jonkonnu, whose performance groups seldom exceed a dozen people and whose performers always play specific character types, Trinidad's Carnival performance groups (called "mas bands") can include as many as 4,000 people and their costume styles change yearly according to the theme chosen by the group's leaders. Like Fancy Dress Jonkonnu, each group has its own King and Queen, but few individual characters are repeated every year. The few individual characters such as Moco Jumbie and the Midnight Robber who appear yearly usually do not belong to mas bands.

MASK 63

Unique to Trinidad are the two-week staged competitions held before and during Carnival, culminating on the stage of the city's largest park, Queen's Park Savannah. There masked and unmasked kings, queens, and individuals dance across the stage to the music of the soca beat, while crowds cheer them on.

Following pages:
3.12 Pitchy Patchy from Jonkonnu in Jamaica. *The Saint Louis Art Museum.*

3.13 Fancy Amerindian costume from Masquerade in Saint Kitts–Nevis. *The Saint Louis Art Museum.*

3.14 John Canoe costume made by the Garifuna people in Belize. *The Saint Louis Art Museum.*

3.15 Ireme dancer's costume for the Abakuá society's celebration of Carnival, Cuba. *The Saint Louis Art Museum.*

3.16 Pierrot Grenade from Trinidad Carnival. *The Saint Louis Art Museum.*

In 1983 I witnessed the stirring and emotionally compelling band River, designed by Peter Minshall. This band, which was protesting the environmental pollution created by industries in Trinidad, featured a masked king named Mancrab and a queen called Washer Woman. The king represented pollution and the queen purity and environmental sustainability. Each night of the festival competitions Mancrab danced and spun to the violent rhythm of the East Indian–derived tassa drums (fig. 3.18). Twenty-five square yards of white silk canopy waved in the wind above the masquerader. As the dance continued I could see a few drops of what appeared to be blood being sprinkled on the pure white canopy. Soon the canopy turned into a blood-stained shroud, a signal that the king of environmental disaster, Mancrab, had completed his horrifying mission: the "River" that his rival queen Washer Woman had protected was now polluted.

On the first day of Carnival the 3,000-member band dressed in white costumes. Each costume represented a band section, a "river" that led to the main river symbolized by the half-mile-long white canopy suspended by poles above the heads of the costumers. The whiteness was an indication that the band was pure and had not sold out to pollution. However, on the last day of Carnival the band members danced along the streets to the savannah under the canopy of white parachute cloth, now symbolically polluted with the colors of the rainbow. This indicated that the River people had turned their backs on the environment; they now worshiped Mancrab, the industrial king.

The dead queen, covered with "blood," was carried to the stage while the Mancrab danced victoriously to the tassa drums as a blood-stained umbilicus issued from his gut. Meanwhile several black priestesses dressed in white turned to the southern stands of the savannah stadium and poured calabashes of "blood" over their white costumes, a sacrifice to the King of Industry and Pollution. By this time all of the band members crowded the stage and danced to the soca music. Hidden compressors of paint spewed the colors of pollution onto the band and members of the press. The River people had been corrupted, the power of good was defeated. The image of Mancrab was indelibly imprinted in my brain, as well as those of audience and participant alike.

Completely exhausted, I returned to my hotel room all covered with paint. As I stepped into the shower, the paint on my body fell to the bottom of the shower stall. I watched this pool of polluted water swirl down the drain as I contemplated its journey down the reservoir to a river and then to the oceans of the world. This final personal

3.17 Moco Jumbie from St. Thomas. *The Saint Louis Art Museum.*

3.18 Mancrab king in the River band during Carnival in Trinidad. *Courtesy John W. Nunley.*

experience was the intention of the mas designer. The automaton half-man, half-machine Mancrab gave warning of future danger and challenges posed by the renewing years ahead which Trinidadians would have to face throughout their lives.

Renewal rites around the world play to the sensual and ludic nature of humanity. Roasted corn, millet beer, sausages of all kinds, breads, wines and stronger spirits, and ceremonial cakes are prodigiously consumed, and the smell of renewal flavors the air as participants, onlookers, and "second liners" celebrate the new year and its new growing season. The senses are overloaded, desire contains the promise of satisfaction. In the receding hours of the last dance, the last song, and last bite, the old year, the ancestors, and the newly deceased are let go. The spinning earth on its journey around the sun has set another cycle of renewal: the world goes 'round.

men as women

MASK 66

MASK 68

MASK 70

MASKS 72, 73

CHAPTER FOUR

Men as Women

JOHN W. NUNLEY

AT TWILIGHT THE SUN WAS MOVING DOWNWARD at about ten degrees when two masqueraders performed for the Gelede society, an association whose membership helps its individuals both financially and emotionally in times of stress. The maskers appeared in a vacant lot off Duke Street in Freetown, Sierra Leone, following a man shaking a bundle of rattles bound at the center. Musicians played the three drums known as *ako, etu,* and *agboi,* and the sounds provoked the masking pair to perform an erotic swing of hips at once tempered and loose. The samba dance brought the couple—two men, one dressed as a woman—ever closer together. A female attendant of the Gelede society cooled the maskers in their heated states, and if they drew close to touching, a fan was placed between them (fig. 4.1).[1]

This scintillating performance was intended for the pleasure of the elder women, Ajé, who are believed to affect the fertility of females by controlling their menstrual cycles. One of the attendants sang and walked into the dance circle carrying a large calabash on her head. It contained a carved baby, called *bankelu,* painted dark brown and covered with gold costume jewelry from the head to its exposed breasts, which symbolize the future fertility of the infant. The "baby" was taken from the calabash and handed to two men, both of whom hugged and held the sculpture. Others in the audience, both male and female members of the society, held the baby, while onlookers deposited donations in the calabash or upon a fan held by another attendant. As the crowds gathered, more masqueraders appeared for the night's entertainment.[2]

This February 1, 1978, masquerade was held in honor of a deceased member of the society, forty days after her death. The fertility ritual involving the carved baby figure and the Gelede masked dancers would ensure that new offspring would replace the older, dying generation. Throughout the week the masqueraders performed for the entertainment of the Ajé. Crowds gathered to watch, eat, drink, and exchange gossip. The last night of the performance a three-

4.1 Male dancer, dressed as a female, of the Gelede society in Lagos, Nigeria, 1971. *Courtesy Henry Drewal.*

horned, snake-faced masker named Aladigo darted wildly and unpredictably at the crowd. Turning on a group of children seated on a bench, Aladigo so frightened them that they fell over backward. Aladigo was in search of the old crone, who was believed to inhibit fertility. This man masquerading as the fertility snake sought to outwit the powerful crone. Finally, Aladigo said farewell to the Gelede society ancestors, and the celebration came to an end.

Men have long played women in masquerade performances. As has already been discussed in earlier chapters, most masquerades are performed exclusively by men, and men thus play the female roles in addition to the male ones. Through the transformation of the mask, men discover and explore aspects of the feminine. In certain cultures men even perform the couvade, in which they act out aspects of pregnancy, childbirth, and nursing behaviors. In certain societies in Papua New Guinea men will lie next to their wives feigning the pains of pregnancy; the fathers then sleep alongside their newborn children and pretend to feed them.

The fascination expressed by men in playing women is nearly universal. A very different example of men seeking female attributes is seen in an ancient Roman helmet featuring the face of an Amazon. In this case the male wearer hoped to channel the extraordinary martial ability of a member of this famous tribe of women warriors. Through countless centuries men have considered the mask their prerogative. Hopi Kachina masquerades of the American Southwest, Swiss New Year masking traditions, the masquerades of the Igbo (fig. 4.2), Makonde, Dogon, Yoruba, and Chokwe peoples of Africa, the Kukeri and Souvrakari masquerades of Bulgaria, Chinese New Year festivals, the Carnival masquerades of Mexico, and the Baile de la Conquista ("Dance of the Conquest") of Guatemala all include instances of men masking as women.

However, men masked as women are involved in a complex act of appropriation and representation. Men often masquerade as women in rituals to ensure a good harvest and numerous descendants. Thus fertility—both agricultural and human—becomes the "male" responsibility.

In the story of Pygmalion as told by the Latin writer Ovid, the discontented artist viewed contemporary women with scorn. Shocked by their shameful lives and vices, he preferred to be alone. Yet one day,

> He made, with marvelous art, an ivory statue,
> As white as snow, and gave it greater beauty
> Than any girl could have, and fell in love
> With his own workmanship.[3]

MASK 123

4.2 Maiden maskers led by the character Headload among the Igbo people in the village of Iou near Awka, Nigeria, 1930s. *Courtesy G. I. Jones and the UCLA Fowler Museum of Cultural History.*

Enamored with his own creation, Pygmalion festooned the sculpture with flowers, dresses, rings, earrings, and necklaces. On the holiday celebrating Venus, Pygmalion prayed hard to the goddess that he might have a woman as beautiful as his sculpture. Venus turned the statue into a human being, much to the delight of Pygmalion. Later, this unnamed ivory beauty gave birth to a girl, who was named Paphos. Ovid wrote, "[T]he crescent moon fills to full orb, nine times and wanes again, and then a daughter is born";[4] the full moon begets the daughter (the new crescent), the sculpture and the goddess (Venus) beget the young woman.

The English playwright George Bernard Shaw had this story in mind when he wrote his play *Pygmalion.* In the play a linguistics expert, Professor Henry Higgins, wagers that he can turn a lower-class, Cockney-speaking young woman, Eliza Doolittle, into a proper lady of upper-class speech and manner. A musical version of the play, *My Fair Lady,* features the song "A Hymn to Him," in which Professor Higgins asks, "Why can't a woman be more like a man?"

Male appropriation of the female role in fertility is seen in the story of the creation of woman in Judeo-Christian mythology. God creates woman through the agency of man: Eve is created from a rib of Adam (fig. 4.3). She comes from his body, and not from his head. According to the Western philosophy of dualism, which defines the head as the "organ of divine reason" and the body as corruptible nature, Eve is interpreted as inferior because she comes from Adam's body. According to Adam: "This at last is bone of my bones and flesh of my flesh; this one shall be called Woman, for out of Man this one was taken."[5] Adam's birth of

4.3 Michelangelo's *Eve created out of Adam's side*, 1508-12, on the Sistine Ceiling, Vatican Palace, Rome.

the female Eve, by a method that approaches cesarian section, can be seen as an early instance of the couvade.

The first woman of the Judeo-Christian world order, Lilith, was not created out of male substance. God made her, like Adam, from dust. Lilith considered herself to be of equal rank, but Adam disputed her claim to equality. Because of her independent ways, Lilith was eventually replaced by a woman born from Adam. The memory of Lilith, however, has continued through the centuries with a variety of interpretations. In medieval Europe she was pictured as a "she-monster" who avenged herself by eating the flesh of children.[6]

Frequently in societies where matrilocal residence is practiced—husband and wife live in the compound of the wife's relatives—women collectively raise young boys within women's quarters; the boys see relatively little of their biological fathers, who come to visit at the mothers' residences. In these societies cross-sex behaviors such as the couvade are frequently expressed. However, male initiation and the couvade are mutually exclusive. The reason for this might be tied to the view that initiation is a process of "social" birth, as boys become men with the help of the men who perform the initiation ceremonies. However, other cross-sex behaviors

MEN AS WOMEN

can still be found. In many traditional societies young male initiates from ten to sixteen years of age are generally circumcised, which results in a flow of blood imitating the menarche of pubescent females. Like the couvade, circumcision is another behavior that simulates female biology.

The reasons why men play women in masquerades in ritual or on the stage also relate to female biological transitions and social expectations. The ancient Greeks considered female genitals to be mysterious and hidden, and the penis to be noble and easily visible. Because of this view, Greek men concluded that women were designed primarily for internal activities such as keeping the home, raising the children, and other occupations, like weaving, which removed them from the public gaze.[7] Thus, cross-dressing on the Greek stage was justified as protecting women, who were simply not built for such roles. Likewise, Mexican men have traditionally played women's roles in masking because they believe that the female's place is before the hearth and involved in domestic activities within the privacy of the home.

Masquerades are men's work. Their performances are indispensable to the patriarchal imagination. Masks act as vehicles and symbols of a transcendence beyond mere physical reality. Philosophically, aesthetically, and religiously, masks consecrate the effacement of immediate reality for the benefit of a vaster reality.[8] That "vaster," male-envisioned reality includes men's conception of womanhood, which is more concerned with biological character than with social and individual identities. Man masked as woman is a foil to the dramatic, male hero plots of masquerade performance.

When men play women, the feminine signs are remade and appropriated within the patriarchal context of the masked performance. As Peggy Phelan concludes,

> A re-presented woman is always a copy of a copy, the "real" (of) woman cannot be represented precisely because her function is to represent man. She is the mirror and thus is never in it. Her narrowly defined but ubiquitous image represents the frenzy of man to see she who makes him.[9]

Men construct women as men see them or desire them, defining a woman in a man's world. MASK 69 In the tradition of the Ude Agbogho ("Fame of the Maidens") of the Igbo people of Nigeria, masked men portray adolescent females who embody Igbo male ideals of female beauty. According to art historians Herbert M. Cole and Chike C. Aniakor, Igbo men declare:

> Physically she "should" be tall and lithe, with upright posture, a long neck, and stately carriage. Light complexions are preferable, in part perhaps so indigo *uli* patterns will stand out boldly. She should have full, pointed breasts and a slim waist. Ideally she will have fine facial features—a thin, straight nose and small mouth—and her hair will be elaborately and delicately dressed in the preferred crested style. Her facial tattoos will draw attention to small, well-placed features, and often these marks will be supplemented with *uli* patterns. These ideals link, too, with the beauty of nature and valued medicines. Her skin is smooth and glistening, like that of a lovely female fish, *asa nwanyi,* she is too delicate to go out in the sun.[10]

4.4 Transvestites at
Mardi Gras in New
Orleans, 1997.
Courtesy Syndey Byrd.

Although real Igbo women do not often embody to these ideals of physical beauty, the authors
note that the masquerade nevertheless reemphasizes these ideals abstractly each year that it is
performed.

An interesting complement to the male construction of the female role through the masquerade is that men masked as women are allowed to behave in ways that women themselves
are not allowed (fig. 4.4). The men of Guzhang village in northern China, for example, play
women, sea creatures, lions, and dragons in masquerades to ensure cosmic harmony and fertility. When asked why only men play female parts, one man responded, "Because if there were
women dancers we wouldn't feel so free to be flirtatious, and flirting is what makes the show
more entertaining. We perform for hours and days on end. Women are just not strong enough
for that."[11] Men as women are allowed to break sanctions that men themselves have placed on
women. This element is seen in the masquerades of many cultures. In the New Year's celebrations in Nuevo San Juan, Michoacán, in Mexico, men masked as women perform sexual antics
forbidden to women.[12]

In European masked drama, the commedia dell'arte eventually did include women actors,
who played a young maiden known as Columbine and a jolly elder woman (fig. 4.5). These
women could play only their *biological* selves, whereas the men were allowed to play complex
cultural beings and heroic figures that required a "persona," a mask. Similarly, female actors in
Balinese theater may play female and even male roles, yet they are not allowed to wear masks;[13]

since 1985 in Papalotla, Mexico, female characters in masquerades have been played by women, but without masks.[14] The fact that men play complex characters, as well as interesting and powerful creatures of the animal kingdom, supports their political and social dominance.

This is tied to a long-standing male view—found throughout many societies—that men are representatives of "culture" and women are closer to "nature" and are therefore more dangerous and need to be controlled.[15] The cultural historian Sherry Ortner states:

> It all begins . . . with the body and the natural procreative functions specific to women alone. We can sort out for discussion three levels at which this physiological fact has significance; (1) woman's *body and its functions,* more involved more of the time with "species life," seem to place her closer to nature, in contrast to man's physiology which frees him more completely to take up the projects of culture; (2) woman's body and its functions places her in *social roles* that are in turn considered to be at a lower order of the cultural process than man's; and (3) woman's traditional social roles, imposed because of her body and its functions, in turn give her a different *psychic structure,* which like her physiological nature and her social roles, is seen as being closer to nature.[16]

An additional explanation for why men mask as women centers around the fact that men on the whole are usually bigger, stronger, faster, and more aggressive, and thus women masqueraders included in men's groups could risk some harm. Many masked performances are physically strenuous, characterized by violent and aggressive behaviors. Women simply do not fit the masking team, just as female basketball and rugby players do not play on men's teams.

4.5 Columbine, Harlequin, and a Venetian, with their masks, engraving after an 18th-century painting by F. Maggioto. *Reprinted from Pierre Louis Duchartre,* The Italian Comedy *(London: George Harrap), 1929.*

MEN AS WOMEN

4.6 Statue of kneeling Hatshepsut, represented as a king offering jars of wine to the god Amun, 18th dynasty (1490-1480 B.C.), Thebes. *The Metropolitan Museum of Art.*

For another insight into why men play women, we can examine the phenomenon of cross-dressing among men and women. Women usually cross-dress to gain status. Although Egyptian women did not traditionally rule, Queen Hatshepsut became pharaoh because neither of the lineal heirs (her husband and half-brother, Thutmose III, and his brother, Thutmose II) was old enough to rule. To sanction her role as pharaoh, she was depicted in male dress, complete with a beard and at times a phallus (fig. 4.6). The pronouns that accompany the texts describing her life, however, are all female. Thus, her cross-dressing represented greater power and an upward move in status.[17] The nineteenth-century French author Amandine Lucile Aurore Dudevant changed her name to George Sand and cross-dressed to gain status as a writer, a profession then monopolized by men.[18]

When men adopt female roles, they tend to lose status and power because they are playing females who have been marginalized from the arena of power. Recent Hollywood films exemplify that theory. In *Mrs. Doubtfire* (1993), for example, Robin Williams plays a comical older woman in a mask who becomes the "old maid" to his children in his divorced wife's home. Because of his cross-dress he has taken a fall in status, and his ex-wife treats him like hired help.

Men cross-dress to ridicule and parody women and to create images of them that fit into men's views of the world. In the realm of the American stand-up comedian, men usually play the old hag or the young woman: Milton Berle, Jonathan Winters, Johnny Carson, and Flip Wilson often had fun with the roles of old women; Carson, Wilson, and Shelly Berman have played the role of the sexy female or the maiden. The famous British comedian Benny Hill made his reputation by playing both the consummate sex kitten and the old hag.

The female characters most commonly played by masked men are directly related to female biological stages: puberty, motherhood, and cessation of menses. The most frequent portrayals are of the maiden and crone, with the mother role far down the list. The maiden, as the object of desire and attraction, and the hag, as the object of revulsion and fear, require definition by men.

The Three Stages of Womanhood

The different ways in which women's roles are appropriated and defined, and the limitations on them crossed, are reflected in the different female characters featured in male masquerades. As described in chapter 3, the moon has often served as a metaphor for woman, and its three phases—the new, full, and waning moon—have sometimes symbolized the "three stages" of womanhood.[19] Men masked as female characters generally fall into one of three categories: young woman, mother, and crone. The moon is also associated with lunacy, magic, and evil, qualities that are often ascribed to the crone.

Maidens

The maiden masquerader appears in many societies. Usually noted for her great beauty, she is most importantly a virgin, and she has suitors of all ages, including the elders. She is glamorous in a way defined by men, and she may even be bewitching. Yet, most of the time she is passive and meant to be looked at by men. Her masquerade communicates what men define as feminine, and what they want in a female. The maiden mask is widespread, seen for example among the Haida of the Northwest Coast, the Swiss in the Alpine regions, the Hopi of the Southwest, various Mexican Indian groups, and in many ethnic groups in Africa, including the Chokwe of Angola and the Igbo of Nigeria.

The Igbo "Fame of Maidens" masquerade is performed in many villages during the dry season. The wood slit gong and flutes are played as local villagers and invited guests from other towns gather in the clearing where the masquerade is to be performed. Frequently three "maidens" will appear in a warm-up dance. They are accompanied by a "mother" masker who sits and watches the performance. The maiden masqueraders execute several dances that successively increase in tempo and dramatic presentation. The polyrhythms produced by the musicians are reflected by each maiden's dance; arms, legs, and hips move to the different rhythms. Although the "female" body is in a panoply of rhythmical motion, the head and mask remain nearly motionless in order for the viewer to see the impassivity of the ideal facial features. After several dances, the "mother" masker performs with much slower movements, in a restrained manner appropriate to her status as an older, accomplished woman. At times a male masked character will perform with amorous and bawdy behaviors around the maidens to entertain the audience.[20]

This male masquerade commemorates the feminine spirit of maidens, mothers, and female ancestors. Among the Igbo, the female spirits are also linked with Ani ("Mother Earth"), and the masquerades are viewed as part of a sacrifice in her honor; in return, she will make certain that life on the individual, social, and agricultural levels remains satisfying and meaningful.

The Hopi people enjoy one of the richest masking cultures in the American Southwest. At the top of steep mesas of northeast Arizona, the Hopi have maintained their language and rites of fertility, which are centered on the production of corn. Corn itself is called "the Great Mother." The Kachina spirit masking cycle is nearly a year-round event. The spirits are said to reside in the San Francisco mountains in the American Southwest. The cycle starts with the ceremonial planting of beans in the kivas in February, soon after the sun has reached its southernmost point and begins its return for new life. The cycle ends with the harvests in September and October in which women, as well as men playing women, have active roles. However, although the Lakone Mana and the Palhik Mana Kachinas are played by women, appearing in elaborate headdress and costumes, they do not wear masks. These maidens celebrate the harvests and the nourishing contributions they will make to family and society.[21] During the Niman performances in July, the Kachinas are bidden farewell with songs and dances for which male masqueraders play percussion by striking a notched sheep's scapula over a dried and hollowed-out squash, creating "a very weird and most interesting sound."[22] The Ankwanti festival includes Tasap Mana characters, who are males dressed as Navajo maidens who perform by grinding corn and dancing before other Kachinas. The Navajo have been the Hopi's rivals for at least 700 years. Playing upon a Hopi perception of Navajo females, the masqueraders wear masks with a curious buildup around the protruding snout, which represents the fact that the Navajo use their pursed lips, rather than index finger, to point directions.[23]

In Nuevo San Juan, Mexico, in the state of Michoacán, the Tarascan Indians perform masquerades in honor of the saints and Christ. This New Year's Day festival is also held in honor of the exiting and newly elected officers of the local community organization. Some of the main masquerade characters include blacks (*negritos*), the "old ones" (*viejitos*), buffoons and clowns (*feos*), and "little Marys" (*maringuillas*) (fig. 4.7). During the procession from the church through the village, men don pink face masks whose delicate features contrast with their bright red painted lips. They also wear wigs, colorful blouses, and skirts with lace borders. However, while they keep step in their men's boots, the *guares* (women in festive dress) carry the heavy flower stands that bear images of the saints.[24] The men play women, and the women, laboring under the weight of the heavy stands, do the "men's work."

4.7 Little Mary costume Mexico, 1987. *Museum of International Folk Art, Santa Fe, New Mexico.*

MASK 68

Other young females represented by men in masquerade are prostitutes, who are also portrayed as objects of desire. The Yoruba peoples of Nigeria masquerade as "Cash Madames" in the ancestral masquerades of the Egungun societies (fig. 4.8). Egungun maskers perform secondary burial rites of the dead and honor the ancestors on a yearly basis. Dressed in the latest fashion and accessories, their figures transformed with overstuffed artificial breasts and bustles, males take on the role of the whore.[25] Indulging in provocative body movements while counting cash or checking a purse, they quickly get the crowd's attention.

In the real world of prostitution, the female body moves in the marketplace like other goods and services. A prostitute is subject to a different set of rules from those that govern the domestic scene. In Laza, Spain, in the northern region of Galicia, men commonly dress as young women and prostitutes during the pre-Lenten Carnival. A blue-and-red dress stuffed with fruit or rags for breasts, scarves, and thick rouge have been used to dress the part.[26]

The prostitute masquerader is a recent addition to the Bulgarian Souvrakari and Kukeri masquerades, where the incidence of prostitution has risen in recent years. For young men who perform the rites of passage in Souvrakari masquerades, the image of the prostitute represents access to sexuality, an important part of the adolescent male's transition to manhood. Proper women in these societies should not, of course, act and dress in the manner seen in these various masquerades, but it is viewed as humorous when men—some of whom may visit the prostitutes—imitate them.

4.8 Yoruba Cash Madames from an Egungun masquerade in Ilishan, Nigeria, 1980s. *Courtesy Marilyn Houlberg.*

Mothers

The status of motherhood is recognized among most cultures; in many countries, including the United States, a day has been reserved to honor mothers. During the Upper Paleolithic era, "Venus" figurines, which represented pregnant women with large abdomens and swollen breasts (fig. 4.9), may have been used in rituals to ensure the fertility of women. These objects, made 25,000 years ago, suggest that at this time motherhood was already important within the

MEN AS WOMEN

context of male ritual: men most likely created the objects, because primarily men worked with stone.

In many societies motherhood is acknowledged in the performance arena of the masquerade. Celebrations of Jonkonnu in Jamaica commemorate Christmas and the coming year with masquerades for good luck and fertility. On December 26, Boxing Day, troops of masked characters parade from house to house collecting money and food for the celebration. A major character in the parade is Belly Woman, always played by a man wearing a wire-screen mask, a crown, and a dress stuffed in a caricature of pregnancy.[27]

The Baga people of Guinea along the west coast of Africa have created a masquerade character known as D'mba (Nimba), who, with her long pendulous breasts and elaborate coiffure, represents the female ideal in Baga society (fig. 4.10). D'mba is the universal mother who bore many children and raised them to become contributing members of society. Representing goodness and light, D'mba dances in ritual to give women enough strength to bear children and raise them to adulthood. The masker also performs at weddings to ensure good luck and a big family for the newlyweds and before the rice harvest for the benefit of young men who must learn agricultural skills in order to be successful. Dressed in raffia and imported cloth shawls, D'mba dances in the village and fields, casting an aura of festivity over the day.[28]

MASK 75

4.10 Dance of D'mba among the Sitemu people, Guinea, 1990. *Courtesy Frederick Lamp.*

4.9 The "Venus" of Laussel, Aurignacian period. *Musée d'Aquitaine, Bordeaux, France.*

MASK 74

One of the most striking examples of a mother masquerade is the double-faced Gelede mask that is used by the Yoruba peoples of Nigeria. Gelede performances are enacted primarily to ensure the fertility of women. Although it is a woman who occupies the highest office of each Gelede unit, the masquerade is performed only by men. The maskers perform as individuals, groups, matched pairs, and pairs of dancers—including a male dressed as a female and a male dressed as a female in imitation of a male. Couples perform in elaborate helmetlike masks and wear beautifully constructed costumes made of women's head ties, skirts, and wrappers. In order to emphasize the female form, the costumes of the "female" partner feature wicker bustles and carved breasts or breastplates.

The faces of the Gelede mask are crowned with generously curved coiffures that feature dominant sagittal crests joined by sets of three small braided rows on the sides of the crest. While they may possibly represent the female genitalia, they also symbolize the furrows of the

farmed fields that provide the nourishment upon which human fertility depends. The three braided rows of the coifs echo the three sets of scarification on the forehead and cheeks, each containing three cuts. These scarifications are the standard tribal marks for Yoruba identity.

Gelede masquerade performances are known as "playthings" of the Gelede. If the "plaything" is deemed beautiful and entertaining by the Mothers (postmenopausal grandmothers who are "mothers" to the people), they will grant fertility to young mothers and good fortune for yet another year. The performance cools and soothes the powers of elder females so that they will use their forces in a positive manner. The living tree from which the masks are carved is considered to be part of the sacrifice: the freshly cut wood yields sap that is considered the "blood" of the sacrificed tree. The word *gelede* speaks to the purpose of the masquerade: *g* means "to placate, pet, or coddle"; *ele* refers to the female sex and her secretive, life-giving powers; *de* means "to soften with care."[29] Thus, the word *gelede* in transcription means literally "to soothe the female (sex) with care."

A well-executed Gelede mask features two faces and represents Eyini, the deity known as the "Mother of Small Children." The inner head represents the secretive night dances of the Mothers, and the outer head represents the public display of the Gelede dancers at the marketplace.[30] In a broader context, the double-face motif conveys the Yoruba sense of self: each mature person must develop an inner head, which remains cool and in control, so that the outer head, or social personality, is free to deal gracefully and effectively with circumstances, events, and other personalities in the complex and demanding social web.

The double head also represents twins, which are considered a sign of good luck to the mother and family. The incidence of twins among the Yoruba is about 45 for every 1,000 births, four times the global average; the reason for this phenomenon is unknown.[31] To the Yoruba, as well as to other West African peoples, the presence of four eyes gives one the ability to see into the spiritual world, in particular to see Ajé, witches, or Mothers.

The duality of the two heads, while representing the inner and outer self, positive and negative forces, and the good fortune of bearing twins, even more importantly represents the duality of male and female. Yoruba men acknowledge the fundamental powers of women, especially of the elders; by drawing upon the vital resources of the community, the men produce the masquerade for the elder women.[32]

Crones

Some of the most remarkable mask images by male artists are inspired by the old woman, or "crone." Across cultures and throughout time, she has been credited with awesome powers drawn from the world of spirits. She is often associated with witchcraft, and in many societies, including the Hopi of the American Southwest, the Kwakwaka'wakw of the Northwest Coast, the Balinese of Southeast Asia, and, from time to time in various European societies, she is said to eat children.

In patriarchal societies elder women tend to be marginalized and defined as the powerful but wicked crone. In her early years she had been the object of desire for young and old males, and in her motherhood her nourishing and hardworking ways had been indispensable to the survival of society. Her role in reproduction and her major role as nourisher and mistress of the house assured her a protected status. Because women are seen in a biological rather than cultural role, when their reproductive role ends, men do not know how to "define" them. Elder female status was and remains threatening in many societies because elder women exist outside of the set social order for men and women.

Like the waning phase of the moon, the crone begins to lose her luster, wither, shrink, dry out, and crack like decaying fruit. From voluptuous virgin to nurturing mother to elderly woman, she is viewed as the embodiment of nature's life cycle. Elder women often serve as the heads of secret societies concerned with healing and fertility. They may be the keepers of powerful ritual medicines and strict controllers of the society's masquerade performances. Men are often ambivalent toward such women. As mothers they may have been less assertive, but as crones they become dominating.[33] The crone's close association with the raw forces of nature is what society fears and devalues. As a result, male anxieties about women are often projected onto elder women in the form of witches.

One of the most daunting witchlike crone figures is the Dzonoqua (Dzonokwa), the wild woman of the woods, who often arrives during the bloody Cannibal society initiations of the Kwakwaka'wakw Indians of the Northwest Coast of North America. The ritual songs declare:

> Here comes the great Dzonokwa who carries off humans in her arms, who gives us nightmares, who makes us faint. Great bringer of nightmares! Great lady who makes us faint. Terrible Dzonokwa![34]

This character has swaying breasts that are so weighted down that they sometimes drag on the ground. The mouth of the Dzonoqua mask is pushed forward in a pout, and the Dzonoqua is often sleepy and nearly blind; she moves awkwardly, stumbling and falling into things. Like witches in other cultures, she appears only at night and resides in the forest or mountains, which strengthens her identification with nature. Dzonoqua spirits are asocial and not ancestral in nature. As kidnappers of young children, they threaten the continuity of the generations and thus pose a threat to the ancestors as well as the descendants. This old female is marginalized, yet she is indispensable to the welfare of society because she can bestow wealth on those she favors.

Many myths and stories about the Dzonoqua abound, but the different narratives all have similar plots. In most stories there is a confrontation in which the Dzonoqua kidnaps children, and a hero sets off on a rescue mission. In one variation the Dzonoqua also steals salmon from the people, or she denies them goat and bear skins, meat, and berries, all terrestrial products. The hero may trick the creature to regain the food resources or the children that she has kidnapped. Most significantly, the hero takes the Dzonoqua's wealth, including the huge coppers (large, flat, milled, and decorated copper plates that exemplify wealth), which are at the heart of the give-away potlatch feast that the sponsor of the masquerade hosts to enhance his social status. Often the powers of the Dzonoqua will be used to heal a victim in the story or bring someone back to life.

Following men's perceptions of elder women in many other societies, the Dzonoqua is viewed with great ambivalence. She is a source of wealth for men, who seek to move up the social ladder, yet she steals salmon and children, their sustenance, and their future. The

4.11 Koskimo chief hold-
ing a copper, 1894.
*American Museum of
Natural History.*

Dzonoqua also appears during female initiation ceremonies, during which young virgins wear
a Dzonoqua's dress. The reason for this might be explained by the marriage ceremony and the
relationship between parents and children. A maiden offers coppers and other sources of
wealth to her prospective husband, thus stealing from her own family (fig. 4.11). Yet by giving
him the coppers and concluding the marriage agreement, she steals from him in advance the
future children who will belong to her side of the family. As Claude Lévi-Strauss concludes:

> Looked upon from a certain perspective, the opposition between the two roles filled by
> the ogres (giving coppers, stealing children) underlies her unsociable character; but,
> from a different perspective, the young girl would seem to fill a social role and an eco-

nomic function that give her the appearance of a *tamed Dzonokwa:* upon entering the conjugal state, she behaves toward her own kin in the same fashion as Dzonokwa, but reverses the direction of the exchanges in their favor. The ogre steals children from humans and, willy nilly, cedes the coppers to them; by contrast, the young bride takes her family's coppers away from them, and brings the children to them.[35]

Among the Hopi of the American Southwest, the yearly ritual cycle addresses fertility of the staple crops, mainly corn and beans. Through Kachina masquerades, the annual rituals are performed to guarantee the return of the rains; with the power of the sun and the regenerative power of water, new life and survival are assured. During the months of January and February, following the New Year (*Soyal*), the ritual events of Powamu unfold. Many dances are held at this time, during which the primary responsibility of the Powamu Chief is to see that the beans that have been planted inside the "hot house" kiva will germinate, thus by metaphor assuring the future harvest. Within the kiva the participants smoke, sing, and tell stories.[36]

In this cluster of ceremonies, children from ages seven to ten are initiated into the Kachina cult. The boys and girls are brought into the kiva before the Chief, who impersonates the god of germination, Muyingwa. He instructs the initiates about tribal mythologies and proper conduct. Soon, Crow Mother (a crone figure) and two Kachinas appear. Crow Mother hands each whipper a yucca switch to strike the children across the shoulders four times. Afterward, the Kachinas whip each other, and they reveal to the children that the maskers are really their relatives and other village members who are actually playing the Kachinas. Upon penalty of great punishment, the initiates are warned never to reveal this secret.[37]

Later, the Hahai Wuhti Kachina warns the children that many old women ogres, known as Soyokos, will visit them at their homes. To each boy she gives a tiny snare for capturing birds and to each girl she gives corn to grind. With these goods the children may be able to ransom their escape from the Soyokos, who will otherwise kidnap them. Eventually, the grotesque ogresses, with disheveled feather headdresses, long snouts, and large, bulging eyes, make their appearance. Soyokos stop at each house and call out to the child, demanding that he or she admit to bad behavior. The parents counter with arguments that demonstrate the innate good of their child. During this time, the cornmeal and birds may be offered to the ogresses in an attempt to appease them. Protesting the meager food given to them, they nevertheless carry it back with them to the kiva. Upon entering, they are spellbound by the men's dance; under this condition, and given their natural clumsiness, they are immediately subdued. The men jump on the unsuspecting monsters, strip them down to their headgear, and drive them off the mesa.[38]

The chthonic monster-crone of Bali, known as Rangda, shares some qualities with the crones discussed above. She is associated with the wilds of nature, she threatens to eat children, and like the other crones, she must somehow be appeased so that her chaotic devices do not destroy the village. She has large, globular eyes, extended fangs, and a huge disheveled head of hair. Rangda, which literally means "widow," is also the name of a masquerade performed by men within the ritual play *Calonarang.*[39]

MASK 81

The witch in European stories is also associated with nature, as she lives deep within the forest. In the story of Hansel and Gretel, for example, a boy and a girl wander too far into the forest and come upon a house made of gingerbread. They enter inside and are captured by the

MEN AS WOMEN

4.12 Men in New Year's
costumes for
Silvesterklausen in
Urnäsch, Switzerland,
early 20th century.
*Courtesy Stefan
Frischknecht and Theo
Nef.*

witch. The hag cages Hansel and forces Gretel do all the chores, including some of the cooking, while the witch fattens up Hansel so that he will make a tasty feast. In many illustrations, this crone has a deeply lined face and irregular skin surfaces that include warts and other blemishes, like the Swiss masks. MASKS 76, 77

In general, most crones appear to live alone or to be widows. As such, their connection to the patriarchy has been diminished, which destabilizes their status overall. That state of social limbo makes them dangerous to the patriarchy and means that they must be ritually reckoned with, in many cases with masks.

The nineteenth-century English poet Alfred, Lord Tennyson concluded, "Woman is the lesser Man."[40] His judgment anticipates Professor Higgins's complaint, "Why can't a woman be more like a man?" Throughout the development of human society men have often objectified women and have attempted, through material culture, to define them and control them, at least in the public arena. In the social forum of the masquerade, the values and qualities that men assign to women are passed down to the next generation. One wonders how much of the male mythology is taken seriously by women. I believe that the answer to this question is twofold: women both believe and do not believe what men say about them. Women seem to observe with great discernment what the men are doing. They listen to what men say often in order to strategize cross-gender relationships and to preserve their own sense of identity unimpaired by the judgment of men. In Sisala society in northern Ghana, the woman's place is supposed to be in the home, practicing hearth skills. She may prepare foods and pottery to sell at the market, but her station is in the family compound. In reality, however, Sisala women do not conform to this male myth. They often have affairs, which their husbands will tend to ignore, if they are not completely unaware. And while women usually obey men's commands—gathering firewood or bringing home beer from the local bar or village store—Sisala women maintain a surprisingly independent life. Sisala men make judgments about women and order them around, but after the women listen and respond they go about their own business. In general, however, masquerades are powerful tools of inculcation, sending strong signals about social behavior to both men and women: in the public forum of the masquerade, the man's world persists (fig. 4.12).

Masquerades provide structure to societies. Through the narratives attached to particular performances, masking helps to invent and establish a social identity, including gender roles and expectations. Masking as women helps men, and to some extent women, define who or what females should ideally be within the community.

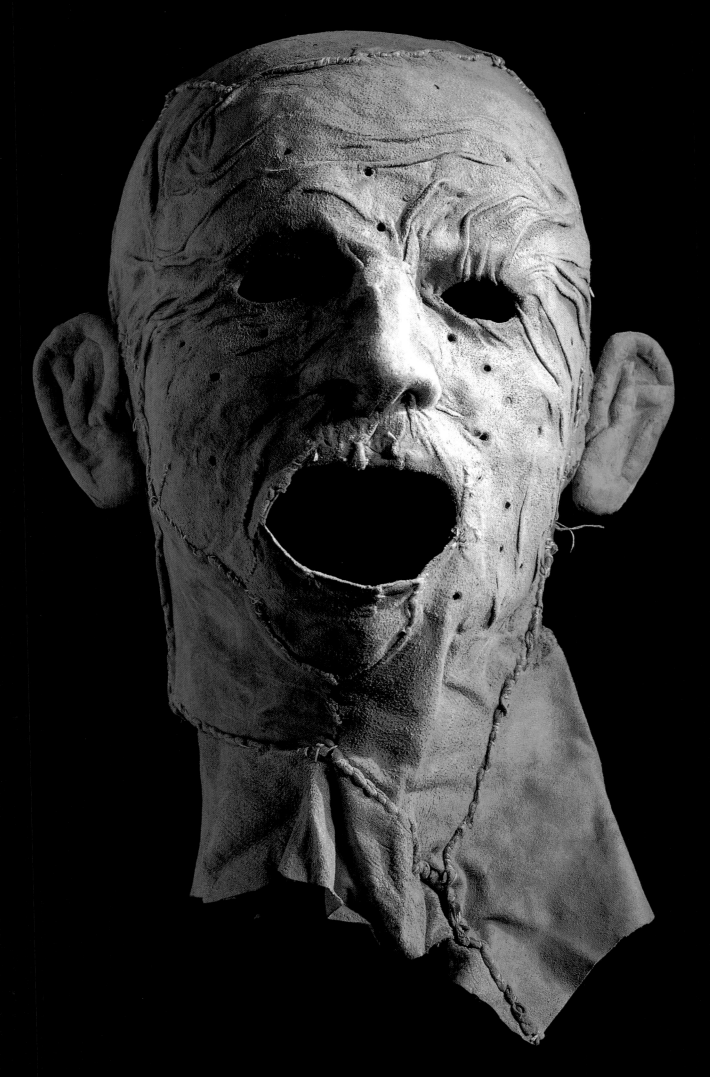

theater

MASKS 82 TO 115

MASK 84

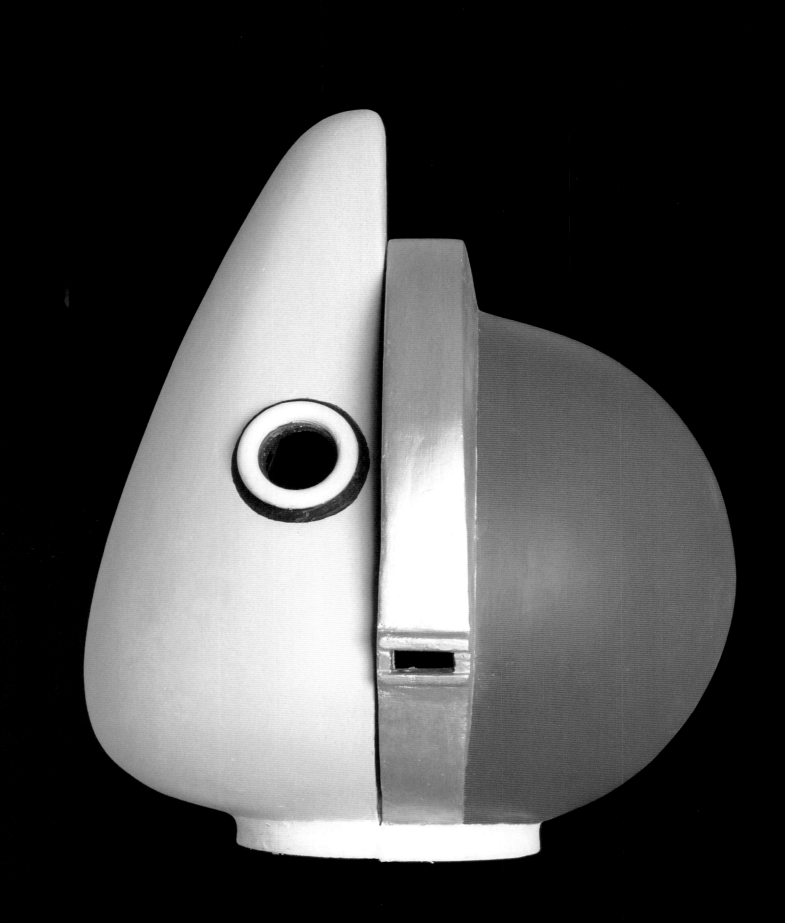

MASK 86

MASK 87

MASK 88

MASK 90

MASK 93

MASKS 96, 97

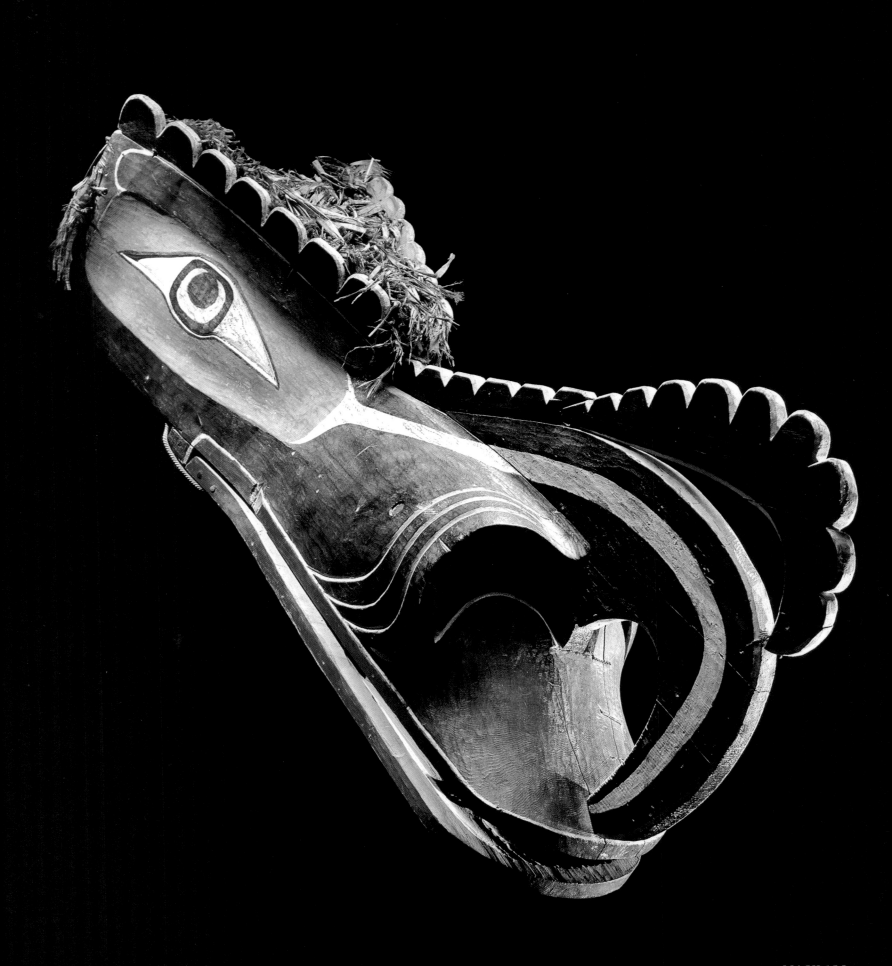

MASK 102

MASK 103

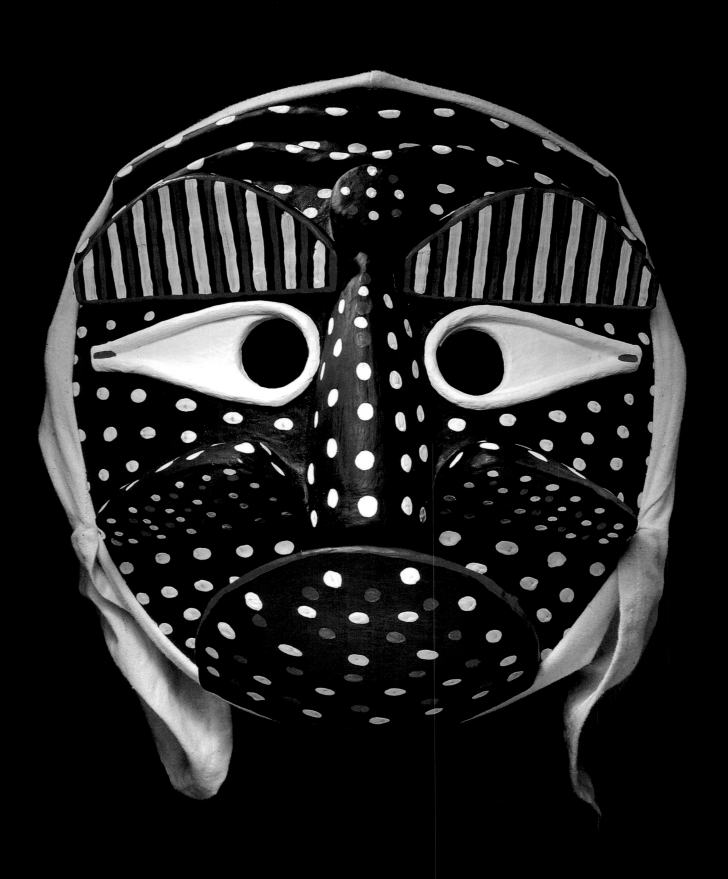

MASK 105

MASK 107

Mι

MASK 111

MASK 114

CHAPTER FIVE

Theater

The Mask in Asian Theater: Ritual and Entertainment

JOHN EMIGH

To APPRECIATE THE RICHNESS AND DIVERSITY OF MASKS in Asia, it is first necessary to comprehend the various Asian contexts and underlying traditions that have given rise to and sustained the use of the mask. To do so requires considerable effort. The performance genres of Asia, although subject to integrating influences, are maintained in many locally based traditions, each with its own history, social functions, patterns of patronage, and aesthetic constraints. Moreover, in Asian traditions of performance—with or without masks—the boundaries between the familiar binary categories of theater and ritual are particularly permeable, and the application of such distinctions can be misleading. Our use of these terms in Western discourse, and our faith in their power to discriminate, have been shaped by understandings of sacred and secular behavior deeply embedded in the religious and cultural history of Western societies, which, especially since the Renaissance and Reformation, have tended to separate "secular" from "sacred" practices along more or less clear lines. This tendency has deep historical roots. Throughout their complex and intertwined histories, the monotheistic faiths that spread outward from Asia Minor—Judaism, Christianity, and Islam—have frequently been characterized by a strong iconoclastic strain. The stronger the resultant distrust of graven images and idols, the greater the resistance to the mask and its implicit celebration of divine multivalence and epistemological ambiguity. These religions have also frequently distrusted the human body as a vehicle of celebration and have accordingly been loathe to use masked performers as instruments of revelation or conduits for divine powers—functions that underlie many Asian masking traditions.

With significant exceptions, then, the enjoyment of the body in motion and the exploration of alternative modes of consciousness—phenomena often associated with masking—have

209

come to be divorced from traditions of ecstatic worship in the West; instead, they have found expression within social (and antisocial) recreational and artistic modes of behavior. This was particularly pronounced in the post-Renaissance period, in which a positivist worldview linked to scientific inquiry further undercut the mask's power to present unseen worlds of forces and forms. The rich masking traditions of the Celtic and Greco-Roman worlds have survived principally in the contexts of Carnival and All Hallow's Eve, occasions specifically separated from and sometimes even framed in opposition to acts of worship. Where masks have persisted in Western religious contexts, they have tended to represent the devil and his minions, perverse comic anti-heroes allied with creatures from the wild during Carnival season and villains in morality plays for the rest of the year.

5.1 Chinese rock paintings in Fujian province, c. 5000 B.C. Drawing after Chen Zao Fu. *Reprinted from Michel Lorblanchet, ed.,* Rock Art in the Old World *(New Delhi: IGNCA), 1992.*

The mask as revived in the Italian commedia dell'arte and on the modern Western stage has derived its power from the ability to portray "character"; it signals a fictional self, or persona, that shadows and supplants the performer's own person. These theatrical traditions depend upon the mask's ability to provide satiric commentaries on social behavior by simplifying, amplifying, and ossifying human expression into grotesque features and stereotypical actions. Such satiric traditions are found in Asia as well. The Asian traditions, however, are more complexly related to divine pantheons and cosmologies, ancestral histories, and shamanic practices. The mask is used as a means to move among divine, human, animal, and ancestral domains, bridging separations that are otherwise thought to cause illness or social dysfunction, and revealing complexities and ambiguities in the ways in which worlds are constructed.

The variants of Hinduism and Buddhism that spread eastward from the Indian subcontinent—reinventing themselves many times over as they encountered, contained, and were transformed by local animist and shamanic traditions—have often found it useful to deploy masks in order to reveal a world of forces and forms outside of direct human control, as well as to represent and comment upon different human roles and lifestyles. Hinduism is a religion with many gods, representing disparate and sometimes contradictory aspects of a divinity which is, ultimately, beyond names and forms; Buddhism is a religion with no gods, but with multifaceted conceptions of reality. Both religions have a natural affinity to the implicit messages of multivalence and layered identity that come with masking. In these contexts (as in those of African,

Oceanic, and Native American traditions that share similar animist and shamanic roots), masks provide images of the divine, human, and chthonic domains of the cultural imagination.

Asian traditions of masked performance—in their history and in their current practice—exhibit a particularly complex interplay among secular and religious contexts, local and regional traditions, village, court, and temple patronage systems, concerns with narrative and aesthetic display, and verbal and gestural modes of communication. The result is a broad array of performative genres, and these genres include rituals that deploy multiple theatrical means, theatrical forms that retain strong traces of ritual origins, and not a few traditions that slip back and forth between "ritual" and "theater" from moment to moment and from context to context, sometimes stressing efficacy and other times entertainment. What follows is an attempt to reveal some of the complex interplay between ritual and theater in Asian masked performance, beginning with some performance genres that, while ritually based, contain striking prototheatrical elements, and moving on to consider some genres that, while seeming to be comfortably within the orbit of theatrical entertainment, still retain strong reminders of contact with sacred domains.

Early Evidence of Masks and Prototheatrical Forms

Masks both conceal and reveal, and the opportunities for mystery and play inherent in this doubled nature lend themselves to a mixing of efficacy and entertainment that is already hinted at in the Mesolithic and Upper Paleolithic cave paintings of central India, which clearly indicate the use of masks in South Asia since at least 15,000 B.C., and possibly much earlier. Dancing figures—some wearing animal masks and carrying bows and arrows, others wearing what seem to be more abstract masks—appear, for example, in the rock art of Ladi-ki-karar and Bhimbetka, providing intriguing parallels to the masked figures depicted in European caves.

Although the dating of these images remains tentative and the function of the masks highly conjectural, the zigzag lines radiating out from some of the masked figures are a possible clue to their meaning[1]: such "entoptic" patterns are commonly envisioned in trance states; they could have either been drawn while in trance or re-created afterward. Their appearance suggests shamanic dances of exorcism and renewal. To judge from the depiction of some of the masked or helmeted dancers, whose bodies are linked together and arrested in exuberant motion,[2] at least some of these dances were communal and celebratory in nature. The rock art reveals a rich and playful imaginative power focused on mask and movement and suggests performances both for human enjoyment and for establishing contact with extrahuman powers. Rock paintings in northern China from about 3000 B.C. augment this picture, depicting either masks or painted faces in ways that are startlingly like those in traditional Chinese theater (fig. 5.1).[3]

Prototheatrical forms of entertainment abound in Asian ritual practice, and many of these make use of the dual nature of the mask. Lifelike yet intrinsically static, poised between the animate and the inanimate, the quick and the dead, the mask offers a bridge between the past and the present, between all that is seen and experienced and all that is imagined or willed into existence through acts of faith or the cultural transmission of forms and values. Life-cycle events are prominent occasions for Asian masked performance, as are ceremonies of renewal: funerary rituals, initiation rites, and the rituals attending the cultivation of rice in irrigated paddies are all frequently marked by masking. As ritual specialists empowered to move among the realms of the divine, the human, and the chthonic in order to communicate with ancestors, animals, and demons, to thereby cure the sick and heal rifts in the community, shamans use masks in many Asian settings, from the frozen tundra of Siberia to the steaming rain forests of southwestern India.

Buddhist Theater and Ritual: Sri Lanka, Korea, and the Himalayas

Although very different in tone, the Sri Lankan and Korean performing traditions mix local traditions and practices with a Buddhist worldview that is skeptical of appearances, revels in paradox, and ultimately punishes evil and rewards virtue. One of the most elaborate ritual uses of masks is seen in the Sanni Yakuma curing ceremonies of Sri Lanka. This tradition (also known as Thovil), exemplifies both the strong shamanic underlay to Asian theatrical masking traditions and the fusion that makes the separation between theater and ritual so difficult in a discussion of Asian masking.

A complete performance of Sanni Yakuma lasts several days. It employs a company of ritual specialists who make use of masks, trance, showmanship, and humor. The patient is placed in an exquisitely decorated temporary enclosure of elaborately carved banana leaves, and a vision of the world as the patient experiences it—menacing and debilitating—is paraded before him or her. As many as eighteen sickness-causing demons and their leader, Maha Kola Sanniya, are summoned with music, blazing sticks of fire, and ritualized incantations. Their masks are illuminated by flashes of fire, and the bodies of the dancers are sometimes caught up in violent trance. In this way, the spirits thought to be involved in causing physical and mental distress are acknowledged and given powerful form. As the performance continues, though, the spirits evoked are put in their proper place by means of both comedic play and ritual. Their control of the patient's mind and body is eroded, and their power shown to be illusory: not only are icons of evil ritually consumed by fire, but the "spirits" are duped into receiving dummy sacrifices in place of the patient; and, eventually, the terror acknowledged by the masked display yields to clowning and laughter, as a masked "holy man" intrudes with irreverent comments and actions. The Sinhalese word for illness (*tanikama*) also signifies alienation or "aloneness"—the malignant influences over the afflicted patient's mind and body are weakened through theatrical play and reinclusion within a caring community.[4]

In the same areas of southern Sir Lanka where the Sanni Yakuma is performed, a more secular form of masked performance is enacted, sometimes by the same performers. This form of performance, known as Kolam (derived from a word in the Tamil language for "disguise" or "mask"), has historical and iconographic links to the Sanni Yakuma and other rituals of exorcism, but it functions more definitely as theater. In the myth of origin of Kolam, a pregnant queen in the prehistory of Sri Lanka became heartsick with the desire to see masked performances; the gods obliged by providing a set of masks hanging from the trees in the palace courtyard, and the queen's mood improved greatly as fanciful narratives were given theatrical life. This more secular theater, then, is considered a gift of the gods, and its ability to engage and entertain is linked by legend to the well-being of the community (or at least the denizens of the palace). Despite these associations, though, Kolam has moved some distance from the shamanic functions of the Sanni Yakuma. After an elaborate ritual beginning, songs recount the histories of the entering characters, and dances by those characters are followed by sections of dramatic dialogue. Masked demonic figures, some of whom also appear in rituals of exorcism, are brought into the orbit of narrative play through engaging story lines that invoke royal families, commoners, animals, and demonic enemies, all set in an ancient, fictionalized version of Sri Lanka's past.[5]

A complex web of connections among rites of exorcism, agricultural cycles, and theatrical play, as well as links between court and village traditions, are similarly significant in the history of T'al Chum, a generic term for Korean masked drama. *T'al* means "disease" as well as "mask," and the shamanic links to Korean village theater are strong, often combining with elements derived from the Chinese-influenced traditions of the Korean courts. Here, though, the narrative emphasis is not on gods, demons, or royal personages, but on social behavior. The central themes involve abuses of power by aristocracy and clergy, familial tensions, and the plight of the poor.[6]

The Pyolsin-kut ritual theater of Hahae village, dating back to the eleventh or twelfth century, combines satiric entertainment with exorcistic elements and invocations for fertility. The nine extraordinary wooden masks extant from this ongoing tradition present comic types while maintaining a deep sense of humanity. The originals, carved from alder wood by a man known as Hur, are now housed in the National Museum Collection in Seoul and have been designated national treasures by the Korean government. As the word *kut* ("shamanic séance or ceremony") indicates, the masked drama in Hahae originally had an exorcistic function and served to encourage good crops, as well as to entertain. Until 1928 these exorcistic comic performances, using the original masks, were held at Hahae every ten years or on the advice of an oracle as part of fifteen days of ritual activities. The dance drama is now performed frequently for tourists, for village pride, and at regional festivals.

The issue of fertility lies at the core of the occasion, and thus the spare dialogue and slapstick comedy appropriately center on sexual matters. The characters span the ranks of Korean society, offering a satiric community portrait: a plain village bride, a flirtatious young courtesan, a crotchety old woman, a venal landowner, a lascivious monk, an idle scholar, a crude butcher, and two unreliable servants. Several of the masks are made so that the expression can vary markedly by changing the angle of the attached jaw (a string is attached to the movable jaw and held in the mouth) or by tilting the angle of the mask to the viewer. The resulting depiction of humankind is thus both humorous and complex, revealing contradictions in character. The tricky servants, overreaching old men, and flirtatious young women are reminiscent of the characters and situations of the Italian commedia dell'arte (which may itself have drawn upon Persian and Turkish popular comedy, as well as the remnants of Greco-Roman farcical traditions, for inspiration), but here the antics are linked to pleasing a local deity who died a virgin and to a system of justice based on Buddhist values.

More abstract masks from Yangju, Songp'a, and Pongsan are used in regional variations of satiric folk plays enacted by farmers and inspired by touring Sandae-dogam players of the seventeenth century. Although related in theme and satiric intent to such earlier forms as the Hahae Pyolsin-kut, the Sandae-dogam plays developed along regional lines after troupes of palace entertainers housed at Seoul were disbanded in 1634 and the performers returned to their native homes in the provinces. The style of these masked dance dramas is even more broadly comic, the masks highly caricatured, and the depiction of human hypocrisy, pretentiousness, corruption, and greed pointedly satiric. These are primarily entertainments, yet ritual elements pervade the tradition. Mythical lions, associated with renewal throughout East Asia (compare the Shi-shi in Japan, the New Year's lion in China, and the Barong Ket in Bali), frequently appear to chastise apostate monks. The gourd and papier-mâché masks are often ceremonially burned after traditional performances, which are still loosely linked to religious holidays and the agricultural cycle.

MASKS 104, 105

Yangju, a small town to the north of Seoul, was a thriving market center in the seventeenth and eighteenth centuries. It is home to one of the regional variants of Sandae-dogam mask dances that developed during that time. Performances of Pyolsandae by farmers and low-ranking officials of Yangju date back at least 200 years. The plays are traditionally performed as part of the celebration of Buddha's birthday, the May festival, and the Autumn festival, and during droughts. These events are supported by the village at large and performed amid feasting and drinking. With their broadly satiric portrayals of rich landlords, apostate monks, lustful old men, and wayward women, the plays have served well as a vehicle of protest against figures of authority and moral hypocrisy. Although less ritually centered than earlier forms, connections with agricultural cycles and with exorcism persist: red-faced masks represent the summer and black-faced masks the winter; in this sense, the plays still celebrate summer's fecundity and mock winter's cold authority (fig. 5.2).

Buddhism as practiced in Central Asia has also been receptive to masked play that doubles as theater and ritual. Here, the faith has adapted a quintessentially theatrical sense of the cosmic struggle between good and evil and has generated a vast array of exemplary enlightened beings (Bodhisattvas) who return to earth in various guises to help counter the deceptive allure of wrongdoing and hasten the enlightenment of the faithful.

Following the Himalayan range from Ladakh in India, through Nepal, Bhutan, Tibet, and then westward all the way through Mongolia into Siberia, one finds variations on a common mask tradition: the Tsam. This pan-Himalayan tradition is based upon a fusion of the ancient regional Bon-po religion of shamanic practices and animism with a strand of Tantric Buddhism, which developed through the efforts of the remarkable Buddhist monk Padmasambhava in the early ninth century A.D. and was carried into the outer reaches of Mongolia by the early nineteenth century. Variants of the highly theatrical Tsam ceremony are found throughout this region and have provided rich arenas for masking. With the loosening of winter's grip on the region, seasonal performances by the lamas of Buddhist monasteries feature Padmasambhava in his various moods; horrific masks of Yama, the Hindu god of Death, and of his deathly (and frequently comic) cohorts; ferocious Bodhisattvas and local deities with the power to conquer or contain the forces of death and disease; an impressive array of animal helpers; and comic old monks. The performances bring together the lamas and the laity in a celebration of faith, while the masks both embody and serve as a means to transcend projections of fear, hatred, anger, desire, and the ultimate illusion, death.[7]

5.2 Corrupted Monk, a character in the Korean drama of Pyolsandae in Yangju, wears a scarred mask to reflect his disease-ravaged skin and the state of his corrupted soul. *Courtesy Young-eun Kim.*

Hindu Theater and Ritual: India and Bali

Hindu religious practice and mythology, characterized by an acceptance of multiple truths, a love of paradox, and a worship of diverse and sometimes contradictory aspects of the divine, have also often deployed masks as a way of giving form to godly and chthonic forces. As Wendy Doniger has noted, "By refusing to modify its component elements in order to force them into a synthesis, Indian mythology celebrates the idea that the universe is boundlessly various, that everything occurs simultaneously, that all possibilities may exist without excluding each other . . . [that] untrammeled variety and contradiction are ethically and metaphysically necessary."[8] The use of theatrical masks, imbued as they are with a sense of paradox and duality, would seem an ideal complement to this worldview and its pantheon of gods and goddesses and proliferation of narratives. It is worth noting, however, that masking in India usually takes place in areas where Hindu mythology has both subsumed and accommodated to local animist and shamanic religious practices already rooted in masking.

Masks of various materials—gourds, wood, cloth, leaves, clay, and papier-mâché—are still used by the Dravidian and Mundari peoples, who have been living in India since before the arrival of Aryans and their gods more than 3,500 years ago. As these local traditions interacted with variants of the pan-Indian Hindu tradition, masks and masked performances became both significant sites and powerful agents in complex processes of integration and adaptation. Many of these earlier animist and shamanic traditions were based on nature-goddess worship, and these goddesses were subsumed into Hindu mythology and practice. Perhaps as a result, the more active, vengeful, and dangerous aspects of divine power are generally represented as feminine in Hindu iconography and narrative, and masks representing these dangerous but very necessary "feminine" energies have been important to Hindu ritual and theater. While many such goddess figures—some more benign, others more ferocious—are recognized by Hindu peoples, they are all considered aspects of Shakti, a term that refers both to Shiva's consort in mythology and to a more abstract notion of divine power in female form. Drawing upon regional traditions as well as the vast repertoire of the Puranas (ancient narratives that tell stories of the gods and goddesses), the use of these Shakti masks is widespread throughout the subcontinent.

5.3 The Gambhira mask performance of Jhantakali in West Bengal, India, 1983. *Courtesy John Emigh.*

Entertainment and efficacy are often intertwined in the use of these masks. The Charkhelaini Chandi mask used by the Rabha people in the jungle-covered hills of Jalpaiguri in the Indian state of West Bengal, for example, is considered to be a powerful container of Shakti's energy. It is treated with great respect during its preparation and is ritually cut into pieces and thrown into the river after the performance, both to enhance the singularity of the occasion and to protect the villagers from the mask's residual power. In performance, the mask is worn by a male dancer considered capable of containing its fearsome energy; the containment and harnessing of this energy for the good of the community is a serious business. Yet, in the midst of the performance, a dancer with the wooden mask of an old man frolics comically with the dangerous Chandi to the delight of the village audience. The prototheatrical encounter of the foolish old man with the spirit of Chandi both entertains and, because of his foolishness, ironically underscores the danger and ritual significance of the deity.

The interaction of the Hindu tradition of Shakti masks with local traditions of goddess worship seems to have been particularly volatile and productive between the seventh and the tenth centuries A.D., as Tantric Saivism (a strand of Hinduism focused on the worship of Shiva and Shakti) rivaled and eventually eclipsed Buddhism in India. An old and well-preserved form of Shakti masked dance that may well date from this period is seen in Gambhira, now limited to the Malda region of West Bengal. The name *Gambhira* is thought to derive from an old term for the inner sanctum of a Saivite temple, and its dances are traditionally part of a series of ceremonies honoring Shiva and Shakti that are performed in the four days leading up to the spring festival of Chaitra Parva, which follows a busy period of agricultural labor. The oldest items in the repertoire are solo dances, performed by men in masks, representing and invoking various aspects of Shakti. These dances are extremely energetic and are marked by rapid shifts of weight, sudden drops to the knees, and the flailing of arms and pointing of fingers.

The masks used for these Shakti dances are thought to provide a conduit for visitation, as the energy and spirit of the represented goddess take over the dancer's consciousness. The possession of the dancer by an aspect of Shakti is facilitated by the driving rhythms of the drum and cymbals, and the possession of the performer provides a model for the erasure of the duality between the worshiper and the worshiped, the individual and the cosmos. The performance also serves a shamanic function; dancers have been employed to ward off smallpox and cholera, as well as the effects of black magic, and some Gambhira performers have traveled as far as Delhi to partake in healing ceremonies (fig. 5.3). Gambhira performances, though, also constitute occasions for entertainment, and the terrifying signature mask of Narasimhi provokes gales of laughter when it points to the children in the audience.[9]

By the second century A.D., and especially between the seventh and tenth centuries, Southeast Asia came under the profound influence of Indic civilizations. Buddhism and Saivism came to the Indonesian archipelago with missionaries, traders, and settlers arriving from eastern India and Buddhist scholars and traders from China. These faiths were fused, adapted, and reshaped to local needs and desires. The zoomorphic masks and costumes used in exorcisms in Java, Bali, and Kalimantan are cousins to the snapping dragons and lions of China, Korea, and Japan, as well as festive animals used in the hills of eastern India. The Kirtimukha and Murti traditions of horrific protectors in Indian temple art found receptive homes throughout Southeast Asia, and, under their influence, the Shakti tradition was reworked in the apotropaic figure of Rangda (a figure associated with Kali and Durga, both aspects of Shakti), used in Bali for exorcistic ritual performances and grafted onto narratives such as *Calonarang*—a story that deals with the suppression and containment of black magic (fig. 5.4).

5.4 Rangda character in a Barong dance drama, Bali. *Courtesy John Emigh.*

MASK 81

Several of these masks and costumes in the forms of animals, called Barong, are worn by two men and used in Balinese exorcistic rituals and celebrations of renewal. The most famous and popular of these is the Barong Ket: a mythical lion-dragon with a beard of human hair, who has been won over from the chthonic world to serve as a protector of humankind. In Balinese temples of the dead and at many temple ceremonies, the Barong is housed together with Rangda and her equally fierce-looking daughter, Rarung. These three figures are complementary and are worshiped together as protectors of the village. In performances, however, the Barong Ket is frequently pitted against Rangda and her daughter in a strategy that serves to empower all three masks. The narrative most frequently used for this purpose is that of *Calonarang*, in which the Widow Witch of Girah (played by Rangda) lays siege to the Balinese

5.5 Ganesha, the
elephant-headed god of
propitious beginnings,
dancing in a Purulia
Chho performance, India.
Courtesy John Emigh.

countryside, accompanied by young women who have been turned into terrifying demons (*leyak*). The performer (always a man) playing Rangda enters into a deep trance and, as Rangda, is able not only to withstand the stabbing of the king's men but also to place the villagers in a trance state that both enrages them and protects them from harm. In this state they frantically attempt to stab themselves and, sometimes, each other with serpentine swords known as *keris*. Although she seems to represent evil, Rangda's appearances are in fact designed to lessen the power of those in the audience who may practice black magic, as she challenges them to pit their skills against "hers." In the process, *Calonarang* provides thrilling theater, in addition to a ritual of protection, containment, and reconciliation.

While some performances of *Calonarang* use minimal dialogue and stress the confrontation of Rangda and the Barong and its ritual significance, others employ an elaborate text and also introduce improvised comic scenes. Conceptually, the tradition slips and slides along a ritual–theater continuum, and in a given performance, ritual may first seem to yield to theatrical storytelling and diversion and then, with the emergence of the entranced Rangda performer, overwhelm the theatrical elements altogether. To make matters even more complex, the theatrical appeal of these figures is sometimes deployed in more purely secular contexts. Although *Calonarang* troupes still perform in Bali for exorcistic purposes, nonconsecrated masks are often used in "Barong and Keris Shows" performed for tourists, in which the trance is usually feigned.[10]

Not all Hindu performances involve trance, real or feigned, nor does mythology and its offshoots provide the only narratives. Alongside local, ritually based performances, India maintained an active tradition of theater performed in Sanskrit and regional languages (*prakrits*) under court patronage throughout the first millennium A.D. The tradition is described in the *Natyasastra*, a lengthy treatise on theatrical arts written sometime between 400 B.C. and A.D. 200. The theater drew upon dramatic elements in Vedic rituals, as well as traditions of epic storytelling, devotional dance, and mimetic play. Designated as a gift of the gods for the enjoyment and instruction of humankind in troubled times, the theater (*natya*) takes shape both through a highly embellished presentation of the voice and body through song and dance (*natyadharmi*) and through mimetic representations and dialogue adhering more closely to the daily use of the body in the social intercourse (*lokadharmi*). Although preceded by an elaborate ritual paying homage to the gods, only some of the plays involved religious myth; others were based on quasi-historical events, and still others were set in the contemporary world. As in so many theatrical traditions, music was essential to the performances. Both narrative and dramatic modes of speech were included, interspersed with sequences of pure dance, and comic commentators interacted with the principal dramatic characters. All of these features have had a lasting impact on masked as well as unmasked theatrical traditions throughout Asia, such as the Topeng theater of Bali and the Noh theater of Japan, to be discussed below. Unlike the Greek classical theater, the pan-Indian Sanskrit theatrical tradition only used masks selectively, usually to represent gods, animals, and demons.

As regional languages came into prominence, the pan-Indian theater yielded to a host of regional forms, many with closer ties to devotional practice. The selective use of masks that marked the Sanskrit theater found its way into many of these traditions, while others instead made elaborate use of highly stylized makeup, creating the effect of a "pliant mask." Of particular note among those regional forms of theater making selective use of masks are those based upon the story of Narasimha, the man-lion avatar of the god Vishnu. In cultures as widely separated as ancient Egypt and the Northwest Coast of America, masks have proved particularly apt in portraying beings that feature the head of an animal on the body of a man. An elephant-headed human figure is evident in a 1000 B.C. Indian rock painting, and the elephant-headed Ganesha is to this day similarly portrayed; as the god of propitious beginnings, Ganesha is summoned at the start of many devotional plays (fig. 5.5). With the head of a lion, the body of a man, and the power of a god, Narasimha is within this tradition. Many devotional forms of theater throughout India depict his emergence from a pillar to defeat the world-conquering demon Hiranyakashipu and to save the demon's devout son Prahlada.

The Bhagavata Mela of the Indian state of Tamil Nadu and the Prahlada Nataka of the state of Orissa are two theatrical performances that feature the story of Prahlada's faith, his rebellion against his demon father, and Narasimha's vengeance on Hiranyakashipu. Bhagavata Mela is performed once a year, on Narasimha's name day, by males of certain Brahmin families in the village of Melattur, in Tamil Nadu. The performers gather from wherever they are employed—often from other countries—to perform the drama as an act of devotion and of ritual obliga-

5.6 The mask of
Narasimha honored in
the temple of
Hugulapata village,
Ganjam, in Orissa, India.
Courtesy John Emigh.

tion. The genre employs a rich range of South Indian classical music and draws upon the highly refined and codified Bharatnatyam dance techniques of Tamil Nadu.[11] The Orissan Prahlada
Nataka has moved from palace to town to village over the past 100 years; now over fifty troupes
drawn from all castes perform on temple-sponsored occasions that extend throughout the
night, pitting one troupe against another in more or less simultaneous performances that can
last as long as twenty hours. Elements of South Indian classical music are mixed with folk traditions, and the performances feature extraordinary acrobatic displays as Hiranyakashipu and
Prahlada whirl up and down a makeshift set of "royal" stairs.

The popularity of the form grew during resistance to British rule, and the drama came to take
on new uses and significance: as a protest against the usurpation and misuse of political power,
a nightmare vision of family dynamics gone awry, a chance to demonstrate devotion and theatrical skill, a parable that teaches endurance through faith, a cathartic display of rage, and a
source of entertainment and laughter. While the dialogue, spectacle, jokes, songs, and dances are
all highly theatrical, the play culminates with the entrance of a performer-priest who wears a
ferocious mask and is possessed by the spirit of Narasimha (fig. 5.6). The theater has in this case
provided an elaborate platform for the staging of a ritual act of devotion; but it may also be said
that the traditions borne by that devotion have given rise to a remarkable form of theater.[12]

Complex relationships among mythological narratives, social circumstances, and theatrical
displays are also evident in the masked variants of Chhau and Chho dances in southern Bihar and
West Bengal in India. Growing out of tributes to the power of Shakti and associated with exorcistic practices performed at the Chaitra Parva festival, these related but very distinct traditions
have developed over the past 200 years under very different systems of patronage to include the
enactments of other tales. The Chho dances of the Purulia District of West Bengal are support-

ed by funds collected from village households. The defeat of the demon Mahishasura by Durga (an aspect of Shakti particularly popular in Bengal) is still a staple in the repertoire, but this repertoire has expanded to include other tales about Hindu gods and martial stories from the Hindu epics *Mahabharata* and *Ramayana*. Often, even in small villages, there is an active competition among "teams," sometimes supported by rival political parties.

The dry and barren land of the Purulia District is difficult to farm, and the people living there have had little power in the hierarchical systems of Indian society. Particularly important to the repertoire, then, are stories that deal with the struggles of the underdog and reversals of power, as when the powerful god Shiva comes to earth in the guise of Kirata, a "tribal" hunter, and bests the hero Arjuna in battle, or when Abimanju, Arjuna's young son, dies a hero's death while fighting the Kurava warriors against overwhelming odds. The papier-and-cloth-mâché masks are modeled so as to boldly display aspects of character and are adorned with glittering bits of tinsel, feathers, and other colorful materials. The dances are vigorous, even athletic, featuring drops to the knees, spins, and backflips, and it is not uncommon to find groups of young boys mimicking these movements in play.[13]

MASK 106

5.7 **Prince Suddhendra Singh Deo of Seraikella on tour in 1937.** *Courtesy Kedar Nath Sahoo.*

In nearby Seraikella, now in southern Bihar, the related Chhau tradition of ritual and theatrical performances has been fostered under palace patronage. Here, the movements used are based on the martial art of swordplay, Parikhanda, that was previously used by the palace-trained militia. While rituals addressing the power of Shakti still frame the performances in April, and the theatrical repertoire still includes martial episodes from the *Ramayana* and *Mahabharata,* other narratives were introduced in the 1930s under the active patronage of the Singh Deo royal family, who formed a palace troupe that toured Europe in 1937 to great acclaim (fig 5.7). The new repertoire included dances based on such metaphysical themes as the dance between moon and night, the struggles of a boatman and his wife ferrying across life's difficult waters, or the fragility of a butterfly. From 1933 on, the masks, as well as the movements, became far more delicate and subtle under the expert hand of master mask maker P. K. Mahapatra. The delicacy and vulnerability of Chandrabhaga, a young maiden (danced by a man) who worships the moon and is driven to suicide by the lustful attentions of Surya, the sun god, contrast strangely with the aggressive "feminine" power of the Shakti rites that frame its enactment.[14]

5.8 A menacing ten-headed Ravana character in a Ramlila performance, Orissa, India. *Courtesy John Emigh.*

Mask and Myth: The *Ramayana*

The Indian epic of the *Ramayana* has been especially receptive to the use of masks. The story concerns the birth of Rama as a human avatar of the god Vishnu, his unjust expulsion into the forest, the kidnapping of his wife Sita by the demon Ravana, and the rescue of Sita through Rama's alliance with a monkey kingdom and the friendship of other animals. Possibly based on a historic incident, the epic was first given written form by Valmiki sometime between 200 B.C. and A.D. 200; it has been retold, rewritten, and restaged innumerable times, with varying treatments of the complex moral issues confronted by its characters, and still serves as a touchstone for moral and political debate in India. Often, as in Sanskrit theater practice, the deployment of masks in theatrical versions is confined to the animal and demonic characters in the epic. Thus, the ten-headed Ravana and his demonic family and followers, as well as Rama's monkey army led by Sugriva and Hanuman and the giant Garuda bird Jatayu, are frequently portrayed with masks (figs. 5.8, 5.9). The Indian masks range from the relatively simple papier-mâché helmet masks of Desia Nata in the Koraput region of Orissa to the elaborately decorated cloth-and-metal masks used in Ramnagar, near Varanasi.[15]

Performances based on the *Ramayana* are by no means confined to India; the story has been a significant carrier of South Asian traditions and values into Southeast Asia and has provided the basis for numerous traditions of masked theater. By A.D. 850 in Java and A.D. 882 in Bali, roving companies of masked players were described in administrative records; of particular note are the traditions of performance that evolved around the *Ramayana*. Based on Javanese adaptations of Indian Sanskrit texts, dramatized versions of the epic were developed side by side with shadow plays and temple friezes on the subject in both Java and Bali. The resultant genres retain traces of these influences in their stylistic constraints and in the concept of theater as a form of *wayang*, a "shadow" of the mythic world. The Balinese Wayang Wong, derived   MASK 108 from a tradition of East Java, is a particularly rich version of the *Ramayana*, featuring scores of demons and monkeys and vivid scenes of battle. Although now rare, whole sets of Wayang Wong masks—with over fifty masks in each set—are still found in a few villages in Bali. Wayang Wong performances are today especially associated with the holidays of remembrance and renewal, Guningan and Kuningan, which lay particular emphasis on cultural heritage and are celebrated every 210 days in the Balinese calendar.[16]

5.9 The character Hanuman, commander of the monkey host, in a Wayang Wong performance, Bali, 1998. *Courtesy Tom Ballinger.*

Masked dances depicting events of the *Ramayana* also developed in mainland Southeast Asia, adapting influences that were arriving both directly from India and indirectly from Java. Masked forms of the *Ramayana*, known as the *Ramakien* in Thailand and the *Reamker* in Cambodia, developed between the ninth and fifteenth centuries in Cambodia, thriving even after Theraveda Buddhism became the dominant religion in the thirteenth century. In 1431 Thailand conquered the Cambodian capital of Angkor, and performers were brought to the Thai court, leading to the development there of the Lakon Khon masked dance drama. The culture of the victors was shaped in the image of the vanquished, and, since then, the Cambodian and Thai traditions have developed along parallel lines, with Thai practices also having a powerful impact on Cambodia.

Over 100 elaborately decorated helmet masks of   MASK 107 gods, heroes, monkeys, and demons appear in these dance dramas. The narration is provided by separate performers, allowing the dancers more freedom of movement. Contacts with European colonial powers and the cosmopolitan life of modern Bangkok have also had their affect on Khon. Originally performed outdoors, Khon performances in Thailand now take place on a proscenium stage, with scenery inspired in part by Western practice. Thus, it continues to be a dynamic form capable of absorbing new influences, even as it remains a testament to the enduring legacy of the past.[17]

Masks of the Human Face in Indonesia

Masks representing human characters are rare in traditional South Asian practice, although the related Chho and Chhau traditions of northeastern India are important exceptions. This is not true, however, of the masked theaters of Indonesia, which have a long and deep tradition of honoring ancestors through masks and puppets. The Balinese tradition of Topeng draws upon this heritage and uses half masks as well as full masks to comment reflexively, and often comically, on the relation of the past to the present and of the present to the past. The resulting theatrical presentations delight in virtuosic character creation along a continuum of refined (*halus*), strong (*keras*), and crude (*kasar*) presentations of human behavior (fig. 5.10). The present tradition of Topeng dance drama in Bali seems to date back to the seventeenth century, when I Gusti Ngurah Jelantik Tusan is reported to have used masks taken from East Java by his ancestor a century earlier.

MASK 111

Developed through an active interchange between court patronage and village participation, the mask makers and masked dancers of Topeng are drawn from all of Bali's four traditional caste divisions. Although the tales used in the repertoire range chronologically from the defeat of the demon ruler Mayadanawa by the gods under Indra to the mass death by suicide of the court at Denpasar when faced by the guns of the invading Dutch colonial army in 1906, most Topeng stories are drawn from the *Babad Dalem*, or "Chronicles of the Kings," which detail the struggles of the Majapahit Empire (which came to include Bali in 1343) and the troubled history of the later Balinese principalities as they vied with each other for dominance.

In the oldest form of Balinese Topeng (Topeng Pajegan), one man portrays all of the characters—alternating full masks used for dancing with half masks that allow for improvised storytelling and commentary. This one-man format is exemplary of the Upanishadic principle of *Tat Twam Asi* ("Thou Art That"), which holds that the microcosmos of the individual contains all that exists within the macrocosmos—a principle still important in the beliefs and practices of Balinese Hinduism. Thus, the elegant king, the strong warrior, the demonic adversary, and the eccentric fool are all aspects of the self revealed through the medium of performance. Topeng Pajegan is commonly presented at temple anniversaries (*odalan*) and at Balinese life-cycle events, such as tooth filings, marriages, and cremation ceremonies. The more sacred performances end with a public offering of a bowl with flowers, food, incense, thread, and old Chinese coins prepared and blessed with holy water by a priest for the

5.10 Gusti Pande, a crude and comic villain, dances in a Topeng performance, Bali, 1930s. *Courtesy Beryl de Zoete.*

benefit of the family or village and presented by the performer in the mask of the character Sidha Karya ("He Who Makes the Ceremony Complete").

Around the turn of the twentieth century, it became more common to present Topeng with troupes of players, allowing characters to interact more immediately with each other. That change encouraged comic byplay among the performers, as well as more theatrical depictions of battles and dramatic confrontations. Although they may also be presented as entertainment for men and gods at temple festivals, these company forms of Topeng (Topeng Panca and Prembon) are considered less sacred and do not involve the appearance of Sidha Karya or a public ritual blessing at their conclusion. After a series of introductory dances featuring proud warriors and befuddled old courtiers, the story of a Topeng performance is introduced, framed, and commented upon by servant characters (Penasar), who improvise Kawi (Old Javanese) dialogue for the principal characters and translate the meaning and import of that dialogue to the audience in contemporary Balinese. The main characters appear in masks that cover almost the entire face of the dancer-actor, while the masks of the commentators fit the face in such a way as to allow free movement of the lower jaw. Near the end of the story, a series of comic *bondres* masks emerge. These eccentric, humorous masks can be highly individual: every performer has a small stock of them, and the performers have often helped in their design. Like the Penasar masks, these are cut so as to allow free movement of the lower jaw or are otherwise designed for easier speaking. Although the demand for masks by tourists has encouraged shortcuts in carving and the use of acrylic paints, most of the masks used for performance are still colored with pigments painstakingly ground from bone, roots, and other natural sources by the mask maker or his apprentices and then applied in multiple coats, involving sanding and repainting as many as fifty times.[18]

5.11 Topeng Babakan dancer as Panji in Cirebon, Indonesia. *Courtesy Museum voor Volkenkunde, Rotterdam.*

Rivaling the importance of the Indic epics in Southeast Asia are the romantic *Tales of Panji*, which portray characters and situations drawn from stories about the legendary Javanese Hindu prince Panji and his search for his lost love, Candra Kirana. As in Balinese Topeng, the characters in the several local variants of this narrative present a continuum of human behavior, from the extremely refined Panji to the lustful and crude Klana, his ogrelike jealous rival. Central Java, East Java, Sunda, Madura, and the Cirebon region at the northeastern edge of West Java all have distinctive styles of masked dance drama that revolve around the *Tales of Panji*. Although these regions have been Islamic since the fifteenth century, the masks hearken back to earlier times in Java's many layers of cultural history, and the dramas have frequently come under active court patronage.

The Cirebon region, which had a central role in the spread of Islam in Java, has a particularly active Panji-cycle tradition, known as Topeng Babakan. The masks of this tradition are

MASK 110

especially elegant in their painting and carving. Long solo dances alternate with dramatic incidents in performances lasting as long as eight hours and held most frequently at circumcisions, weddings, and funerary ceremonies. It is customary for the performer to dance first without the mask, only placing the mask in front of the face and biting onto a leather thong to hold it in place once the character has been established and entered into the body of the dancer. Both men and women dance in this tradition, and women frequently perform both strong and refined male roles (fig. 5.11). This is a rare instance of traditional performance in which women mask as men.[19]

Human Masks in East Asian Theater

Topeng and Topeng Babakan deal primarily with local history, not religious mythology; they relate the tales of men, not gods. This ability to use masked theater—with still-evident links to ancestor worship—as a means of representing and reflecting upon the past is also exemplified in some little-known but theatrically fascinating forms of Chinese theater. Although supplanted by elaborate makeup in the better-known Beijing Opera, masks are still used in China in the regional ritual-theater forms (Nuoxi and Dixi) of Guizhou and Kweichow provinces. Most impressive among these variants is the "Earth Opera" of Anshun, which uses hundreds of masks in elaborate processions to reenact episodes in a folk history of China, from about 1000 B.C. to the mid-fifteenth century. The narratives of these folk "operas" center around highly romantic tales of martial deeds, but the performances are staged to coincide with the rice crop's flowering. The agricultural context, along with specific rituals attending these outdoor performances, serves to imbue the ceremonial opening of the box of masks at the start of a performance with an aura of sacred significance. After bowing to the four directions (strengthening the bond between history and geography), masked actors representing famous warriors of the past are joined by a diverse cast of hermits, barbarian soldiers, old ladies, clowns, earth gods, and various animals (fig. 5.12).[20]

5.12 Dancing hero from Anshun Earth Opera, Guizhou, China. *Reprinted from Fu Shin Shen,* The Masks of Anshun's Earth Operas *(Taipei: Shu Hsing Publishing),* 1994.

Forays across the permeable boundaries between folk, festival, and ritual performances on the one hand, and court-sponsored theatrical entertainments on the other, are central to the remarkably rich history of East Asian forms of masked theater. From the seventh to the tenth century A.D., the Tang Dynasty court of China became a venue for performers traveling over the silk routes from Tibet, Manchuria, India, Indochina, Indonesia, Iran, and the Mediterranean provinces of the fallen Roman Empire. One result of this theatrical eclecticism was a highly syncretic form of masked dance drama that spread first to Korea and then to Japan, where it took the name of Gigaku. The dramatis personae included

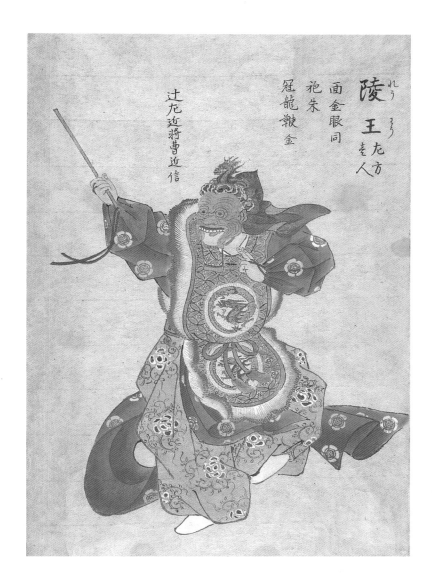

陵
王
左
壱
人
左
方

辻
㢠
近
将
曹
近
信

面
金
眼
同
袍
朱
冠
龍
鞁
金

5.13 Ryōō the dragon king, depicted in *Record of a Bugaku Performance at Nikkō in the 4th month, 1815. Courtesy The British Museum.*

Brahmin and Buddhist priests, drunken revelers from central Asia and Iran, a beautiful woman and comic old men, the mythical Garuda bird from India, and the magnificent Shi-shi—yet another variant of the mythical lion-dragon that has taken many forms throughout southeastern and eastern Asia, encountered both in the theater and in festivals of exorcism and renewal, symbolically chasing away malingering forces clinging to the old year.[21]

Influenced by Chinese and Korean models, masks of the more refined and stately Bugaku supplanted Gigaku in the imperial palace of Japan between the ninth and twelfth centuries. Bugaku masks range in appearance from the sublime to the humorous to the demonic.[22] Danced in foursomes reminiscent of the Chinese custom of honoring the cardinal directions, some of the later Bugaku masks have detached or hinged jaws in the manner of the Hahae Pyolsin-kut masks of Korea mentioned above (fig. 5.13). Over the same period of time that Bugaku was becoming more and more refined in the imperial court, rural forms were also incorporating masks: Kagura, a Shinto form of ritual entertainment focused on the power exercised by the dead in the world of the living; Sarugaku, an acrobatic form of comic theater based on Chinese and Korean models; and Dengaku, a tradition of "field play" blending aspects found

227

in rural dramas of Korea and China. All three provided elements that were drawn together in the late fourteenth century by the master performer and playwright Kan'ami and his son Zeami, who subsequently received the active patronage of the young shogun, Yoshimitsu. The mask of Okina, dating back to the twelfth century and frequently worn in the opening segment in Noh performances, has traces of this complex history.

The tradition that Kan'ami and Zeami created and further developed in Yoshimitsu's court brought masked portrayal to a new level of subtlety and artistic accomplishment. Zeami, especially, is credited with adding a focused concern with Zen Buddhism and a stately decorum to his rural ritual and theatrical precedents. Through a unique blend of movement, stillness, music, and poetry, Zeami was able to create a delicate balance between the mimetic portrayal of character (*monomane*) and a quality of transcendent grace and beauty (*yugen*).

MASKS 112, 113, 115

The stories of Noh theater, like those of Topeng in Indonesia and the Anshun Earth Opera in China, deal with human history, but often with a far more personal and intimate focus. Typically, the stories involve an encounter that reveals an unresolved issue in the past. Masks are usually worn only by the principal actor (*shite*), who unfolds these personal histories with the support of a chorus who sings and chants poetry famous for its complexity and beauty. Frequently, the *shite* wears two masks in sequence, the second of which reveals a long-suppressed secret buried in the past that is crucial to an understanding of the story (fig. 5.14). Although performances are usually shortened now, originally five Noh plays would be performed in sequence. In order, these would be a stately play presenting a god, a play focused on the deeds of a warrior, a "wig" play centered on a beautiful woman, a "miscellaneous" play based on contemporary events or incidents of madness, and a play about demons or other supernatural beings. These plays, revolving

MASK 114

around the lingering ghosts of past events, would alternate with comedic Kyōgen plays based on events in the contemporary world, sometimes using whimsical masks for gods, demons, and clowns. The entire evening and all of the units within it proceed by a *jo-ha-kyu* structure, based on rhythmic patterns of opening, intensifying, and releasing.

Although Noh theater has no specific ritual function, its connections to Shintō practices of ancestral worship and to Zen Buddhist philosophy run deep. Its narrative and performative structures mirror the pattern of Kagura rituals, in which conjuration leads to a visit by a being or beings from another temporal or cosmological dimension, and the performance then serves to entertain both the otherworldly visitor and the assembled community. Some of the old Noh masks are among the most beautifully finished and subtly expressive masks ever made, while the Kyōgen masks humorously play with the face's expressive range.[23]

Asian Masks and Western Theater

Asian traditions of masked performance, in their complex negotiations between ritual and theatrical practice and court, temple, and village systems of patronage, present a staggering array of images that respond to different religious and philosophical conceptions of human life. Broad categories of usage can be identified and influences traced, yet these traditions are all imbued with specific regional and local cultural values and functions. The power and vitality of these masks, however, have attracted attention well beyond the specific cultures that gave rise to them. Throughout the twentieth century, playwrights and directors of the Western stage, including William Butler Yeats, Vsevolod Meyerhold, Jacques Copeau, Antonin Artaud, Eugene

5.14 The character
of The Woman in a
performance of the
Noh play *Sumida River.*
*Courtesy of the Japan
Society.*

O'Neill, and Bertolt Brecht, and a host of more contemporary theater artists, have looked to the Asian theater with its many masks as exemplary in its imaginative range, its precision and physical commitment, its vitality and intensity, and its enduring links to ritual and myth. The traditions have often been misunderstood, and sometimes stylistic elements have been usurped without regard to the underlying meanings, but the masked Asian performer has often been used as a model in the attempts of Western theater artists to transcend the limitations of naturalism and the positivist worldview that gave birth to that aesthetic, in order to more fully express the conditions of human life.

The Mask in Western Theater: Transformation and Doubling

LESLEY K. FERRIS

Throughout history, theater has been a powerful means for people to communicate and define themselves. Theatrical communication occurs through transformation: an essential function of the actor is his or her ability to transform, to play the role of another, to create a fictional persona. In the earliest examples of theater in the West, in Greece, this act of transformation took place when the actor donned a mask.

Masks are central to the notion of transformation in theater, but they are also the essential markers of theater's innate quality of doubleness: theater represents two worlds, the fictional and the real. Samuel Taylor Coleridge, the British poet and writer, wrote about the duality of art as part of his theory of the imagination. He believed that art was a mediator between nature and man. Although he was referring specifically to poetry, a well-known phrase that he coined in 1817 has been used over and over again to describe an aspect of the spectator's response to a theater event. He talked of "that *willing suspension of disbelief* for the moment, which constitutes poetic faith."[24]

Coleridge recognized an inherent duality in humankind: the ability to know something is not real, while simultaneously experiencing emotions as if it were. An audience can become utterly involved in the fictional performance and the characters on stage as if they were real people; part of being an audience member is suspending one's disbelief and giving credence to events on stage. Theater does not exist without the collaborative interchange between the performer and the spectator. Garland Wright, a recent artistic director of the Guthrie Theatre in Minneapolis, has said, "For me, the theatre is an act of the imagination which is shared between actors and audiences."[25] The double consciousness of the audience member is of course also felt by the actor, who must transform him or herself into the theatrical character. Different actors—perhaps depending on their school of training—experience this in different ways. The Victorian actress Fanny Kemble explained that she maintained an awareness of both herself and the role she played:

> The curious part of acting, to me, is the sort of double process which the mind carries on at once, the combined operation of one's faculties, so to speak, in diametrically opposite directions; for instance, in that very last scene of Mrs. Beverly, while I was half dead with crying in the midst of *real* grief, created by an entirely *unreal* cause, I perceived that my tears were falling like rain all over my silk dress, and spoiling it.[26]

5.15 The two bird figures and piper on this red-figure calyx krater c. 415 B.C. probably represent a scene from Aristophanes's play *The Birds*. The J. Paul Getty Museum, Los Angeles.

This doubleness emerges most clearly in the use of masks in the earliest forms of Western theater. To wear a mask is to literally put on a second face, a second identity—a theatrical identity removed from the everyday world. The word *person* derives from the Latin word *persona*, meaning "mask" or "role," and the Latin word comes from an even older root word, the Etruscan *phersu*, which means "masked dancer." A mask blots out the actor's face, the primary way that we identify people, and substitutes another identity. The mask simultaneously hides one identity while revealing another, providing the actor with a doubled self.

Ancient Greek and Roman Theater

The classical Greek theater was a theater of masks. Our knowledge about this comes from surviving scripts, a minimal amount of written commentary, and visual material such as vase decoration, sculpture, and painting (fig. 5.15). In 534 B.C. the Athenian government officially sanctioned and gave financial support to a theater contest for the best tragedy presented at the City Dionysia, a major religious festival. The government record of these events has provided additional facts and details.

The City Dionysia took place in the spring and celebrated the god Dionysus. Dionysus was a fertility god associated with birth and death. The only god whose parents were not both divine, Dionysus was born twice: his mother, the Theban princess Semele, died before he was born; Zeus, his father, removed the unborn child and deposited him in his thigh, allowing the fully developed offspring to emerge later. "Dithyramb," a religious hymn sung and danced by a chorus to honor Dionysus and often considered a precursor to tragic drama, literally means "double birth."

Doubleness infuses the imagery and myth surrounding Dionysus. In addition to his role as a fertility god, Dionysus was celebrated as god of the vine. Wine, considered a gift from the god, had the ability to elevate human followers of Dionysus into an ecstatic, religious rapture. While singing and dancing under the influence of the sacred drink, men believed their exalted feelings changed them into satyrs, creatures that were half man, half goat. Some Greek scholars believe that the dithyrambs were first performed by dancing and singing around a sacrificial goat, the sacred animal of the god. The followers of Dionysus wore the skins of the sacred animal, masks or other types of facial adornment, ate the sacred meat, and drank the god-given beverage, throwing themselves into a spiritual ecstasy to effect a direct union with the divine. Like the god himself, humans could become half human, half god for a brief moment. The legacy of this early connection to the sacred goat of Dionysus resides with us in the word *tragedy*, derived from the Greek *tragoidia*, which means "goat-song."

Aspects of Dionysiac worship thus required disguise to transform the individual into a higher, divinely inspired being. The significance of such masking and its celebratory nature led the Greeks to develop a dramatic form. The very act of wearing a mask and transforming oneself into another character was considered a form of worship. How the transition from this kind of singing in praise of the god developed into what we now know as tragedy remains unclear. One theory is that Thespis, credited as "the first actor" and from whom we get the word *thespian*, stepped away from the singing, dithyrambic chorus and began to speak his own role, creating a dialogue between chorus and character. This initial convention of the single actor changed in the early fifth century B.C.when Aeschylus, the earliest tragic writer known to us, introduced a second actor. Later Sophocles changed the dramatic tradition again by adding a third actor, and this became the standardized arrangement for classical Greek drama: three actors and a chorus.

The City Dionysia, which lasted for one week, was extremely important to the citizens of Athens because it not only celebrated religious and artistic achievements but was also an effective display of the wealth, power, and public spirit of the Athenian city-state. The tragedies were considered the centerpiece of the festival. They were performed on the fourth, fifth, and sixth days of the festival week, each of the three days devoted to a single playwright who presented three tragedies, sometimes linked together as a trilogy, sometimes as separate plays. This triple bill was followed by a fourth piece called a satyr play, a short comic piece that made fun of the tragic characters. The actors for this final work dressed as satyrs, thus demonstrating the connection between the practice of theater and the worship of Dionysus.

Festival performances took place outdoors in large amphitheaters. In the first theaters the spectators probably sat or stood on the sloping hill looking down on a circular space known as the orchestra. Wooden "bleacher" seats were eventually erected, and more permanent stone seats were added later. The Theater of Dionysus, located on a hillside that sloped down from the Acropolis in Athens, was completed in stone in the fourth century B.C. The theater had a seating capacity of 14,000 to 17,000 spectators, and thus the masks of the actors and chorus had an important function: the enlarged, exaggerated expressions of the masks made it possible for the audience to see the faces. The gestures and movement of the actors were probably also very expressive and physical, enabling audiences to view them and complementing the large masked face.

All actors wore masks that covered the entire head and depicted hairstyle, facial features, beard, and decorations. The masks were made of perishable material such as cork and covered with linen. The chorus members in a tragedy all wore the same mask, thus clearly identifying them as a group and keeping the visual tone contained and somber. For example, the chorus in the *Agamemnon*, the first play of Aeschylus's *Oresteia* trilogy, consisted of the old men of Athens who were too old to take part in the Trojan War. Their masks would have been bearded, their features old and shriveled.

Comedy as a dramatic genre did not receive official sanction in Greece until 487–486 B.C., when it was accepted into the City Dionysia. One day of the festival was set aside for the comedy competition, featuring five plays written by five different dramatists. The comic chorus was usually varied and differed greatly from the tragic chorus. In Aristophanes's comedies, such as *The Birds, The Frogs,* and *The Clouds,* the chorus masks represented the titles. The masks for human roles often had exaggerated features and grotesque qualities such as extreme baldness, long beards, or ugly noses. Several of Aristophanes's plays featured well-known contemporary Athenians, such as the philosopher Socrates and the playwright Euripides. The masks for these roles were known as "portrait masks," and the audience could easily identify their likenesses.

A significant aspect of Greek masked theater is that within the "three-actor rule" playwrights could double their three actors in various roles; in some cases, the same role might be played by more than one actor. The versatility of the masks and the fact that they covered the entire head made it possible for actors to switch masks off stage and quickly enter as a different person. Women were not permitted to perform—it is not clear whether they even attended the performances—but full-headed masks made it easy for men to assume the roles of females.

The significance of the mask in Greek culture is considerable. It was considered a civic duty to perform in a festival chorus. During the three days of tragedy, one day of comedy, and one day of dithyramb competitions, well over 500 citizens performed. This pervasive use of the mask reflected the Greek notion of a participatory democracy as well as a participatory religion.

5.16 Fragment of a Roman vase, probably from the 4th century A.D., depicting a tragic actor contemplating his mask. *Courtesy Martin von Wagner Museum, Wurzburg.*

The mask offered the chorus a corporate personality that projected a dominant emotion visually underscoring the play's meaning. The mask was not a substitute for the human face but a powerful creative tool that removed the citizen from everyday life and offered contact with the god. Thus the knowledge and experience of wearing a mask was part of what it meant to be a Greek citizen (fig. 5.16). The mask also had a potency beyond the actual festival performance. It was common practice to dedicate the masks to the god and hang them in the temple after a performance. Thus the masks were on display in the sanctuary and accrued additional religious potency over time through their contant visibility to the community at large.

The classical age of Greek theater ended in 336 B.C., when the reign of Alexander the Great began. Despite the relatively short time he was in power (he died in 323 B.C.), Alexander conquered the Persian empire and extended his realm into Egypt and as far as India. His "Hellenization" of the eastern Mediterranean took Greek culture and theater far beyond the Peloponnese. However, instead of maintaining theater's connection to the religious festivals from which it had developed, Alexander created victory festivals to celebrate military accomplishments. The number of theatrical events grew to celebrate his many victories, and the need for actors increased. The City Dionysia, which occurred once a year, had utilized numerous local citizens and a handful of dedicated actors who performed the main roles, but the victory festivals of Alexander were too numerous for the performers to be volunteers. Acting became a profession, and the first actor's guild, which included actors, playwrights, chorus members, musicians, and costume and mask makers, was created.

Whereas playwrights had formerly been the center of the theatrical event, now individual actors became famous. A shift of focus occurred in the area of genre as well; although tragedy was still performed, comedy increased in popularity. New Comedy, as it came to be known, centered on middle-class Athenian life, love, and family relations.

5.17 Marble relief of
Menander holding the
mask of a youth, with
masks of a woman and
an old man on a nearby
table. Probably a 1st- or
2nd-century A.D. Roman
copy of a 3rd-century
B.C. Greek work. *The Art
Museum, Princeton
University, Caroline G.
Mather Fund.*

The writers of New Comedy were prolific, but only one complete work, *The Grouch* by Menander, has survived, although there are numerous script fragments by him as well as other writers (fig. 5.17). Menander was known for varied character portrayals and complicated, ingenious story lines. Over time, however, New Comedy plots became repetitious and similar characters continually reappeared. Masks were conventionalized into a restricted number of easily identifiable types.

Greek theater continued throughout the Roman era, during which time Menander's plays were extremely popular. Late in the Roman Empire, Pollux, a Greek lexicographer working in the second century A.D., produced a catalogue of forty-four masks in a work entitled *Onamasticon*. He identified four major categories: old men, young men, young women, and slaves; a smaller fifth group consisted of old women. Each group has several mask descriptions: for example, there are nine old men masks, including "first grandfather," "principal old man," and "pimp"; four young men; seven slaves; and five young women, including "talker," "curly," and "virgin." This division of humanity into four major classifications may seem simplistic, but the categories corresponded closely to the plays,[27] which required representatives from these four types.

Archaeological remains support Pollux's catalogue descriptions. During the period of New Comedy, masks and images of masks proliferated in a variety of forms: mosaics, frescoes, and full-size and miniature terra-cotta (figs. 5.18a–d). The masks that actors actually wore in performance, however, were lightweight and perishable. They were also extremely important to an actor's work and no doubt jealously guarded. Over time and after many performances the masks themselves accumulated an aura of spirituality, a tangible means of connecting to the god. Actors did not forget their bond to Dionysus, and many of them dedicated their masks to him.

Numerous miniature masks have been found throughout the ancient world. The popularity of these terra-cotta miniatures seems to be the result of souvenirs of productions or perhaps small symbolic gifts dedicated to Dionysus. As theater scholar David Wiles states, "Terra-cotta masks helped familiarize the Hellenistic world with the tradition of New Comic performances, so that the masks became a common currency within a far-flung culture."[28]

Part of that far-flung culture included the fledgling Roman Republic. However, before the Romans became acquainted with Greek masking traditions, the dominant influence on Roman theater was from Etruria, in the northwestern Italian peninsula. The Etruscans made extensive use of masks, music, and dance in their religious festivals as well as civic ceremonies. One

5.18a–d Miniature New Comedy Hellenistic terra-cotta masks from Lipari. *Glasgow Museums: Art Gallery and Museum, Kelvingrove.*

5.19 A 9th-century manuscript showing a range of character masks from Terence's comedy *Andria. Biblioteca Apostolica Vaticana.*

particular form of Etruscan theater, described by the Roman poet Horace in the first century B.C., consisted of improvised, often obscene, dialogue performed by masked clowns at harvest or marriage ceremonies. Another form of improvised farce came from the southern Italian peninsula. Called Atellan farce, this performance utilized type characters with fixed masks and costumes. The Latin word for actor, *histrio,* from which we get the word *histrionic,* comes from the Etruscan word for "masked player." Thus, masks were central to Roman theater even before the Romans copied and replicated many elements of Greek theater.

A major difference between Greek and Roman theater was the social position of the professional actor. In Greece acting had religious and political importance, and certain actors served the city-state as trusted ambassadors. In Rome, however, acting was primarily the work of foreigners and slaves. The Greeks believed that dancing and performing in mask was part of what it meant to be a citizen, but in Rome such activity was hardly a source of pride for a family of good standing; in fact, it was inconceivable.

Unlike the Greeks, who used masks as celebratory, life-affirming religious worship, the Roman preoccupation with masks centered on death. Wiles points out that the most important use of the mask in Rome was associated with funeral rituals. When a Roman nobleman died, he was privileged by rank and class to receive a death mask. Each noble family would display their lineage of masks in a special area of their home; the masks would also be on public display at special state events. These death masks had a performative aspect, as Wiles explains:

> A person who had the same physique as the dead man, and had been trained in life to imitate him, sometimes a professional actor, would participate in the funeral as the living incarnation of the dead man. Others would wear the robes of office and masks of the deceased man's ancestors, and would take their places on ivory chairs mounted on rostra, so that the whole family line was, as it were, brought back to life on stage.[29]

This worship of the dead through funerary masks had a bearing on how masks were used in the theater. Theater mask makers had to avoid at all costs the "portrait masks" of Greek comedy, because creating a likeness of a real figure would seem to mock the funeral performances of a noble family. The avoidance of portraiture, or any attempt to make a mask look like or suggest a living person, reinforced the usage of character types that already existed in Atellan farce and, later, in the New Comedy from Greece. Character types were the staple in Roman comedy (fig. 5.19). Plautus's much-produced *Menaechmi,* in which the mistaken identities of two sets of identical twins cause comic mayhem, is one example of a play that might have made good use of masks.

In terms of the sheer volume of spectacle and the numbers of performances, the Roman theater was most productive during the fourth century A.D. Although it continued to be active for an additional 200 years, the rising opposition of the fledgling Christian Church would soon gain momentum and overwhelm it. Theater was heavily denounced by early Christian fathers for a variety of reasons, including its association with pagan gods and festivals and the violent spectacles in which early Christians had been tortured and killed. Initially the critical onslaught by the Church had little effect: during the latter years of the Roman Empire more than half of the calendar year was officially dedicated to various kinds of theater festivals. Roman actors had plenty of opportunity to retaliate by ridiculing and mocking Christian ritual and symbols on the stage, much to the delight of the audience. However, in 393 Theodosius I made Christianity the state religion. After 400 theatrical activity went into decline, and gladiatorial contests were abolished in 404. In the sixth century the emperor Justinian closed all the theaters; the last definite record of a Roman performance is in the year 549. Rome did not survive the Lombard invasion in 568, after which state support of theatrical performances definitively ended and with them the long tradition of masked theater.

Medieval Theater

The Catholic Church succeeded in suppressing the theatrical art form for centuries, but in the Middle Ages the Church reintroduced performance as liturgical drama to teach the scripture to its numerous illiterate converts. First staged inside churches by priests who exchanged simple dialogue from the New Testament, this kind of performance was essentially maskless. As the audience size increased and the performances became more elaborate, these events were forced to move outdoors into the streets. The Passion Plays, a series of plays telling the story of the life of Christ, became extremely popular throughout Europe and often relied on spectacle for their scenes of heaven and hell. Certain key characters, such as the devil and his minions, wore masks to create a frightening, horned visage. These theater masks used to depict evil became transmuted into a grotesque form of punishment: women accused of witchcraft were forced to wear twisted, comic masks, not unlike devil masks, at their trials. A lasting tradition of devil masks, however, was in medieval performance rituals such as Carnival, or Mardi Gras, where even today the devil is a perennial favorite.

Masks also appeared in certain folk dramas and ritual entertainments, such as mummeries, processions of disguised characters who visit various private houses during the Christmas or New Year's celebrations (fig. 5.20). These mummings are most likely a survival of pre-Christian ceremonies or even the Roman Saturnalia, a December festival celebrating the god Saturn and featuring unrestrained merrymaking. By the year 1500 mummeries and disguisings were primarily court entertainments, and although masks were used, this tradition did not develop into a sustained theater of masks.

5.20 An illustrated manuscript page with figures wearing a variety of animal masks and dancing in a mummery procession during Christmas or New Year's celebrations, from the *Li Romans d'Alixandre*, c. 1340. *The Bodleian Library, Oxford.*

Commedia dell'Arte

Masked theater did not reemerge in the West until the Italian Renaissance. Commedia dell'arte, literally, the "comedy of the profession," flourished beginning in the mid-sixteenth century, entertaining most of continental Europe. Improvised and nomadic, this was a grassroots form of comedy, performed in the streets and town squares, and only later invited into established theater buildings or the courtyards of wealthy citizens. Unlike the masked theater of Greece and Rome in which only men performed, commedia introduced the first professional actresses in a major theatrical form. The commedia companies were family-based structures in which husband-and-wife teams often handed down their roles to sons and daughters. Evidence exists of such "inheritances" lasting three or four generations. The family structure of the companies, linked with the precarious and unpredictable earnings of traveling players, made it economically necessary for the women to take part in both running the company and acting.

Despite the important role of women in this masked performance art, the actresses of commedia did not wear masks, and their roles were confined to young lovers or servants. Traditional scholars have given two explanations: first, that the female roles never developed into a clear, consistent "type"; and second, that the female face was exposed so as to exploit the women's visual appeal and beauty. More recent feminist scholarship has suggested that within the society of the time there was a pervasive belief that artistic creativity precluded women, part of the ongoing prejudice against their work in all artistic arenas. The unmasked actress in a theater of masks reinforced the assumption that true, lasting art was found in the male masks.[30]

MASK 87 The four major masks of commedia are Harlequin, Pantalone, the Doctor, and Brighella. In the beginning, various roles were identified by the actor's name or by various character names. But, over time, the major male characters became stabilized. Likewise, each of the characters originates from a different region in Italy, providing ample opportunity for the actors to mimic local dialects to comic effect. The Doctor, a pompous professor type, comes from Bologna; Pantalone, the greedy, lecherous old man, hails from Venice; Harlequin, the crafty clown, and Brighella, the intriguer, are both servants who come from opposite ends of the town of Bergamo.

A unique aspect of commedia is its improvisation. Unlike actors in the Greek or Roman traditions, commedia actors were responsible for composing their own lines. Although language was important, it was not as important as in other kinds of theater in which linguistic imagery

5.21 This late 17th-century engraving, *L'Harlequin Bergamasco*, illustrates the characteristic mask, slapstick, and diamond costume of Harlequin. *Courtesy Deutsches Teatermuseum, Munich.*

5.22 *Pantalone Serenades His Mistress,* an early 17th-century Dutch oil painting, shows the unmasked lady, Harlequin, Pantalone, and a Zanni. *Drottningholms Teatermuseum, Stockholm.*

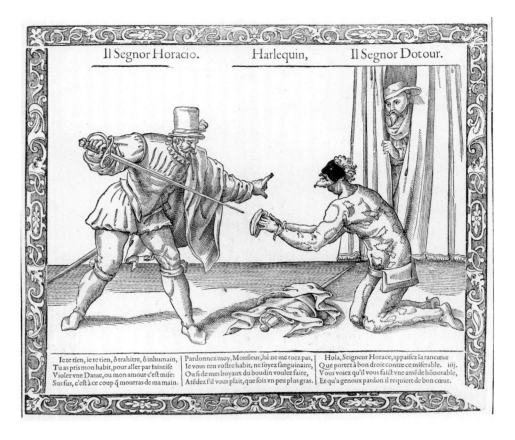

Il Segnor Horacio.   Harlequin,   Il Segnor Dotour.

Ie te tien, ie te tien, ô trahitre, ô inhumain, | Pardonnez moy, Monfieur, hé ne me tuez pas, | Hola, Seigneur Horace, appaifez la rancœur
Tu as pris mon habit, pour aller par faintife | Ie vous ren voftre habit, ne foyez fanguinaire, | Que portez à bon droit contre ce miferable. iiij.
Violer vne Dame, ou mon amour c'eft mife: | Ou fi de mes boyaux du boudin voulez faire, | Vous voiez qu'il vous faict vne amêde hônorable,
Sus fus, c'eft à ce coup q̃ mourras de ma main. | A tédez fil vous plait, que fois vn peu plus gras. | Et qu'a genoux pardon il requiert de bon cœur.

5.23 This 16th-century woodcut by Fossard shows Harlequin with Signor Horatio and the Doctor. *Nationalmuseum, Stockholm.*

and poetry are central. Instead, commedia was a highly physical theater: it relied on gesture, sight gags, and easily identifiable characters in masks and costumes. The term *slapstick* actually derives from commedia: a slapstick was a mock sword or bat made of two thin pieces of wood attached at one end; when the stick was struck against something—such as the rear end of a fellow actor—it made a loud, clear smacking sound. The slapstick was part of Harlequin's costume, and most drawings of him depict him with one tucked into his belt (fig. 5.21).

Although the characters of commedia would have been recognizable to Plautus and even Menander, there is no clear line of descent between Roman comedy, the Atellan farces, and commedia. If anything, the use of the mask in Italian comedy was decidedly different (figs. 5.22, 5.23). Commedia utilized half masks, covering the top half of the face, but leaving the bottom half—the mouth and chin—visible. This half-mask approach allowed the actor a specific physical presence, as opposed to the Greek actor, whose mask covered the entire head. The commedia masks were molded out of leather on carved wooden forms. Leather, unlike the cork or wood used by the ancients, absorbs a good deal of sweat, and over time the mask adjusted itself to fit the actor snugly. Commedia performers became identified with one mask and acted with it throughout their careers; the characters of the commedia players stayed more or less the same, but the stories or situations changed according to which scenario they would decide to play at any given performance (figs. 5.24a, b). Each company had a selection of scenarios, basic plot outlines that they had developed—or stolen—from others, one of which would be tacked up at the back of the stage and consulted before the performance. Over a period of time these scenarios were refined and passed on from one generation to another.

Commedia was immensely popular, and it rapidly created a demand outside its homeland. One famous Harlequin, Drusiano Martinelli, took his family of performers to England in 1577 and to Spain a decade later. By 1600 the various companies had toured all over Europe, influencing a multitude of theater artists along the way. In the middle of the seventeenth century, the company of Tiberio Fiorelli took up permanent residence in Paris, sharing a theater with the playwright (and actor) Molière. The company's physical performances and visual clarity through mask and costume made it easy for the French-speaking audience to understand their improvised art. They were so successful with Parisian audiences that Louis XIV placed Fiorelli's troupe under royal protection, and in 1680 they became known as the Comédie-Italienne (in order to distinguish them from the newly established Comédie-Française). In 1697, however, the Italian actors were expelled from France; a performance that offended the queen is the most cited reason for this action. The Italian troupes did not return until 1716 when they abandoned Italian in favor of French and began performing exclusively in scripted plays, gradually abandoning their masks.

The troupes suffered a similar fate in their homeland. In the mid-eighteenth century Carlo Goldoni, a Venetian playwright, began a personal crusade to reform Italian comedy by cleaning it up and ridding it of what he considered rude, licentious material. He removed the slapstick crudities of the improvised form and sought to establish a more genteel, realistic style, stating that "comedies without masks are more natural and pithy." Although he admitted that masks had been essential to Greek theater, he pursued his view that "the emotions and sentiments had not been brought to such delicacy as is demanded today; we now want the actor to have a soul, and a soul under a mask is like fire under ashes. That is why I conceived the idea of reforming the masks of the Italian comedy and of substituting comedies for farces."[31] Finally, he eliminated the masks and all vestiges of improvisation and succeeded in establishing a middle-class comedy focused on local morals and manners. His playwriting reforms were frequently attacked by various theatrical figures who wanted to retain the vibrancy and rawness of masked theater.

Goldoni's bitter rival in this debate was Carlo Gozzi, who vehemently opposed the bourgeois watering down of traditional commedia. He attempted to restore the masks and improvisation through a series of fantastic, visually spectacular scripts. Gozzi's work did little to restore commedia, but instead created a scenically arresting style of theater that became known as *fiabe*, or fables. The well-intentioned Gozzi ignored the crucial role of improvisation in commedia—this was a form of theater that defied conventional notions of stability; the masked characters, often subversive and always adaptable, could not be trapped in the confines of a preordained script.

5.24a, b Commedia dell'arte characters Harlequin and Pantalone as represented in engravings by A. Manceau. *Reprinted from Maurice Sand,* Masques and Bouffons, *vol. 1, Paris, 1860.*

Although some form of traditional commedia survived until the late eighteenth century, the cultural atmosphere was such that written dramas and comedies were valorized over the impermanence of improvisation. Commedia began as a grassroots theater of the streets. As it became more and more popular, it was appropriated first by royalty and later by an emerging middle class that wanted its theater indoors, in the comfort of large, imposing theaters. The gritty, streetwise comic players, who originally survived on handouts and income derived from passed hats, moved inside to larger single audiences and royal patronage, and box-office takings that offered financial stability. Masked performers eventually disappeared, and with them went the last remnants of a viable and vibrant masking tradition in Western theater. Despite the pervasive influence of the form—until the nineteenth century Harlequin continued as a character in English pantomime, sometimes referred to as "Harlequinades"—the idea of a living, continuous tradition is gone.

How is this possible? Many people have tried to understand the decline and eventual loss of this once popular theatrical form. By the late eighteenth century the focus shifted from characters that reflected the hierarchical span of society (as commedia did at the basic level of masters and servants) to more realistic characters emerging from a growing middle class. During the late nineteenth century theatrical realism was firmly entrenched and naturalistic theater was seen as the goal to which all theater forms aspired: stripping and laying bare "truth" to an audience. Commedia performance, which was overtly theatrical and extremely physical, and featured masked players, was contrary to this striving for realism. Instead of creating an illusion of reality, the commedia production constantly reminded the spectator that he or she was taking part in a performance.

Another change was the way in which the actor was regarded. Over time the actor's own face became very important to his career; famous male actors became known for their impressive range of facial expression. The unmasked public face became part of the "cult of personality" that began to overtake the profession at the time commedia was in decline. A mask erases the personal, the specific, the details of the self—those very aspects that the public now wanted to embrace. With the advent of film early in the twentieth century, naturalistic theater seemed to have found its own medium, and acting became associated with the success and popularity of film stars whose faces were shown in close-ups.

5.25 Masked performers in Jean Genet's *The Blacks* at St. Mark's Playhouse, New York, 1961. *Courtesy Time-Life Syndication.*

Twentieth Century

In the twentieth century, however, there was a burst of theatrical activity in which masks were again featured. Many theater artists wanted to break free from the confines of naturalism and return to older theater traditions; the theater mask was seen as a means of restoring a sense of overt theatricality to their work. These artists were fascinated by the

5.26 Scene from Eugene O'Neill's *The Great God Brown* at the Greenwich Village Theater, 1926. *Courtesy Billy Rose Theater Collection, New York Public Library, Performing Arts.*

mask's inherent doubleness: the mask's duality allows it to function as both a metaphor in the performed text and as a device on the stage (fig. 5.25).

Edward Gordon Craig, a British theater designer and director, spent much of his creative career arguing for an abstract and ritualistic theater that would have a spiritual significance equivalent to Greek tragedy. Between 1908 and 1929 he published a quarterly journal entitled *The Mask* in which he articulated his theories. Writing in 1911 he stated:

> The mask must return to the stage to restore expression . . . the visible expression of the mind . . . the inspiration which led men to use the mask in past ages is the same now as it ever was and will never die. It is this inspiration that we shall act under and in which we trust. Therefore let no one attempt to put this thing aside as being of the antique . . . .[32]

Despite the fact that the masking tradition had faded from the dominant forms of Western theater, Craig and other theater artists sought ways to revitalize the use of the mask. In her study *Masks in Modern Drama,* Susan Harris Smith identifies over 225 plays written since 1896 in which playwrights employed masks.[33] These works of modern dramatists, often marginalized as avant-garde or experimental, have rarely been seen in mainstream commercial theater. Bertolt Brecht, the celebrated German playwright and director, wrote several plays to be acted with masks. Both Craig and Brecht were affected by the continuing use of masks in Asian theater and looked for ways to revive those traditions that seemed lost in Western culture. As a Marxist, Brecht found naturalistic theater's "illusion of reality" to be politically suspicious, lulling audiences into passive spectatorship, and passive citizenship. Brecht's usage of masks

5.27 Douglas Campbell
in *Oedipus the King* at
the Stratford Festival,
1954. *Stratford Festival
Archives.*

was specifically intended to make the theatrical experience more "strange," as he sought to jar his viewers.

The American playwright Eugene O'Neill found masks to be a liberating means of creating visual metaphors on stage and used them extensively in a range of plays in the 1920s. O'Neill employed African masks in *The Emperor Jones* to ensure ethnic authenticity; in *Lazarus Laughed* masks distinguish a chorus composed of various races, ages, and temperaments. In contrast, *The Great God Brown* features masks that each portrayed four characters; these masks perform a symbolic function, transforming through the course of the play to visually suggest character conflict and development (fig. 5.26). O'Neill, in an essay entitled "Memoranda on Masks," articulated his fascination with masks:

> The use of masks will be discovered eventually to be the freest solution of the modern dramatist's problem as to how—with the greatest possible dramatic clarity and economy of means—he can express those profound hidden conflicts of the mind which the probings of psychology continue to disclose to us.[34]

Whereas O'Neill focused on serious drama, W. T. Benda, a Polish immigrant to New York City, designed masks for satirical, decorative reviews such as the *Greenwich Village Follies* in 1920. Benda did much to popularize the mask in America, and his masks began a craze, as the fashion industry even used his designs on fashion models and mannequins.

William Butler Yeats, the Irish poet and playwright, was introduced to masks by Craig and later influenced by the Noh theater of Japan. Like many theater artists committed to a mask revival, Yeats eschewed commercial theater as crass, demoralizing, and having little artistic sensibility. His mission was to restore an Irish theatrical tradition: he believed that his use of masks in his plays would elevate Gaelic folk heros to mythic stature because of the mask's inherent imagistic and ritual power.

Twentieth-century directors have also advocated the use of masks. Giorgio Strehler, one of the major figures in Italian post–World War II theater, founded the famous Piccolo Teatro in Milan, which he dedicated to the revival of a specifically Italian repertoire. On numerous occasions he reworked Goldoni's play *Arlecchino, Servant of Two Masters,* attempting to recuperate the masked tradition of commedia. The classical tradition received a major revival with Tyrone Guthrie's 1954 *Oedipus the King* at Canada's Stratford Shakespeare Festival (fig. 5.27) and Jean-Louis Barrault's 1955 *Oresteia* in Paris, both fully masked productions. Peter Schumann, the

MASK 83   director and mask maker, has created theater pieces that employ masks and puppets for over thirty years with his company Bread and Puppet Theater.

In addition to the playwrights and directors committed to masked performance, choreogra-
MASK 85   phers such as Mary Wigman and Oskar Schlemmer have worked with masks (fig. 5.28). Wigman created masked dances in order to subsume her identity into that of an anonymous "ceremonial figure." Schlemmer used masked mechanic figures in his dance pieces, exploring the fascination with technology and machines.

In order to use masks effectively, many directors have found that they need to train actors in mask performance. This has led to another element of mask work: the use of masks in actor training programs. In the early part of this century, the innovative Russian director Vsevolod Meyerhold used the principles of commedia to develop a strong physical training system for actors. Jacques Copeau founded a theater school in 1921 in France that was an early center of mask work. Copeau's nephew, Michel Saint-Denis, established several actor-training schools in Europe and the United States that required masks in their program of study. Jacques Lecoq, a leader in mask-work training, starts with the concept of a "Neutral Mask," a simple, symmetrical, full-faced mask with no hint of character or expression. The purpose of the Neutral Mask is to depersonalize the actor, to strip away the facial identity so that the actor can experience a physicality not defined by the face. Peter Brook, the celebrated British director, has noted the importance of such mask work for the actor:

5.28 Oskar Schlemmer, watercolor study for *The Abstract,* c. 1920. *Staatliche Museen Preussischer Kulturbesitz, Kunstbibliothek, Berlin.*

5.29 Scar and Mufasa from the original Broadway production of *The Lion King*, 1997. *Masks by Julie Taymor. Courtesy Disney.*

The moment you take someone's face away in that way [such as with Lecoq's Neutral Mask], it's the most electrifying impression: suddenly to find oneself knowing that that thing one lives with, and which one knows is transmitting something all the time, is no longer there. It's the most extraordinary sense of liberation. It is one of the great exercises that whoever does for the first time counts as a great moment: to suddenly find oneself liberated from one's own subjectivity.[35]

Other forms of mask training include the "Life Mask" in which an actor's own face is cast as a mask. The mask thus made is then worn by participants other than the original actor. The "Character Mask," made in the commedia tradition of a half mask, allows actors to physicalize a character based on the look of the mask. Masks are incorporated into actor-training programs in the strong belief that such training will enhance the skills and artistry of the emerging actor-artist.

Masks are still with us in Western theater, but the thrust of contemporary work with theatrical masks has been to retrieve a lost tradition, to utilize masks to give imagistic, metaphorical resonance to a playwright's ideas, or to serve as a training device for actors. Although this has created some wonderful and exciting performance work, it has not been able to reinvigorate a form of mask performance comparable to the earlier traditions. In contrast, Asian masked theater, still so strongly linked to ritual, has maintained a continuous performance tradition. Nevertheless, a recent experiment synthesizing Asian and African masking and puppetry with Western theater has produced an incredible commercial success. Julie Taymor's visionary work in *The Lion King* on Broadway, which received great critical acclaim and tremendous popular success, has for the first time in the twentieth century produced a widely accessible work that employs masks. Perhaps this success will offer us new options for the future (fig. 5.29).

MASK 84

Masks in Western Film

CARA McCARTY

STORYTELLING HAS ALWAYS BEEN A PART OF HUMAN SOCIETIES, and there is a continuing need for people to retell and update familiar tales from ancient times. Today, the primary medium for reincarnating traditional myths is film; it is also our myth maker. Like dreams, film's fantasies reflect our enduring quest to reinvent ourselves, to transform ourselves in new ways. Movies continue to address our ongoing search for truths and self-discovery, and they push our expectations as well as define our limitations. Science-fiction movies in particular cater to our need for fantasy and have proven cinema's great potential to create new creatures, masks, and worlds that do not even exist. As a powerful, almost universal form of mass entertainment, film reflects contemporary ideals and cultural values. We go to watch films in movie theaters, specially designated spaces whose cavelike interiors create a ritual setting. The darkened environment lets us forget the outside world, and for two hours we sit suspended in time and space, absorbed in the spectacle played out before us on the larger-than-life screen.

Our fascination with movie stars and emphasis on the individual actor have relegated masks to very defined cinematic roles. Films are judged by how realistically, how convincingly, an actor portrays a character. We often go to a movie just to see a certain actor or actress. Close-up shots bring us even closer to the individual performer. The close-up, in which the huge face on screen allows us to see nuances in facial expression, reveals emotions and personality traits of the actor. The closer we get, it seems, the more real the film becomes. This calculated form of character development is important in propelling the narration of the story, and it yields information that a mask would conceal.

Masks are associated primarily with horror and science-fiction films, and occasionally adventure dramas. Such films deal with the fantastic, with supernatural issues that allow the audience to suspend disbelief. The masks in these movies often occupy alternate worlds that actors cannot, and their presence in a film sends a symbolic message. Villains, monsters, and superheroes are the predominant wearers of masks—the Phantom of the Opera, Batman, Darth Vader, the Lone Ranger, to name a very few—and their masks rather than their faces instantly identify them to audiences (fig. 5.30). Their masks hide disfigured faces, conceal identity, or help transform them into someone with superhuman powers. In the 1994 film *The Mask*, the actor Jim Carrey uses a mask to transform himself into a tycoon.

Ever since the 1930s, when the Universal film studio began to specialize in producing such famous movies as *Dracula* and *Frankenstein*, horror has had mass appeal as a film genre. Many of the stories revolve around similar themes that were popularized in nineteenth-century gothic novels and are continually recycled, with variations on the gimmicks that generate terror and suspense. Early horror films featured melodramatic villains, mad scientists, eerie settings, bats, vampires, ghosts, and ominous black birds.

With the demand for realism, horror films have escalated to unprecedented levels of shock value, depicting grisly details with gut-wrenching impact. Because many of the thrillers and suspense films are competing with scenes from live television news, videos, and special effects, they need to be edgy in order to have full impact. The audience expects more and more, and scaring them has become harder and harder. Unlike the brutish creatures of early horror flicks created by mad scientists, today's monsters look like ordinary citizens. The graphic realism and seductive emotionalism in contemporary cinema approximates Roman theater, which was ultimately banned by the Church in the early Christian era because of public rapes, spectacle murders, and other gruesome violence.

Masks in film are often used to arouse suspense as well as feelings of pity or sympathy. In one of the earliest horror films, *Phantom of the Opera* (1925), we ultimately empathize with the masked Phantom, who is both monstrous and human. The Phantom was born with a seriously misshapen face, which has been hidden by a mask all his life. The film's arresting moment of terror comes when the Phantom turns toward the camera and removes his mask to expose the horrific skeletal face beneath. Removing his mask not only reveals another person, but it also forces us to look at ourselves and perhaps expose a hidden part of our own persona and think about what it means to be human. We become more understanding and tolerant of the world through the masked monster or villain on whom we take pity.

5.30 George Clooney as Batman in *Batman and Robin*, 1997. *Courtesy Warner Bros.*

The lure and magic of the unknown, of outer space and aliens, have nourished science fiction for decades. George Lucas's spectacular space epic *Star Wars* (1977) transports us to "a long time ago in a galaxy far, far away. . . ." But regardless of how far away the galaxy is, the film refers to themes and characters that are familiar to all of us, that connect us, in myths that have persisted through time because of their relevance to many cultures. The myths deal with the fundamental underpinnings of human behavior, no matter who we are and where we live. *Star Wars* is not just about the clash of good and evil, heroes and villains, but about principles and self-mastery.

The most celebrated cinematic mask in recent years is worn by the black-robed Darth Vader. As part of his life-supporting body armor, the mask contains the breathing apparatus necessary for him to function. But it also represents a human turned monster. Seduced and corrupted by the dark side, he was transformed into a monster; his goodness is imprisoned behind his ominous black mask and armor. The epitome of evil, despair, and an unrelenting quest for power, Darth Vader has become one of the most infamous villains of our time. Throughout the saga his vaporous breathing and props, including the mask, amplify his destructive force. Our dislike and mistrust of him is increased because we cannot penetrate the forbidding black mask. Recalling *Phantom of the Opera,* another great moment in cinematic unmasking occurs at the end of *Return of the Jedi,* the third film in the trilogy, when Luke Skywalker removes Darth Vader's helmet and reveals a deformed face, an undeveloped human being. Darth Vader's mask has become the lasting symbol for *Star Wars* (fig. 5.31).

Our insatiable demand for fantasy, for make-believe, is pushing filmmakers to achieve unprecedented levels of movie magic and shock value. The special-effects industry is using revolutionary technological innovations and computer animation to create spectacular masks and creatures that were previously unimaginable. These masks often correspond to known character types, but their fantastic forms and dazzling abilities, like Jim Carrey's mask, can only be accomplished on film and with computers. In traditional theater, the mask amplified the character, but today we depend on special effects and unnatural settings to rejuvenate these familiar masked character types, giving them a credibility palpable to contemporary audiences. These technical achievements permit us to integrate conventional filmmaking with computer animation in order to create seamless transitions between the real and the magical. We witness characters on screen transforming convincingly from one character to another, as shamans do when shape-shifting to negotiate with spiritual forces.

There is a direct link between a culture's fantasies, dreams, and its artifacts. Cinematic masks externalize many of our fears, desires, and passions. Masks have always been the products and mirrors of the human imagination. Like earlier rituals in our human history for which masks were created, they will continue to undergo transformations that make them more pertinent to our times. Movies are one of the ways contemporary society can collectively experience secret dreams and heightened moments of emotional tension. Although the use of masks in film is limited, the fact that they continue to enthrall directors and audiences confirms their enduring ability to stimulate our sense of wonder and astonishment, to allow us to suspend disbelief, and to transport us away from daily life and out of the ordinary.

5.31 *Star Wars* **movie poster, 1977.** *Courtesy The Everett Collection.*

offense | defense

MASK 116

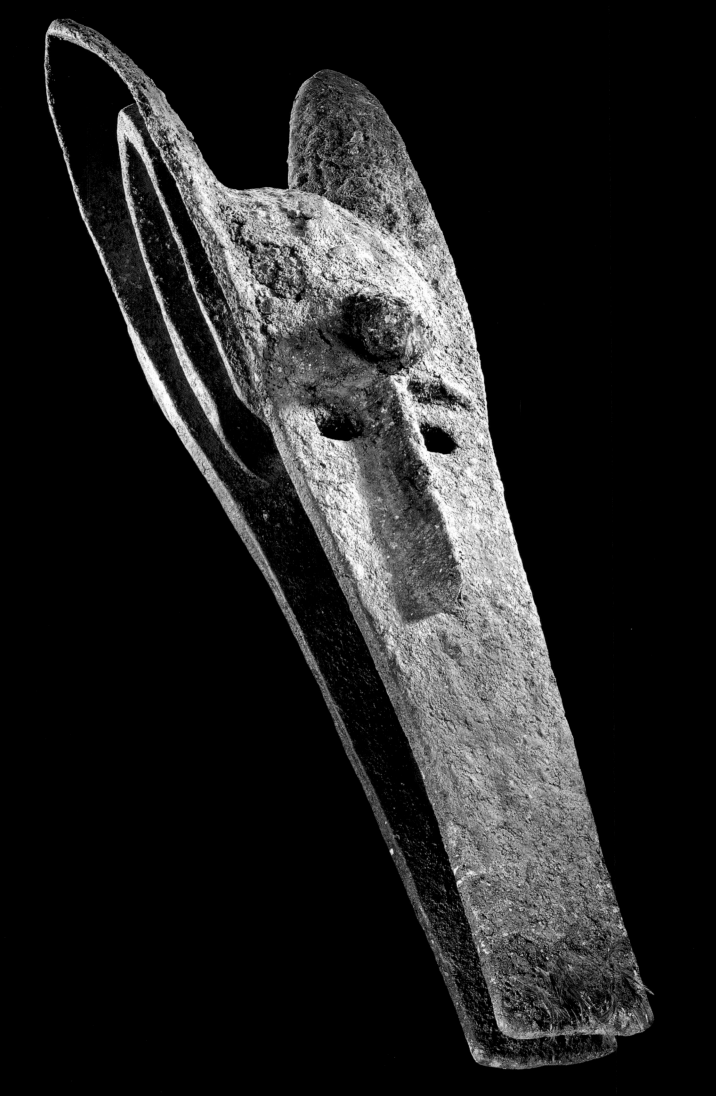

MASK 119

MASK 128

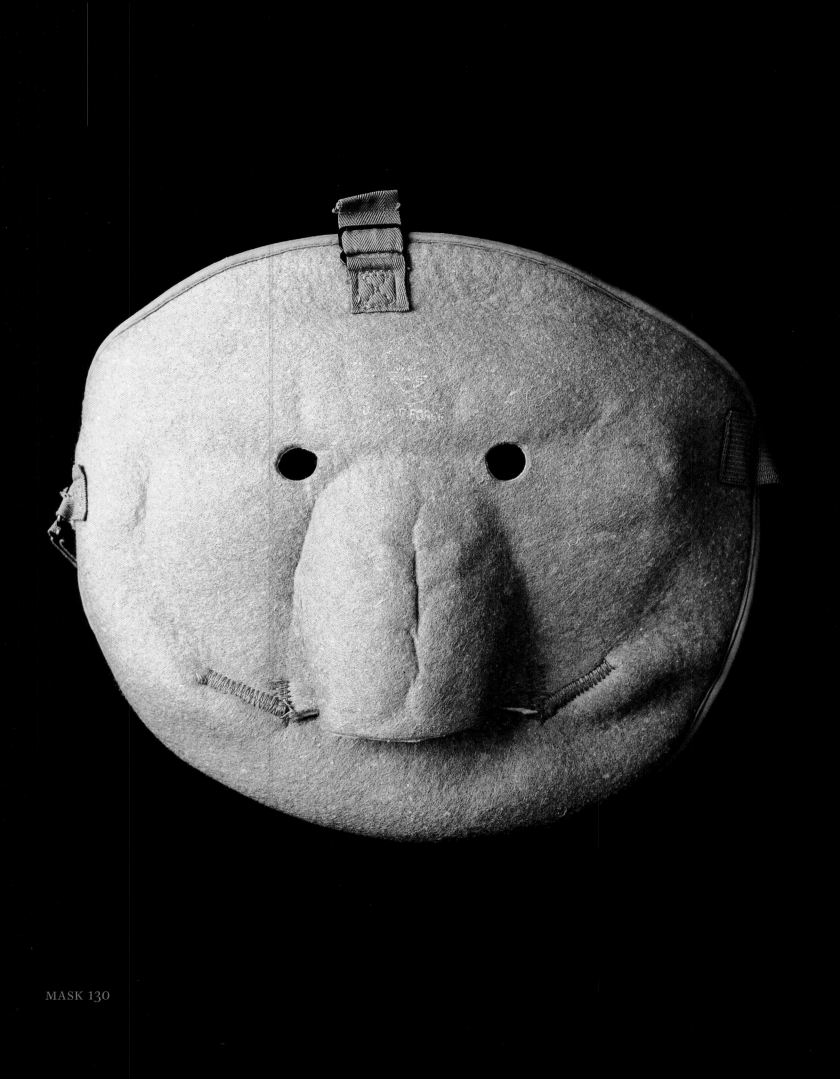

MASK 130

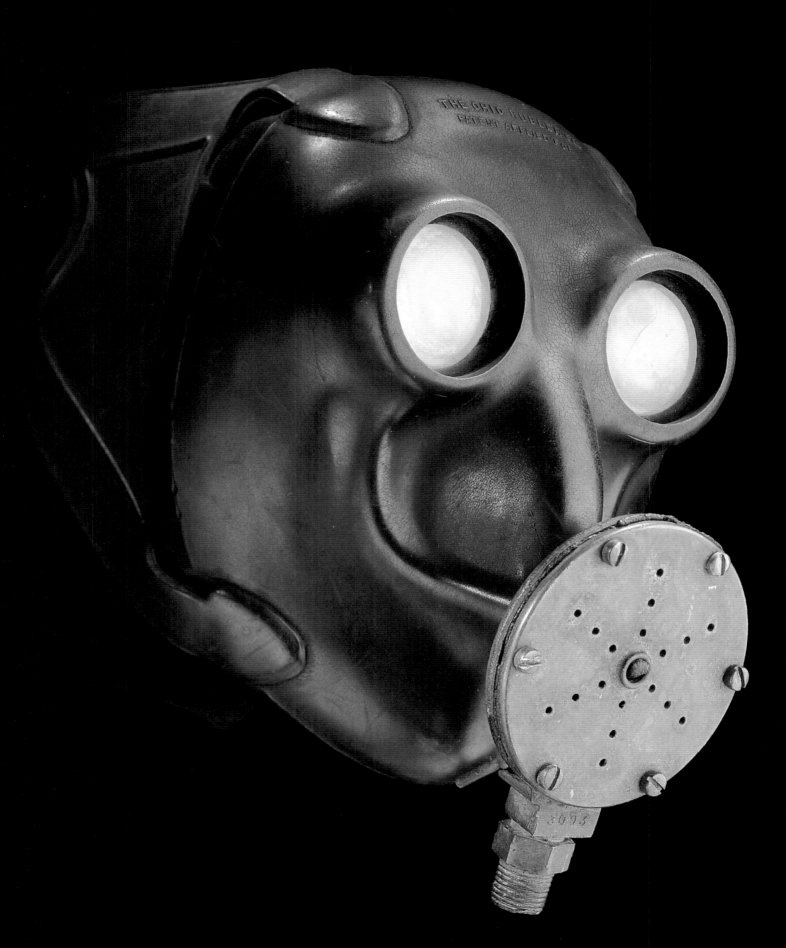

MASK 134

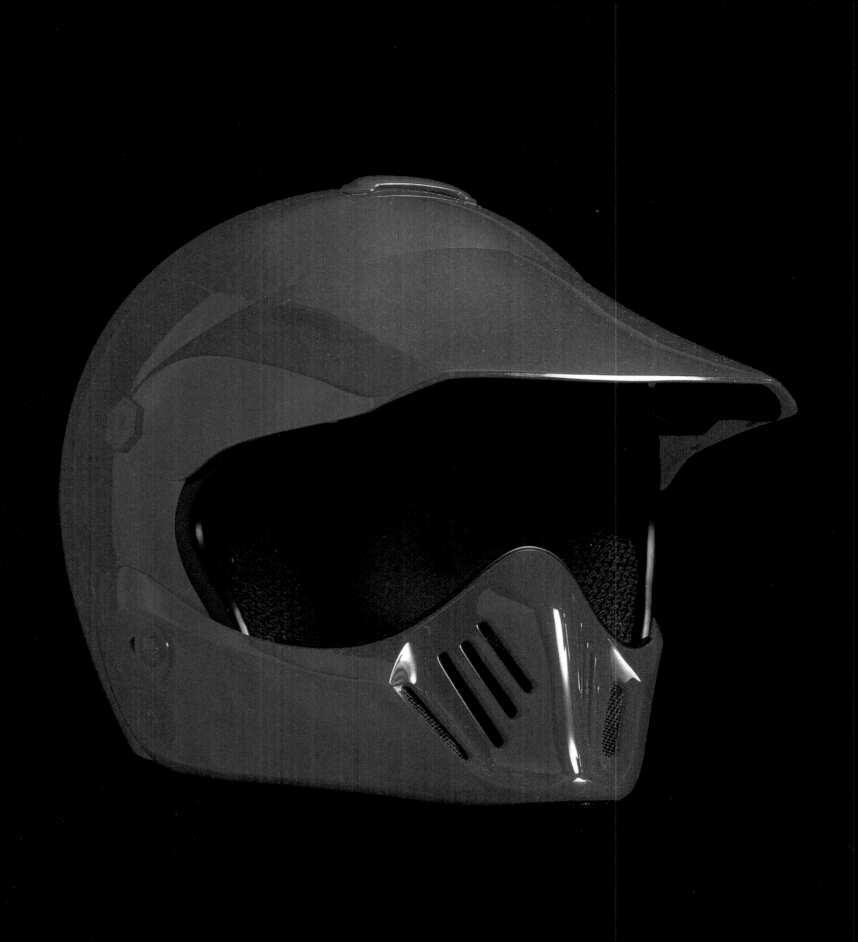

MASK 136

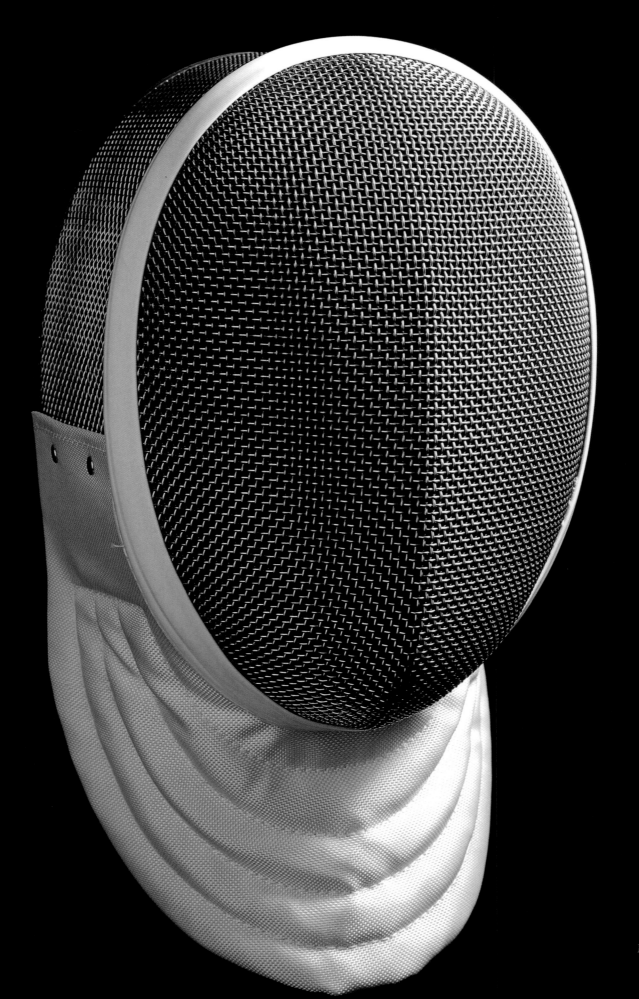

MASK 137

MASK 138

IRWIN

APOLLO 15
SCOTT WORDEN IRWIN

Offense | Defense

CARA McCARTY

Recently as I was leaving for a trip I bought a copy of *The New York Times* to read aboard the plane. By the time I finished it I had counted five photographs of masks used to illustrate that day's articles—the New York City bomb squad, a beekeeper's hood, a baseball catcher's mask, and masks worn by two protagonists in new movie releases. The previous chapters in this book have discussed masks used in rituals, masquerades, and theater, but a looser definition of the word *mask* is simply "a protective covering for the face": something that keeps dust from our eyes or a hockey puck from severing our nose, allows us to see and breathe in an alien environment, or prevents us from being recognized.

Images of athletes, terrorists, and rebels shrouded in camouflage and protective face coverings routinely make front-page news or prime-time television. Many of our activities today are extensions of those practiced by our ancestors, and what is often a precarious relationship between civilization and its enemies is demonstrated with few artifacts as effectively and persuasively as weapons, body armor, and masks. Whether these masks protect against the elements, diseases, malevolent spirits, or other humans, or whether they are worn to conceal or bring forth one's identity, they attest to some of the fundamentals of human existence: the dangers and hostility of the surrounding world.

The masks described earlier in this book were created for rites of passage and renewal; they deal with the transformation of time, with the cycles and changes that take place in the heavens and on earth. The masquerades are performed to mark the biological and seasonal rhythms of life, changes that are repeated over and over again; something ends that must be rejuvenated through ritual and repetition. Even funerary masks, which memorialize the dead, reactivate past time. However, masks created for protection are worn when dealing with space, primarily with spatial boundaries. Our perpetual conflicts with one another are initiated by acquisition of territory and revenge, competition for resources, trading rights, even the power to preserve and perpetuate life or destroy it. Shamans negotiate with spirits for spaces that may offer protection to the community from both physical and spiritual affliction and to empower spaces that can destroy spiritual or physical enemies. Much of human history has been shaped by our struggles with these two forces—time and space. They both set limits and lend structure to our lives.

Aggression is at the root of much human conflict. Motivated by power and control, aggressive acts encourage territorial behavior, causing people to protect both their surrounding space and themselves from invasion. In fact, many sports depend on controlled aggressive behavior. One team attempts to score a goal, while the opponents maneuver to protect their territory. Nowhere is this rivalry more direct than in the military, where the two fundamental strategies of offense and defense are for protection and survival. Depending on the circumstances, one can quickly turn into the other. The crossover between offense and defense rapidly sparks controversy, making international news when a country stockpiles its strategic weapons in the name of defense while neighboring countries interpret it as a threatening offensive maneuver.

6.1 *Phyllium giganteum insect camouflage. Courtesy Christian Schweizer.*

When dealing with adversaries in either the physical or spiritual world, warriors, athletes, diviners, and shamans all wear protective attire with a powerful and forbidding appearance. People have invented fantastic cultures of body protection to ensure their survival ever since they had to learn to compete in the world. Many animals and insects have natural defensive masking capabilities like camouflage to render them invisible, or built-in weapons like claws or venom, but humans have had to devise "second skins" to defend against aggressive acts or threats to their physical well-being (fig. 6.1). Armor has assumed a myriad of forms and has been made of such materials as cloth, leather, vegetal matter, metal, and plastics. The materials used and the degree of protection are dependent on the resources available but also on the sophistication of the technology one needs to combat. As expressions of a society's artistry, technology, and styles of combat, protective masks reveal much about our respective cultures and how we cope.

Shamanic Armor

In many societies, warding off evil and danger is the responsibility of the shamans and diviners, specialists comparable to Western priests, physicians, and attorneys. Healing or problem solving is achieved through the shaman's consultation with, or appeasement of, the spirits. As the society's designated intermediary, it is the shaman who wears the ritual mask and costume.

A shaman's costume is a type of armor that helps protect him or her while negotiating with evil forces of the spiritual world. Often an extraordinary assemblage of appendages, power symbols, and other paraphernalia, the outfit helps the shaman mediate with good spirits, expel or pacify evil spirits, and avert community crises such as illness or bad weather. Shamanic attire constitutes a complete symbolic system that is meant to impress the onlooker with the various problems the shaman can address. A striking example is now part of the Baron von Asch Collection at the University of Göttingen. Collected in the late eighteenth century by the German naturalist Carl Heinrich Merck, a participant in the Billings expedition across Russia of 1787 to 1794, this costume is from the Siberian territory of the Evenki, a Tungusic-speaking group of fishermen and reindeer hunters and herders. Made of reindeer skin, it is decorated with layers of fringe, strips of cotton and silk textiles, glass beads, and a leather pouch containing tobacco and vegetal matter. What makes the outfit a particularly stunning display of power is the nearly thirty kilograms of metal appendages—bronze disks representing the sun and the moon, several life-size copper masks, bronze and iron bells, small iron objects representing reindeer antlers or bones, and leather-covered, copper, doll-like spirit helpers (fig. 6.2). When Baron Georg Thomas von Asch donated the costume to the university, he provided the following description:

> The robe, decorated with magic charms, snakes, masks, and ironwork is put on first. The long sash is wound over the robe and around the body so that the remaining parts lie over the chest and over each other in the shape of a cross and the ends dangle backward over the shoulders. The sash is fastened where it crosses over the chest. At the same time, the other longer piece is fastened over the sash on both sides, the narrower part at the throat, so that the wider end hangs down over the body. The boots are pulled on, and the big copper mask with the knobby beard is tied on to the face to illuminate it at night beside the fire, where the magic occurs. The round brass plate with the inscription is also fastened to one side of the robe. The shaman maintains that this is his diploma. Beneath the masses of charms, snakes, bells, and ironwork on the shaman's robe, are little leather pouches holding pieces of meat. No Tungus would ever dare to touch even one of the charms that hangs from the shaman's clothing.[1]

This costume, believed to be the oldest and most complete extant example of its type, is exceedingly rare because most were burned along with the owner at death.

The shaman's mask and costume are essential elements in the act of transformation. They legitimize the shaman's authority and status in society and bring forth his or her identity. Siberian shamans called their garments "bird skins," through which they attained supernatural vision and a new animal identity to access spiritual forces. The costume's leather fringe, resembling bird's plumage, and the shaman's birdlike trance enabled celestial ascent, the mystical journey to the sky: as the shaman performed dramatically, jumping around in an ecstatic trance with arms outstretched like wings, imitating the movements of a bird, bells and metal amulets jangled to call forth the friendly spirits.

Comparable sacred dress can be found in Africa, where protective attire is worn at times of crisis to combat spiritual aggression. Like shrines, these masked garments are elaborate assemblages that empower the diviner to identify evil sorcerers and witches and to protect the community from their destructive actions. They symbolize the prestigious role religious specialists have in the survival and well-being of their communities. Two visually captivating examples are

MASKS 117, 118   a *juju* masked gown worn by the Ngang associations in the small kingdom of Oku in Cameroon and a Mboli mask from the Guro village of Poïzra in Côte d'Ivoire. The *juju* masked garment, known as *Keghefshio,* is worn by the highest-ranking members of the Ngang associations (fig. 6.3). Studded with a mixture of display and power elements—shells, metal amulets, bones, bird beaks, and magical destructive medicine affixed to its neck frill and headpiece—it is considered extremely dangerous.[2] Rich in its variety of materials, the Mboli mask is crowned with

Following pages:
6.2 Shaman's costume, with
details, from Siberia, c. 1770.
Institut für Ethnologie der
Universität Göttingen,
Abteilung Völkerkundliche
Sammlung.

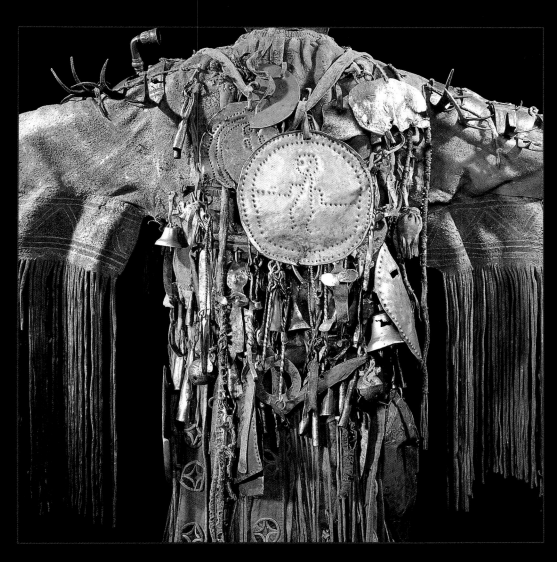

accumulations of monkey skulls, antelope horns, seed pods and other vegetal parts—materials associated with spiritual power coming from the world of the forest (fig. 6.4). Both works are metaphorical medicine kits, which give the diviners access to the spiritual world. They are visual feasts compared with many Western masks and armor designed for physical protection, which tend to be visually austere.

In addition to shamanic masks used for healing, other societies have developed protective masks to ward off illness. Among the Pende in the Democratic Republic of Congo, the Mbangu mask is worn to hunt disease. The mask's characteristic black-and-white asymmetrical features represent the bewitched—people suffering from various disfiguring diseases such as syphilis, epilepsy, smallpox, and tertiary yaws. During a public ritual the masker wears a humpback with a projecting arrow to signify that he has been stung by a sorcerer's arrow representing disease (fig. 6.5). He also carries a bow and arrow to hunt down either the illness or the person who disabled him. The masker performs the dual roles of the hunter and the wounded. In Europe during the Black Death, Venetian doctors wore Carnival-like masks with extremely long pointed noses to ensure they kept a certain distance from their patients or the deceased. Our contemporary equivalents are the hygienic masks worn by surgeons, nurses, and dental technicians to prevent the exchange of germs between themselves and patients.

6.3 Anti-sorcerer's *juju* costume, Oku province, Cameroon, 20th century. *Collection of Charles and Kent Davis.*

MASK 121

Battle Armor

Scientific investigation, technological prowess, and the control of nature have predominated the Western approach to the world; harmony with nature and the supernatural has preoccupied many societies outside of the West. They see the world as populated by a variety of spirits, and everything—including plants, the sky, the landscape—is alive with a spiritual force. This belief in animism is expressed in their artifacts, in their mythology, and in the human interactions with other animals and spirits.

Although masking is prominent in the ritual ceremonies of these societies, masks are seldom worn for physical protection. Success or failure in battle or a hunt is more likely to be interpreted in spiritual or religious terms. As Lucien Levy-Bruhl noted in his studies on Siberian bear ceremonialism, "Whatever the instrument, weapons, tools, or processes employed, [indigenous peoples] never consider success certain or even possible if these alone are used, without the concurrence of the unseen powers having been served. Material aids, although indispensable, play but a subordinate part. The [person] who has a successful hunt-

6.4 Mboli anti-sorcerer's mask, Guro village of Poïzra, Côte d'Ivoire, 1995. *Courtesy Anne-Marie Bouttiaux.*

6.5 Masqueraders dance the Central Pende mask known as Mbangu in the Democratic Republic of Congo, 1989. *Courtesy Z. S. Strother.*

ing expedition or reaps an abundant harvest or triumphs over his enemy in war credits the favorable result not . . . to the excellence of his instruments or weapons, nor to his own ingenuity and efforts, but to the indispensable assistance of the unseen powers."[3]

Tlingit warriors on the Northwest Coast were among the few traditional groups who made protective masks as part of their war gear. Visorlike masks covering the lower half of the face up to the eyes were worn in conjunction with wooden helmets. The wooden visor was secured in place by biting a spruce root pegged to the inside. These helmets were also richly carved with the heads of supernatural beings, part human, part animal, from whom the warrior sought to obtain protection and strength during combat. Such impressive totems must have transformed the battle into an elaborate theatrical display.

In the South Pacific, the Gilbert Islanders were unique in creating body armor that included protective headgear that covered the face. The following observation was provided by Charles Wilkes, commander of the United States exploring expedition in the Pacific, following his visit to the Gilbert Islands:

281

6.6 Warrior in armor
from the Gilbert Islands
(Kiribati), c. 1880.
*Engraving by Hans
Kaufmann, reproduced
in Friedrich Ratzel,* **The
History of Mankind**
*(New York: MacMillan),
1896-98.*

[A] sort of cuirass [was worn], covering the body as far down as the hips, and rising above the back of the head. . . . It was made of plaited coconut-husk fibers, woven into as solid and compact a mass as if it had been made of board half an inch thick, and was as stiff as a coat of mail. For the legs and arms, they have also a covering of netted sennit [cinnet] of the same material, which they put on. . . . However singular the bodydress is, that of the head is still more so: it consists of the skin of the porcupine fish, cut open at the head, and stretched sufficiently large to admit the head of a man. It is perfectly round, with the tail sticking upwards, and the two fins acting as a covering and guard for the ears . . . by its toughness and spines affords protection against the native weapons.[4]

In the same account, written in 1845, Wilkes states that the Gilbert Islanders "believe themselves invulnerable in their armor." Various European visitors to the islands reported the inhabitants to be the most warlike people in Micronesia, for everywhere they witnessed numerous scars on the people's arms and legs. Their densely woven and knotted armor was an effective defense against their principal weapons, formidable swords and spears carved in coconut wood and edged with compact rows of sharks' teeth. This type of armor was probably developed after 1765, when the Gilbert Islanders first came into contact with Europeans (fig. 6.6).

The introduction of the Corinthian masklike helmet in ancient Greece in the seventh century B.C. may mark the beginning of Western combat masks. Beautifully rendered as a single piece, it encased the entire head, cheeks, and jaw, obscuring all but the eyes, mouth, and chin. As the design evolved, the nasal guard became increasingly elegant and elongated, dramatically framing and focusing all attention on the eyes. The sudden occurrence of this masked helmet remains a mystery. The Greeks' primary weapons were swords and spears, and shields could perform many of the protective functions of a mask. In addition, the Corinthian helmets were confining, muffling the senses. Was there an irresistible tendency to convert the helmet into a mask? Helmetlike masks were an important part of Dionysian religious festivals, and armor's distinguished position in Greek society is confirmed by its frequent depiction in vase paintings, metalwork, and literature from the period (fig. 6.7).

Perhaps the Greeks believed that a battle mask would transform a citizen into a fighting warrior, giving him strength and courage for combat. But as Homer's description of Hektor in the *Iliad* shows, when the Greek readied for battle, he was empowered by more than his armor:

6.7 *Achilles slaying Penthisilea*, depicted on a Greek vase painting, c. 540 B.C. *The British Museum.*

The armor was fitted to Hektor's skin, and Ares the dangerous war god entered him, so that the inward body was packed full of force and fighting strength. He went around calling in a great voice to his renowned companions in arms, and figured before them flaming in the battle gear of great-hearted Peleion.[5]

Some of the most magnificent helmets and masks ever to be produced originated in Japan between the mid-sixteenth and seventeenth centuries. Japan was in a process of unification following a tumultuous period of wars and social upheaval. During this brief interlude, creative activity went unchecked. It was also the moment when firearms first entered Japan by way of a Portuguese trader who had been shipwrecked on the southern Japanese island of Tanegashima in 1543.[6] The introduction of the gun changed entirely the way battles were fought. This, coupled with the unbridled freedom of expression, fostered a completely new type of armor and the development of conspicuous helmets.

Created for the samurai, Japan's military elite, these fantastically shaped head sculptures and masks were unique statements of personal identity and taste. They were dramatic departures from the traditional hemispherical helmets that had been used. Their purpose was to aggrandize the wearer and facilitate identification during battle (fig. 6.8). The colorful lacquers,

6.8 The warrior Oda Nobunaga at the Battle of Nagashino (1575) accompanied by a helmet bearer carrying his famous helmet, mid-17th century (detail from an eight-panel screen). *Robert Burawoy collection.*

fanciful crests, and shapes were proud symbols of the military aristocracy. Each helmet was elaborately adorned with designs inspired by various sources—Korean and Chinese metalwork, attributes of Shinto and Buddhist deities, animals whose particular features or strength the samurai wished to be identified with, and references to famous battles. These auspicious motifs were believed to have the ability to protect the samurai while also overwhelming the enemy.

Grotesque, fierce-looking iron masks were worn with the helmets to both frighten the enemy and protect the wearer's face from weapons. As ferocious expressions of terror, the masks symbolized the samurai's power to overcome antagonistic forces. They not only transformed the warrior's appearance but inspired his performance as well. With the peace and stability that characterized the next two and a half centuries, armor became essentially a luxury item intended primarily as artwork for ceremonial display. MASK 127

In Europe, through the Renaissance, incessant warfare forced states to continually improve their systems of defense. Like the fortifications surrounding the towns, armor underwent numerous alterations to withstand the increasingly technical and powerful means of combat. The advent of gunpowder had a decisive impact on the development of armor. Soldiers became increasingly vulnerable to improved weaponry, especially handguns that were introduced in the second quarter of the fourteenth century.

By the mid-fifteenth century, full suits of plate armor replaced mail, integrating what were MASK 125 previously separate components into one lustrous, unified shell. The knight was now dramatically enclosed in an invulnerable steel skin, a second persona. The streamlined contours of the plate armor rendered the cumbersome shield obsolete and provided the glancing surfaces necessary to deflect weaponry. Both as hardware and as treasured art objects, the armor helped transform the warrior: fortified and impenetrable, he appeared ominous, daunting, and invincible, prepared to conquer the world. He exuded a look of rationality, domination, and control, totally disengaged from nature (fig. 6.9).

The evolution of European helmet designs paralleled advancements in body defense. Helmets were particular showcases of an armorer's metalworking skills and construction ingenuity, for in addition to protecting the head, elements were devised that permitted visibility and ventilation during strenuous battle. With the introduction of visored helmets in the late thirteenth century facial protection improved significantly and the rounded visors could effectively deflect a blow aimed at either the face or the top of the head. The most successful design, however, was the close helmet with its single or two-part visor. Its pivoting visor could be kept lifted to expose the knight's face until the moment before attack, when it was closed and locked shut.

Despite this functionality of design, however, a decorative element developed for reasons of identity and status. Knights were proud of who they were and wanted their heroic deeds and identity known. This and quick recognition by one's own forces during the chaos of battle or tournaments led to the art of heraldry. Each knight had his own registered coat of arms whose hereditary marks were passed down through generations. Emblems were painted on shields and incorporated into the crest fixed to the top of some helmets. Their decorative and bold contrasting colors, visible from afar, helped distinguish friend from foe.

The significance of European armor both as protective equipment and as an artistic statement waned from the seventeenth century onward. During that period the intensification of warfare and widespread use of firearms posed serious threats. Armor was in such great demand that it had to be produced quickly and inexpensively: its main virtue depended on its bulletproof capabilities. However, the excessive weight of bulletproof armor was unwieldy, severely encumbering the wearer's ability to fight or even move. New combat strategies and the long distances that armies marched also forced them to shed the armor. Close helmets were eventually replaced by open-face versions; and by the early eighteenth century, armor had virtually disappeared from European battlefields and was worn only as "fancy dress" for ceremonial purposes by high-ranking officials.

6.9 Field Armor in the "Maximilian" style, 1510-25, attributed to Wilhelm von Worms the Elder and others, Germany. *The Saint Louis Art Museum.*

Throughout the world armor has served as an important indicator of rank. For the elite it was a mark of distinction, an ostentatious display of power, possession, and an affirmation of social position. The quality of workmanship and decoration were expressions of the owner's wealth and artistic sensibility. Helmets were worn like crowns, glorifying the leader. Embellishments enhanced a leader's personal image of power and pride not only as an imposing statement to the enemy, but to sustain the morale and confidence of himself and his men. It communicated immediate recognition of the wearer and what he represented. Armor could even humiliate the enemy: as an impressive display of wealth and power or as a reminder of a previous defeat, it could intimidate the rival. The effort lavished on producing battle armor of great beauty was ultimately an advertisement for the armorer's craftsmanship.

In Europe armorers were the most revered and important craftsmen of their time, for in addition to their expert metalworking skills they were entrusted with protecting their leaders in battle. And some of the greatest artists in European history, including Hans Holbein the Younger, Leonardo da Vinci, and Albrecht Dürer, collaborated with armorers on design and decoration. The pristine sculptural forms of battle armor were sometimes enriched with etched decorations, although embossing was kept shallow to avoid creating an edge for the point of the sword or lance to catch on. Eventually, however, the priority for bodily defense was overridden by the patron's indulgence in artistic pursuits and opulent display: the smooth practical surfaces of battle armor were replaced with dense ornamental motifs in high relief.

The prestigious role of armor in many cultures has been prominently depicted in their art. One of the most resplendent battle paintings of the ancient New World is on the interior walls of a temple at Bonampak, in Mexico, where murals vividly depict pageants of Maya warriors in full regalia engaged in combat (fig. 6.10); many famous European paintings and sculptures commemorate a victorious leader, battle scenes, triumphal processions, or are portraits of noblemen dressed in splendid battle regalia. In fact, much of our knowledge of European armor has been gleaned from paintings, manuscripts, sculpture, and tapestries. Few complete examples of original armor from the fourteenth and fifteenth centuries survive intact; the material was so costly that parts were replaced individually, or the armor was recycled and remade over and over again. For a warrior who often owed his life to his armor, it had a particular symbolic significance. Armor has been revered as a memorial of a battle, a competition, or an act of bravery—expressions of human strength, courage, and power.

6.10 Battle mural from Bonampak, Mexico, Late Classic period, c. 800. *Courtesy Peabody Museum of Archaeology and Ethnology, Harvard University.*

OFFENSE | DEFENSE

 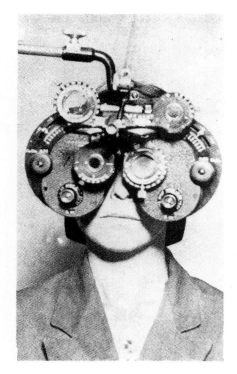 

Masks of Industrial Culture

There is a formal similarity to many masks designed for physical combat, but as artistic state-ments, their appearance and decorative details characterize the prevailing stylistic trends of an era. During the early twentieth century, distinct facial features were commonly depicted on protective masks. Like some Western art of the time, some even appeared to be influenced by the burgeoning vogue of African masks. But by the first world war the spirit of a machine cul-

MASKS 131, 132 ture pervaded mask designs with extraordinary visual impact. Industrial masks portrayed the wearer as a mechanized individual, symbolically equating humans with the strength and efficiency of machines (fig. 6.11). Gas masks became the twentieth century's visage of war. The metaphor of the machine was not inconsequential—at the time artists were either extolling the beauty of modern technology or despairing of an increasingly dehumanized world.

By the middle of the twentieth century facial features were eliminated or became integrat-ed within the mask's overall design, paralleling tendencies in modern art toward complete abstraction. Like the modern artist in quest of the essence of sculptural forms, makers of mod-ern headgear have distilled their designs to abstract featureless forms. Totally effaced, the glis-

MASKS 134, 137 tening mesh of a fencing mask or a contemporary bullet-resistant mask is reduced to a contoured face shield, removing all features but the eyes. The labor-intensive art of fabricating unique armor has now been replaced with standardized forms, mass-produced from molds, with few protrusions and virtually flawless paint finishes.

These modern masks are not only beautiful objects, but their designs enhance the visual expression of their purpose. Each feature provides a visual clue to the mask's function. Not only does a welding mask protect the worker's eyes and face from infrared and ultraviolet rays and

6.11 Protective face masks, illustrated in "Aboutissements de la mécanique," *Variétés* 2/9 (15 January 1930). *Courtesy Ellis Library, University of Missouri, Columbia.*

sparks, but its black impenetrable character represents an indestructible shield against fire.

MASK 138   The aerodynamic wing shape of a bicycle racer's or speed skier's helmet protects the face and skull of an athlete traveling at high speeds while giving abstract form to the concept of flight.

MASK 133   Deep perforations in hockey masks, strategically positioned and shaped to provide ventilation and deflect oncoming pucks, resemble the battle scars one is apt to incur in this physically intense and often violent game.

We tend to associate masks with non-Western cultures, yet rarely do we think of our industrial culture as producing masks. Modern industrial masks have the same psychological impact as their predecessors: they intimidate, mystify, terrify, and can transform the wearer's behavior. As shields that not only hide the face but allow it to move forward in a hostile environment, they are mediators between the wearer and the world.

The history of offensive and defensive equipment has been inextricably linked to an arms race: from the use of stone weapons to nuclear bombs, technology and combat have not been far apart. Makers of defensive equipment are forever trying to protect the wearer against battlefield tactics and the most destructive weapons in use at the time. Today, nonexplosive weapons such as chemicals, radiation, and information-sabotaging computers dominate the technology of offense. Unlike direct hand-to-hand combat, warfare has become increasingly disengaged from the body. Goggles, for example, capable of "blinking" electronically at one tenthousandth of a second, are worn by air force pilots to prevent blindness from the flash of a nuclear explosion. The competition between offense and defense has been ceaseless as each side advances its technological superiority over the other. The quest for combat advantages, for dominance and control, has provided a continual impetus to the development of science, technology, weapons, and body protection.

Some of the fundamental weapons that early armor was intended to protect against, such as guns and knives, still exist; armor endures in the form of bullet-resistant body defenses, riot masks, and shields, for example. Modern industrial masks are designed for physical protection and are usually linked to specific professions or vocations. They are often worn by society's heroes—the police, firefighters, astronauts, athletes, or soldiers—people whose actions are beyond the ordinary, or who risk or sacrifice their lives for others. Most are still worn by men, but as an unprecedented number of women are participating in professional sports, the military, and other activities, this is changing rapidly.

Just as armor from previous centuries revealed important information about its culture, these modern head sculptures are portraits of our technological society. They speak directly and powerfully of our own age. Many are more disturbing than the hoods of the Inquisition or a

6.12 Family Portrait, Ramat Gan, Gulf War, 1991. Photograph by Micha Bar'Am, courtesy Magnum Photos, New York.

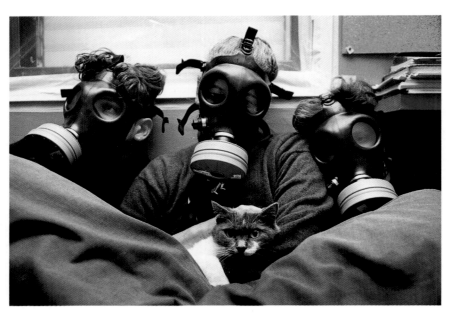

knight's armor precisely because of what true commentaries they are on the dangers and destructive capabilities of contemporary life. For centuries most protective masks were made for armed combat, but in industrial cultures masks are also worn to confront other unknowns: gas attacks, hazardous wastes, outer space, terrorism, chemical and biological, or "germ," warfare, nuclear explosions, sports accidents. Today, for instance, the entire population of Israel is equipped with gas masks, as they live with the perpetual fear of attack (figs. 6.12, 6.13).

Advances in modern weaponry and ammunition, as well as improved health and safety standards, account for the recent proliferation of protective headgear. This headgear helps ensure our safety both in everyday occupations and in recreational activities, like sports, and also preserve us in life-threatening situations. Some kinds, like underwater headgear and space helmets, make survival in alien environments possible. We have been able to explore where no humans have ever before ventured. Through our travels in space and underwater we have penetrated the realm of the nonhuman and have been able to survive for extended periods.

6.13 Martin Fletcher on *NBC Nightly News*, 1991. *Photograph by Arthur Grace, Courtesy NBC.*

Aside from military and sports equipment, the makers of contemporary masks are motorcycle manufacturers, underwater contractors, manufacturers of body armor, suppliers for the fire and police departments, and medical suppliers. The masks are constructed of the most resistant and durable materials available to protect the human face. Made of revolutionary synthetic and composite materials, they provide specific protection against temperature extremes, chemicals, fire, and other harmful elements. In recent years technology has given us lightweight, durable materials such as expanded polystyrene foam, reinforced plastics, and Kevlar, greatly improving the comfort and fit of headgear in addition to its ability to protect. Kevlar fiber, valued for its unique combination of bulletproof strength and heat resistance, is now used in a wide variety of protective applications.

As high-performance gear, these masks have one overriding purpose: to keep the wearer alive. Strict functional parameters dominate the design. Like tools, the sculptural beauty of defensive equipment derives from an economy of design and purity of form. Very little is extraneous, and lightness and ease of mobility are primary considerations. Condensation, heat, and suffocation have always been major drawbacks along with muffled senses. Today aerodynamic considerations and features such as ventilation, noise reduction, and scratch-resistant face shields are integral parts of the design. Full-face helmets become entire head systems replete with visors, breathing apparatus, lamps, infrared binoculars, and built-in radio communication systems. They not only accommodate the senses, they extend the body's capabilities.

Uniforms of Anonymity and Social Control

6.14 The eerie beginning of a David Duke cross lighting, 1976. *Photograph by Mitchel Osborne.*

Although shielding against physical injury is the primary purpose for most protective masks, others are worn to specifically conceal and protect one's identity. Secrecy masks weaknesses, and people feel safer behind a barrier. Donning a mask can give one courage and strength: with inhibitions reduced, the wearer is empowered with greater feelings of security. Anonymity de-individualizes. When a person cannot be identified or judged by others, emotions and impulses usually held in check are more apt to be expressed. The "you don't know who I am and I don't know who you are" psychology, however, carries the great danger that one might not feel personally responsible for one's acts.

The frightening link between anonymity and aggression has led to some of our most egregious acts as humans. In societies where men prepare for war by putting on masks or painting their bodies, the incidence of killing, torturing, or mutilating the enemy is considerably higher than if appearances were left unchanged.[7]

In the United States the robes and pointed white hoods of the Ku Klux Klan symbolize one of the most violent secret societies in the country's history. The simplicity of their hood is a chilling reminder of how little it can take to transform oneself, to even abandon one's humanity. This hooded order's legendary cross-burning rituals and hate crimes are haunting examples of humans turned savage. By operating in an aura of secrecy, the Klan has been able to increase its lawless behavior and minimize the opportunity for informants. In this case, the mask gives evil a safe place to operate. The uniformity of the Klansmen's ritual costume underscores the power of anonymity within a group, hiding their identity not only from their victims but from one another (fig. 6.14). In 1949, when asked why Klansmen wore hoods, their leader, Imperial Wizard Dr. Samuel Green, responded, "So many people are prejudiced against the Klan these days, that members are afraid they'll lose their job, their influence in public affairs, or otherwise be penalized if they are recognized."[8]

In a number of cultures, veiling the face and covering the head is a means of concealing identity. Although not an invention of Islam, the veil stands as an image of the social control MASK 1 and seclusion of women in the Arab world. Unlike most societies in which men are the predominant masqueraders, in Arab cultures men control women through the practice of veiling them. Viewed as a sexual force, the female body is hidden to protect women from external sexual aggression and to protect men from female desire, both of which can threaten or disrupt public order. The veil immures the woman from the world, protecting her sexuality while permitting her to move through society unrecognized. As an extension of the veil, the entire body is usually shrouded beneath tentlike garments that deny all reference to the body's contours. The link between sexuality and the veil is confirmed by the fact that young girls don the veil at the onset of puberty, while women past their childbearing years begin to relax the restrictions (fig. 6.15).

To lose one's inhibitions when disguised behind a mask is akin to surrendering oneself to collective team identity. Emphasis is not on the individual but on conformity, group fidelity, and obedience to authority. In sports, team spirit is a mix of mob psychology, animal instincts, and a sense of worth derived from being part of a group. The individual rises and falls with the

6.15 Veiled woman from the Jiddet Harassi tribe in Oman, 1988. *Photograph by Pascal Marechaux.*

team. As an organized force, the military is structured to carry out missions irrespective of the thoughts and feelings of the individual. Its deliberately authoritative and impersonal style of dress exploits group allegiance: masked in a crowd of uniformly attired warriors, soldiers submit to unit loyalty, abandoning self-awareness and making it possible for them to do things collectively that most people could never do alone.

Sports: Armor for the Playing Field

Protective face masks and headgear are now required in many Western sports. Shoulder pads and helmets, for instance, are the most salient features of a uniformed football player. The sheer size of their padded bodies heightens the drama of intimidation. In addition to its defensive function, the helmet is a football player's most dangerous weapon: more than half of all serious football injuries are caused by blows from helmets.[9] During the past couple of decades, helmets have evolved for a snugger fit, maximum strength, better shock absorption, and lighter weight for optimal protection against skull fractures. Many now incorporate transparent visors and wire masks to guard the face. The increased number of concussions and other debilitating head injuries caused by bigger, faster, and better-

6.16 Goalie Gerry Cheevers, c. 1967. *Courtesy Boston Bruins.*

6.17 a–d Jacques Plante in masks he developed for hockey goalies. *Courtesy Hockey Hall of Fame Archives.*

conditioned players colliding on an unyielding artificial turf will surely lead to further redesigns.

Just as the god of war empowered Hektor when he donned his armor, when an athlete puts on a uniform he or she is transformed into a team player, ready to tread dangerous territory, fight, and win. Much protective headgear is a game face, the face of a fearless warrior that conceals the thoughts, lines of vision, or any expressions of fear from the enemy. Hockey goalies develop "cage courage" when masked: armored and disguised, they feel bigger and protected, confident to play the game more aggressively. Like the demons who guard the facades of buildings, the goalie transcends into a new zone of toughness and defiance as he dons his mask to guard his terri-

tory and make his saves, keeping the evil spirit—the puck—from invading his space. What can be a game of quick-paced finesse and beauty often transgresses into boxing brawls between skate-clad gladiators. Masks amplify the spectacle: as uncompromising targets, their sinister appearance ups the ante of confrontation and intimidation.

We identify hockey goaltenders by their masks—they even achieve celebrity status when masked. Without them, the athletes are unrecognizable. Before the current standardized designs with face cages, hockey masks were customized to each player. Molded to the goalie's face, the skull-like fiberglass shields were hand-painted with team colors and designs that conveyed the personality of the wearer. Gerry Cheevers, goalie of the Boston Bruins, was the first to wear a decorated mask. Each time Cheevers was "wounded" by a puck traveling at up to 100 miles an hour, his trainer painted his mask with stitches (fig. 6.16). Proudly wearing his scars like heraldic bearings, Cheevers made this mask his trademark—a fun yet terrifying reminder of the dangers of hockey. The mask became a metaphor for what his real face could look like if left exposed.

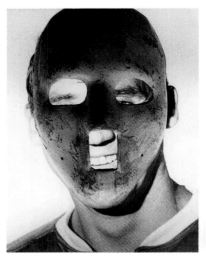
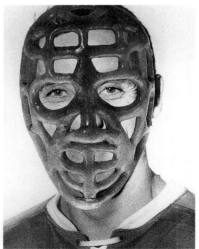
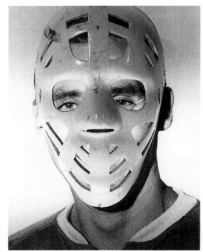

In sports, and sometimes even in combat, the absence of armor was both a tradition and a confirmation of one's manliness, courage, and fearless bravado. Personal pride outweighed the risk of injury, even death. Hiding behind protective gear was a sign of weakness. When hockey masks were introduced in 1959 by Jacques Plante, star goalie of the Montreal Canadiens, coaches objected (fig. 6.17a–d). Plante's coach, Toe Blake, feared that if he wore a mask he "wouldn't be fighting for his life"[10]—a truly vulnerable goalie would have the quickest reflexes. Recently, however, masks have become not only acceptable, but even mandatory equipment in sports. In fact, athletic uniforms today are dramatic colorful costumes that contribute ritual to sport, for both the players and the spectators. Sports is theater, and athletes' accoutrements are rallying devices.

Athletes, too, can be psychologically altered from one transitory state to another. A speed skier's full-face insulated helmet increases his or her chance of survival in a crash while traveling at high speeds, but it also helps to focus concentration by muffling sound and restricting vision as the skier slices through the wind. Speed skiers, whose objective is to ski straight down a mountain as fast as possible, now reach speeds of up to 150 miles an hour. The mental demands of such life-threatening competition are strenuous, and participants strive to elevate themselves into a trancelike state of mind. They study Zen, tai chi, and transcendental meditation to hone their balance and keep their bodies in line against the force of air. Technologically sophisticated equipment and protective gear have made it possible for people to engage in risky activities, pushing their limits to perform human feats in the face of danger (fig. 6.18).

6.18 Speed skier at Snowmass, Colorado, 1988. *Courtesy Shaun Paul Gabbard.*

Sports often have the same level of emotional fervor and enthusiasm associated with religious rituals. They are much more complex than just a recreational or spectator experience. Rich in heritage and meaning, they are integral to our social and cultural values. Their prominence dates back thousands of years to when communities designated a special place to conduct a game, or erected special buildings or arenas in which to play the game and seat the spectators.[11] Like the ritual areas set aside by our ancestors to play out myths, we create playing fields on level grounds where rules of fairness are practiced.

In some societies where certain animals were revered as god figures, rulers often called upon these divine beings for protection and strength during combat or rituals. This was true of both the ancient Maya and Aztecs, whose high-ranking leaders glorified their positions and gained access to divine powers by dressing as gods. During combat rulers impersonated deities by carrying shields with jaguar motifs and by wearing flamboyantly colorful and resplendent full-bodied war regalia made of jaguar pelts and other symbolic elements. Although the rulers personified the divine, artwork commemorating battles shows a distinction was made between a true god and a human impersonator: the Aztec warriors wore eagle or jaguar helmets, but their human faces peered out maskless through the animal's gaping mouth; Maya rulers were depicted in profile showing a cutaway of a deity mask hovering over their human face. Not only did warfare provide them an opportunity to associate themselves with the gods they portrayed, but transforming themselves into divine beings was also an effective way of intimidating the opponent.

Warfare and ritual ball games figured prominently in Mesoamerican attitudes about life, death, and sacrifice. They were frequently performed as ritual acts integral to their mythology and their ordering of the world. Preoccupation with death pervaded Mesoamerican societies who believed human beings were created to nourish the gods through sacrifice. One of the primary motives for warfare and ball games was human sacrifice and decapitation. The renewal of life and survival of the community depended on offering blood to the gods, so constant warfare and ceremonial events were seen as ways to capture sacrificial victims.

The ball games that were played throughout Mesoamerica since ancient times continue to this day. The ball court was a site for both large public spectacles and sacred rituals. The games ranged from a popular recreational sport to violent battles in which players or war captives competed for their lives. In the game, two opposing teams volleyed a solid rubber ball back and forth. The ball was struck with the hips, buttocks, arms, legs, and thighs. Protective padding covered the arms, knees, and legs, and a yoke was worn around the lower waist and sternum to provide a hard surface with which to hit the ball and protect the player. There is scant evidence, however, that the protective equipment included masks. One exception is found in the Oaxaca region, where stone reliefs at Dainzú depict ballplayers in animated positions wearing open-cage face shields that resemble contemporary catchers' masks (fig. 6.19).[12] Clay figurines in static poses with partial face masks have been found in burial sites at other locations, but it is not certain whether they were worn for protection during the game or during postgame festivities.

6.19 Relief at Dainzú in Oaxaca Valley, Mexico, Middle Pre-Classic Period (600-200 B.C.), showing a ballplayer wearing a protective face mask. *Courtesy Rijksmuseum voor Volkenkunde, Leiden, The Netherlands.*

When played in a ritual context the ball games represented a battle between life and death. Stone and ceramic figurines of both Olmec and Tlatilco kings portray them wearing protective ball game equipment and regalia such as headdresses, bichrome face masks, and mirror pendants. The mirror associated the rulers with the sun god, and corn iconography, an Olmec symbol of fertility and life, identified the rulers as priests of the corn god. These masks and headdresses were not worn for physical protection, but they metaphorically empowered the rulers to defeat the forces of death and drought in order to promote fertility and new life for the community.[13] The headdresses, masks, and emblems were spiritual vehicles through which sacred power and protection could be obtained.

In Europe rival groups of knights used to hold dangerous tournaments staged as mock battles in preparation for real warfare. By the Renaissance, these tournaments became more organized games and were accompanied by extensive rules and extravagant pageantry. The most

6.20 Leonhard Beck,
*The Art of Jousting and
Tilting*, woodcut from *Der
Weisskunig*, 1512–16. *The
Cleveland Museum of Art*.

popular games were jousting matches in which two knights dueled on horseback, charging each other on opposing sides of a barrier (fig. 6.20). Initially, there was little distinction between battle and tournament or jousting armor, but by the fifteenth century special jousting armor was devised, reinforced with additional components. Weighing as much as one hundred pounds, it was worn for much shorter periods than battle armor, and the wearer's movement was considerably more restricted. Jousting helmets were formidable, completely impenetrable except for the recessed eye slit. Their smooth, glancing surface, projecting to a sharp ridge, was a critical deflecting element: the objective was to score points but not injure the opponent.

MASK 126

Today an increasingly popular form of mock combat is paintball. An intense team sport played in open fields and forested terrains, it is a contemporary version of "Capture the Flag." The objective is to steal the enemy's flag and carry it back to one's home territory without being hit. As the battle is fought, opponents are eliminated, marked "dead" with paint-filled gelatin pellets shot from air guns. The warriors are primarily teenage boys, adult men, and former soldiers. To get psyched for the game contestants often apply body paint as part of the pregame ritual. Their martial attire includes camouflage vestments and specially designed gear. The most important piece of equipment is the face mask; it is central to the game's rules and rituals, and its purpose extends beyond protecting the eyes. The number one rule in paintball is, Never take off your mask, even if you get hurt; otherwise, you forfeit your game for the remainder of the day. The mask is part of team identity, of belonging, of collectively assuming a new role and behavior. It helps the player to adopt a warrior's facade during the game. Once the game begins, an "us" and "them" camaraderie develops quickly, leading to loyalties and extensive male bonding. Paintball is a game of good guys versus bad guys, and players suspend everyday civilities while indulging in aggressive impulses.

Professional sporting events are aired on prime-time television so that people all over the country, even the world, can tune in simultaneously. Vast sums of money, resources, and social energy are poured into the games, which are hyped with pumped-up spirit and tradition. Sports arenas, once small-town natural sites, have evolved into grand public places. Elaborate stadiums that are often the largest structures in the region are theaters of collective dramatization, emotional outburst, and controlled frenzy. Their colossal size makes them urban status symbols.

Football is one of the most highly aggressive sports, a unique combination of sophisticated strategies and primitive combat. According to NFL spokesman Greg Aiello, "The essential nature of the game . . . is based on hitting and physical contact."[14] When the ball is snapped, bodies and helmets collide as players push, block, and tackle one another. What prevents the game from becoming overly aggressive is the threat of penalties and rules that keep players in check. Even football's martial language implies combat. It is described as a "war" game in which offensive and defensive linemen face off across a trench, the line of scrimmage. Games are played on a level field, the battlefield. Football coaches liken themselves to generals, their assistants to officers, and the players to soldiers. The thrown ball is referred to as the long bomb, the quarterback may launch an aerial attack, the defensive lineman runs to break through the lines to invade enemy territory.[15] Pregame locker room rituals heighten the athletes' sense of transformation, rush of adrenaline, and aggressive inclinations. Prior to the competition, some players collectively bang their helmets against the side of their lockers. They feel invincible in their protective uniforms and helmets—fearless warriors who approach the game like gods. After the contest the players tend to their wounds and inspect their helmets for evidence of battle damage.

To survive in alien and hostile frontiers, people must sometimes take their environment with them. In the second half of the twentieth century, we invented "space-age" armor: the full-face helmet and space suit worn during space missions. For centuries people have pondered worlds beyond our own, and flight has always been the most magical kind of travel to emulate. The flight of souls to the moon and the heavens has been central to the religions of many cultures, East and West. Before the mid-twentieth century, human flight and travel to outer space were relegated to the shaman's spirit journeys, storytellers, science fiction, and visions of freedom and escape. People dreamed of traveling in fanciful spaceships to explore and inhabit the universe.

In the 1950s and 1960s, the United States entered the space race by competing with the Soviet Union for national prestige. This endeavor catapulted our visions into reality, culminating in the space exploration that brought us the indelible image of planet earth suspended in the black void of space. It changed forever our relationship to earth and the universe. It gave us a new unifying perception of the world that has taken us beyond local consciousness to a universal awareness. Astronaut John Young believes that "human exploration of space is the most important endeavor in the world because some day it might lead to our survival. If you want to see an endangered species, get up and look in the mirror."[16] The space suits and headgear physically enabled humans to break from the earth's atmosphere and gravity's bond and make that fantastic adventure possible. The famous photograph of Buzz Aldrin standing on the moon during the Apollo 11 mission, his gold-domed visor reflecting the moon's horizon, is a reflection of the human self, reminding us of how far we have come (fig. 6.21).

The space suit with helmet is a package, a portable life-support system that allows astronauts to exist in an alien environment. The dangerous and deadly situations that threaten travelers at high altitudes increase exponentially in outer space. As armor, the space suit protects an astronaut from nature's hostile forces—assaults from speeding meteoroid particles, temperature extremes, and unfiltered solar rays. Without protection, there would be instant death. Unlike the disturbing impact of many masks designed for physical protection, space helmets evoke an aura of innocence and benevolence. Their innocuous bubble form is purely functional; resembling a colossal eyeball, it permits the eye to see far and wide, while the astronaut floats silently in the solitude of space. Space helmets are not meant to be confrontational; they were designed for exploration intended to benefit all of humankind. Profoundly different from a shaman's bird costume and mask, the space suit is yet curiously related to it in another way: like the shaman's magical power of flight it has allowed us to continue our journey that was begun in Paleolithic times, when humans first began to explore other identities. Like the knights and their armor of centuries past, astronauts take pride in their suits—are spiritually connected to their suits—and some even keep track of their space armor long after they have worn it.

Most of the early pressure suits worn by pilots and astronauts resembled those depicted in space novels by nineteenth-century science-fiction writers like Jules Verne, who wrote about technology's unlimited possibilities. When designing space suits, engineers culled ideas from deep-sea diving equipment, the articulated protective shell of tomato worms, and pressurized inner tubes. As part of their research on articulated joints, engineers also studied armor at the Higgins Armory Museum and the Tower of London.[17]

Many of our dreams derive from myths, which we continue to revive and build upon over the centuries. At the time of the early space odysseys, Western society was invested in viewing itself as the rightful descendants of the Greek and Roman cultures in its drive to dominate the forces of nature. Greco-Roman mythology even provided the narrative roles for space exploration: Mercury, Gemini, and Apollo became the names associated with the early manned space missions. Apollo, the solar deity, the Greek god of light, became the metaphor for space travelers of reason who were launched into the heavens by the Saturn rocket, named for the Roman god of agriculture and the raw forces of nature. Apollo, also known as the celestial archer whose arrows ranged long and infallible, symbolized courage and control, whereas Saturn, the divinity for whom the festival of Saturnalia was named, was a god of wild energy, who taught the Romans about feasting and wine. Like the orgiastic and unrestrained festivities of Saturnalia, Saturn represented the body out of control. The Apollo astronauts sat with the controls atop the thirty-six-story Saturn booster, which together resemble an arrow. Today, because of the frequency of its missions, the grand enterprise is now prosaically termed the space shuttle.

Protective headgear, more than any other mask type, is an index of the technological and cultural developments that have taken place within a civilization. Their creations express the temper of their times. They are both the products and the consequences of technology. But, while the magnitude of destruction and technology have changed dramatically in some societies, the ongoing need for protective masks confirms that human nature has changed very little. The link between masks created for physical uses and masks created for spiritual purposes is protection and transformation. Both symbolize the wearer's power and position in the world. The persistent belief in the spirit world and our ability as humans to impact it continues to nurture shamanic healing and spiritual protective practices. Industrial masks inadvertently send powerful messages beyond their workaday functions, which is one of the reasons we are so captivated by them. As we are faced with new and graver dangers, as the technological sophistication of terrorism increases, and as environmental hazards, allergies, and diseases threaten our existence, so must the protection used to combat them advance. Facial protection and body armor will reappear in new materials and forms as long as manufacturers and designers are challenged to improve their designs.

Although protective masks often have an adversarial quality, they can have progressive and benevolent functions that benefit humankind. As with many of the spectacular epics about voyages to new worlds, travel to space will continue to be one of the frontiers we pioneer, perhaps even inhabit, during the twenty-first century. And while the purpose of contemporary headgear is still to protect, it is no less powerful a form of communication about our ambitions, enemies, fears, and yearnings than its predecessors.

6.21 *Opposite:* Buzz Aldrin on the moon, 1969. *Photograph by Neil A. Armstrong. Courtesy Johnson Space Center, NASA.*

6.22 *Following spread:* Earthrise, as seen from Apollo 8, 1968. *Courtesy Johnson Space Center, NASA.*

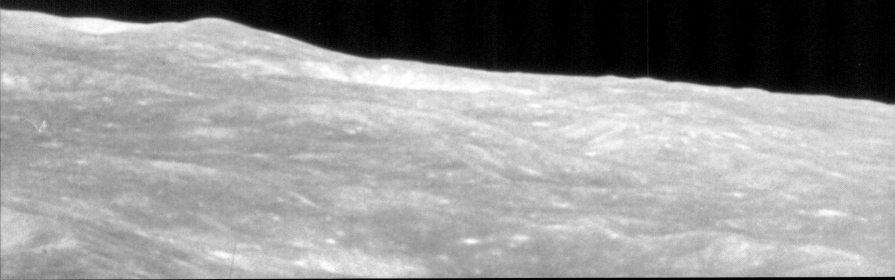

Mask Captions

Images and descriptions refer to the masks illustrated at the beginning of each chapter

CHAPTER 2: RITES OF PASSAGE

1 VEIL, c. 1985
Saudi Arabia; cloth, beads; h: 16 inches (40.6 cm); mask courtesy Sheila Hicks, headpiece courtesy Marion Lowe

One indicator of social status in the ancient Middle East was whether a woman's sexuality was "publicly" or "privately" owned, i.e., available to many or protected by a wealthy family. Veils became a symbol of the seclusion enjoyed by women of the privileged classes. Subsequent Muslim conquests in the Middle East extended the practice, which also corresponded to Islam's association of morality with the sexual female body. According to Muslim beliefs, veils are meant to protect women from aggression and to protect society from female desire, which threatens to disrupt the public order. Veiling requirements fluctuate as women's bodies change. Girls don the veil at the onset of puberty. In many cultures that incorporate veiling practices, the strictness slackens when a woman is past her childbearing years. Veiling often functions as a symbol for ideal social relations and as a "membership card" to signify who belongs to what group. *Meghan Barnes; photograph by Lynton Gardiner*

2 NOWO INITIATION MASK, 20th century
Mende people, Sierra Leone; wood, raffia; h: 15½ inches (39.4 cm); The Saint Louis Art Museum, Friends Fund

Bondo is the only known women's secret society in West Africa whose members are allowed to masquerade. Each year the young women and the officers of the society enter the forests to receive instruction on domestic activities, hearth and marketing skills, and knowledge of traditional medicine. Carved by men for the women who have successfully completed this initiation, the masks display elaborate coiffures, broad, lozenge-shaped faces, and generously curved neck rings. The deep furrows of the coiffure and the large square Islamic-influenced amulet represent and guarantee fertility. A black stained raffia top and skirt complete the costume. *John W. Nunley; photograph by David Ulmer*

3 LAKISI INITIATION MASK, 19th century
Mbundu people, Democratic Republic of Congo; wood, fiber, pigment; h: 30 inches (76.2 cm); The Saint Louis Art Museum, Partial gift of Mr. Thomas Alexander III and Laura Rogers and funds given by the John R. Goodall Trust, the McMillan-Avery Fund, Dr. and Mrs. William H. Danforth, Mr. and Mrs. Sam Langsdorf, Mr. and Mrs. Jefferson Miller, Ms. Jane Stamper, The Gateway Apparel Charitable Foundation, Mr. and Mrs. Charles F. Knight, Mr. and Mrs. William F. Schierholz, and donors to the 1993 Art Enrichment Fund

Masquerades, known as Makisi (Lakisi is the singular form), are part of an artistic tradition embraced by the Chokwe, Lwenda, Mbundu, and Lunda peoples of Angola and Zambia. This kind of mask was originally used in circumcision rites that helped to "steal" young boys from their mothers and move them into the patrilineal system. Currently the Makisi masquerade dance complex is represented by eleven different masked characters, but the nature of these characters is not known to outsiders. These masks are now rarely carved. Today, Makisi dancers are hired for parties, political events, and weddings. Although they perform in secular contexts, the dancers still provide a focus for building a strong identity. Only a handful of early masks have survived. *John W. Nunley; photograph by David Ulmer*

4 INITIATION HELMET MASK, second quarter of the 20th century
Matambu sect, Mungongo society, Sala Mpasu people, Kwilu-Kasai region, Democratic Republic of Congo; raffia, cane, other plant fiber, feathers; h: 47 inches (119.4 cm); The Museum of Fine Arts, Houston, Museum purchase with funds provided by the Alice Pratt Brown Museum Fund

Until the early 1960s, all Sala Mpasu boys were initiated at puberty into the local warrior's society (Mungongo). Thereafter, they could gain status and property by joining more societies and obtaining the rights to wear the masks associated with each. The more types of masks a man was privileged to wear, the greater his status. Upon his death, all the masks to which he had rights were danced publicly at his funeral. Bearded fiber masks, a mark of the Idangani society, were among the most important and highest status masks. Part of a male/female pair, they were worn with a netted shirt of plant fiber and a skirt of animal skins, which were said to empower the costume and its wearer. *Anne-Louise Schaffer; photograph by Lynton Gardiner*

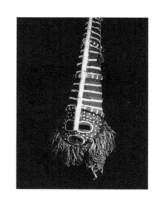

5 **Cikunza Initiation Mask**, 20th century
Chokwe people, Angola; wood, fiber, bark cloth, string, pigments; h: 58¼ inches (148 cm);
UCLA Fowler Museum of Cultural History, Gift of George G. Frelinghuysen

Initiation masks such as this Cikunza headpiece play a vital role in Chokwe society because the masquerades reinforce the teachings of the initiates in the bush camp. Resources are scarce, and the young must be taught as quickly as possible the roles that they must play as adults. The grasshopper that this mask represents embodies the Chokwe worldview. This animal experiences many metamorphoses as it pursues the path of life. Likewise, men and women pass through many stages before their ultimate passage into the world of spirits. Each of the circular rims dividing the headpiece denotes a level of human development. The conical shape of the mask renders each successive rim concentric to its lower counterpart. By such a construction the Chokwe may be offering a commentary on the nature of life. *John W. Nunley; photograph by Don Cole*

6 **Eharo Mask**, 20th century
Elema people, Papua New Guinea; bark cloth, pigment, wood; h: 61½ inches (156.2 cm);
UCLA Fowler Museum of Cultural History, Gift of the Wellcome Trust

Male cults in the Papuan Gulf utilize elaborate dance costumes and enormous men's houses. The men's house, or *eravo,* is the center of all major ceremonial events and the hub of male activities. Dance costumes, masks, and ceremonial materials are assembled and stored within the *eravo.* Construction of the *eravo* is a 10- to 12-year process engaging several neighboring villages. This Eharo mask would have been introduced during the last phase of construction to herald the completion of the new *eravo* doorway. The mask was used to reenact myths and to provide comic entertainment for the visiting women, children, and uninitiated males. This mask represents a totemic seabird crowned by the figure of a young male initiate, identified by his large mop of hair. It was probably made by a visiting male exchange partner in response to a request by one of the men constructing the *eravo,* and enhanced the status of the man who commissioned the piece.
Jacquelyn Lewis-Harris; photograph by Don Cole

7 **Alor Mask**, early 20th century
Tolai people, East New Britian, Papua New Guinea; wood, pigment, fiber, feathers, shell, coconut shell, clay;
h: 30 inches (76.2 cm); Linden-Museum, Stuttgart, Staatliches Museum für Völkerkunde

The Tolai inhabit a wide coastal area that includes parts of New Hanover, New Ireland, and the East New Britain island groups. They maintain control and provide societal guidance through the auspices of two men's societies, the Iniet and the Dukduk. The Alor mask is made and worn by the members of the Iniet society. The word *alor* means "skull" and refers to the main component of a former style of Alor mask, which was literally molded over the facial bones of an ancestor's skull. Both the older and the contemporary masks are considered to be the temporary resting place of the Alor spirit. Wooden Alor masks are carved by several Iniet clan members under the supervision of an elder "big man" or leader, who follows a design he has seen in a dream. This mask was carved to resemble a bearded ancestor wearing a large helmetlike hat. The intertwined snakes—a sea snake and a bush snake—rising to the apex of the headdress represent totems and the Iniet society's spiritual power over both land and sea. *Jacquelyn Lewis-Harris; photograph by Anatol Dreyer*

8 **Coronation Mask**, 20th century
Bamileke, Cameroon; wood; h: 21 inches (53.3 cm); UCLA Fowler Museum of Cultural History,
Gift of the Wellcome Trust

Some of the best-known masks from the Cameroon Grassfields are bold head crests called "Batcham masks," because the first such mask was acquired in the Bamileke kingdom Batcham in 1904. Men's societies, which were linked to the palace and to the noblemen who fulfilled important political and ritual functions in the kingdom, owned these and other masks depicting important royal animals. This type of mask is said to represent the hippopotamus, an animal reserved for the king. During performance the masquerader—dressed in a tunic-like garment, his head covered with a fiber or fabric hood—held the mask securely in place while executing the prescribed steps. Masqueraders performed on rare occasions: for the installation of a new king; funerals of kings, queen mothers, and important noblemen; and during annual harvest and New Year's celebrations.
Christraud Geary; photograph by Don Cole

9 FUNERARY MASK, 19th century

Lega people, Democratic Republic of Congo; leather, feathers, pigment; h: 9⅛ inches (23 cm);
Royal Museum for Central Africa, Tervuren, Belgium

The Lega people organize their social, political, and religious life along the lines of the closed
society of the Bwami, which encompasses numerous levels, some of which are accessible to
women. The society enables individuals to acquire wisdom and prestige through teaching and
the contribution of personal belongings. The Bwami also fulfills the role of art promoter: a number
of cultural artifacts are produced, exchanged, and presented to individuals as they gain access to
the upper echelons. In this context, numerous masks are passed along, most of which are made
of ivory or wood. This unusual specimen is carved from the sole of an elephant's foot. The mask
might originate from the Elanda society, who borrowed techniques from their Bembe neighbors;
if this is the case it could serve as the incarnation of a spirit in charge of social control.
Anne-Marie Bouttiaux; photograph courtesy Royal Museum for Central Africa

10 TATANUA HELMET MASK, late 19th century

Northern New Ireland, Papua New Guinea; wood, paint, opercula shell, lime plaster, plant fiber,
bark, bark cloth, rattan, coral; h: 15¼ inches (38.7 cm); The Museum of Fine Arts, Houston,
Museum purchase with funds provided by an anonymous donor

The most important ceremonies in the religious and social life of northern New Irelanders are
called Malanggan. Held one to five years after the death of an important individual, they not
only commemorate that person, but also provide the opportunity to initiate young men and women
into society. The ceremonies are staged by the clan of the deceased in the presence of invited guests.
Spread out over several weeks or months, they consist of dance performances, speeches, feasting,
and the exhibition of large wooden sculptures carved especially for the occasion. Several types
of masks are made for these ceremonies, but the best known is called Tatanua, derived from
the word meaning "spirit." They are worn by male dancers in combination with a bark shirt
and a leaf skirt as they mimic the movements of birds. *Anne-Louise Schaffer;
photograph by Lynton Gardiner*

11 ELEPHANT MASK, first half of the 20th century

Kuosi society, Bamileke, Cameroon; cotton cloth, flannel, glass beads, raffia cloth, indigo dye, cane;
h: 56¾ inches (144.3 cm); The Museum of Fine Arts, Houston, Museum purchase with funds provided
by the Brown Foundation and the Brown Foundation Accessions Endowment Fund

Elephant masks are among the most flamboyant works of art created by artists in several Bamileke
kingdoms of the Cameroon Grassfields. This mask consists of two flat round disks that represent
the elephant's ears, and two long cloth panels hanging down in front and in the back, depicting
the elephant's trunk. The masks are worn as part of splendid costumes that consist of billowing cloth
skirts, beaded, embroidered bodices, and wide, beaded belts. Wealthy Bamileke men's
societies, such as the Kuosi in Bandjoun, perform elephant masquerades to this day. These
societies support the king and act as his general staff. In precolonial times they defended him
against enemies. The elephant, an animal reserved for royalty, is thus an apt symbol for the role
of men's societies within the kingdom: it is a powerful animal and its ivory is a source of riches.
Christraud Geary; photograph by Lynton Gardiner

12 PARAE MOURNING MASK, early 19th century

Tahiti, Society Islands, Polynesia; shell and feathers; 36½ inches (92.7 cm);
University of Cambridge Museum of Archaeology and Anthropology

The most elaborate funerary ceremonies and the only masking tradition in Polynesia were
reserved for the funeral of the Tahitian high chief. When a leader died, the chief mourner wore this
unique costume during the final funerary rites that signaled the end of mourning and expressed the
grief and rage of the deceased. The entire costume was a collection of the most highly valued
materials; pearl shell, sea-turtle shell, fine bark cloth, human hair, braided sennit (fine coconut
fiber), and bird feathers. The craftsmanship and the design were commensurate with the
importance of the wearer and the rank of the person honored. The mask consists of several
pearl shell halves bound together, with minuscule eye holes drilled into the lower shells.
The mask was attached to a feathered turban of bark cloth, sennit, and braided human hair,
a combination of materials associated with sacred ornamentation. *Jacquelyn Lewis-Harris;
photograph by Lynton Gardiner*

13 MASK OF THE TIMUR-BATAK, 19th century

Batak people, Simalungung, North Sumatra, Indonesia; wood, pigment, palm fiber, horsehair, iron; h: 25¼ inches (64 cm); Royal Tropical Institute, Tropenmuseum, Amsterdam

This mask was worn during the funeral ceremony of an influential individual. The masked dancer carries a pair of wooden hands during the funeral masquerade, which is called "Causing that to dance which is the property of the soul." These ceremonies usually feature various masks representing a man, a woman, and a horse or a hornbill. The masked dancers perform in front of the house of the deceased during the wake, accompanied by a *gondang* orchestra. They follow the coffin to the cemetery, leaving the masks on the tomb or in a small house erected above the tomb. In the past, men and horses were sacrificed, but this is no longer considered necessary: the ceremonies themselves dedicate the dancer's soul to the deceased and assure the deceased that his descendants will continue to serve him. *Elisabeth den Otter; photograph by Lynton Gardiner*

14 FUNERARY MASK, 19th century

Kanak people, New Caledonia; wood; h: 20¾ inches (53 cm); Museum der Kulturen, Basel

New Caledonia encompasses several islands, including Grand Terre, which is the residence of the Kanak people. Kanak communities were organized around the men's clan house, called the Do Moan. Dance masks such as this one, sculptures, and important ceremonial items were stored within the Do Moan. Early descriptions connect the appearance of the mask with the funerals of major clan chiefs. In the northern areas the origin of the mask is based on the story of Azyu, a chief's son who was disfigured by enemies and killed. He sent the mask from the land of the dead, rather than returning to life without his nose. The costume's feathered mantle was thought to relate to powerful forest spirits that wear cloaks of feathers or transform into birds. In several areas of New Caledonia the word used to name this mask corresponded with the word for "bird." *Jacquelyn Lewis-Harris; photograph by Peter Horner*

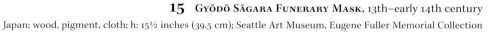

15 GYŌDŌ SĀGARA FUNERARY MASK, 13th–early 14th century

Japan; wood, pigment, cloth; h: 15½ inches (39.5 cm); Seattle Art Museum, Eugene Fuller Memorial Collection

Fierce and demonic, this mask represents the Dragon King of the Sea (Sāgara Nāgarāja). It was part of a large set of ritual guardian masks created for the Gyōdō, a Buddhist ceremonial procession within the precincts of a temple or shrine. The practice of circumambulation, the adoration of a sacred object by walking around it, was introduced to Japan from China during the late Nara period (710–794). On the occasion of a memorial for the dead or the public presentation of a sacred image or relic, the Gyōdō was solemnly performed by richly robed priests chanting holy scripture; they were escorted by attendants wearing masks of the protectors of the Buddhist faith. A long-snouted dragon, the head now missing, surmounted the head of the mask Sāgara; when worn with robes tightly drawn around the neck, it would have given the dramatic impression of a ferocious bestial sculpture come to life. *Steven Owyoung; photograph by Paul Macapia*

16 FUNERARY MASK, Middle Classic period (c. 400–c. 700)

Maya culture, Rio Azul, Petén, Guatemala; fuchsite inlaid with shell, colored with cinnabar; h: 7¾ inches (19.8 cm); Museo Barbier-Mueller de Arte Precolombino, Barcelona

This soft, greenish stone mask has the characteristics of the G-I, a deity of the Palenque triad with strong connections to the underworld. The eyeballs and the incised lines of the "design" on the face are colored with cinnabar, as are the incisions on the tooth. On the forehead is the bloodletting bowl, a symbol of sacrifice. At the sides of the mouth are fish barbels, also associated with the G-I. The back of the mask includes a glyph referring to Rio Azul, where it was probably found. This mask could have been placed on the face of the deceased or on top of a burial urn. As early as 1500 B.C. burial goods were put into graves to accompany the dead during their trip through the underworld. *Ted J. J. Leyenaar; photograph by P. A. Ferrazzini*

17 FUNERARY MASK, Late Post-Classic period (c. 1200-1521), 15th–early 16th century

Teotitlan del Camino, Mexico; turquoise, human skull, shell, mother-of-pearl; h: 8⅞ inches (22.5 cm); Rijksmuseum voor Volkenkunde, Leiden, The Netherlands

In the Pre-Columbian world, there was an emphasis on the dead and their voyage in the afterlife. The "face" of this human skull, doubtless that of an important person, is inlaid with a mosaic of turquoise, shell, and mother-of-pearl. The pattern forms a serpent on the forehead, which suggests that the deceased may have been a priest in the service of the god Quetzalcoatl, the Feathered Serpent, one of the most important deities for the Indians of Mesoamerica. In the Post-Classic period, especially during the cultural zenith in the late 15th and early 16th centuries, Mixtec craftsmen were in the service of their Aztec masters. Only a few items of this type still exist. This piece is missing the nose and right pupil. *Ted J. J. Leyenaar; photograph by Lynton Gardiner*

18 FUNERARY PLAQUE, c. 100–300

Nazca people, Peru; gold; h: 7¼ inches (18.4 cm); The Cleveland Museum of Art, Gift of the Hanna Fund

The Peruvians placed a false head or mask of either wood or precious metal over the mummy bundle onto the head of the deceased. This golden mask depicts a human face in ecstasy with an abundance of serpent symbols: the hair is represented as locks ending in serpent heads, and a writhing serpent is drawn under each eye. The serpent is a symbol of fertility for many people, indicating that the deceased was presumably a priest in the service of a fertility god. The use of gold indicates that the departed must have played an important role in the Pre-Columbian society of the Nazca. *Ted J. J. Leyenaar; photograph courtesy The Cleveland Museum of Art*

19 FUNERARY MASK, 500–600

Moche people, Peru; ceramic; h: 9¾ inches (24.8 cm); Collection of Mr. and Mrs. Meredith J. Long

This mask depicts the Fanged God with a wrinkled face. The mask combines feline imagery—the fangs and the central head in the headband—with serpent heads in the earrings. The use of feline symbols refers to death and indicates high status. Because of the constant shedding and renewal of their skin, serpents in Moche iconography symbolize fertility; they are also regarded as creatures in close contact with the afterlife because they live close to the earth. *Ted J. J. Leyenaar; photograph courtesy The Museum of Fine Arts, Houston*

20 FUNERARY MASK, Early Classic period (c. 300–c. 600)

Teotihuacan, Mexico; stone; h: 6½ inches (16.5 cm); The Art Institute of Chicago, Gift of Mr. and Mrs. Julian R. Goldsmith

As early as Olmec times, in the 2nd century B.C., masks were made to accompany the dead during their trip through the underworld. This mask shows the typical Teotihuacan oval eyes and, as is often the case with Teotihuacan masks, holes in the ear and on the forehead. A thread was probably pulled through the piercings so that the mask could be worn; in other words, the mask was sewn onto the face or breast of the deceased for the funeral ceremony and burial. Although the many surviving Teotihuacan masks resemble each other, they have different expressions, suggesting that each Teotihuacan funerary mask represents the face of a specific individual. This kind of mask has been found not only in Teotihuacan but in other parts of Mesoamerica as well, especially in the federal Mexican state of Guerrero. *Ted J. J. Leyenaar; photograph courtesy The Art Institute of Chicago*

21 FUNERARY MASK OF A QIDAN MALE, Liao dynasty (907–1125)

China; gilt bronze; h: 9⅝ inches (24.5 cm); Collection of Mr. and Mrs. Michael Steinhardt

The Liao dynasty was founded by the Qidan, a powerful federation of proto-Mongolian tribes that invaded China from the northern steppes. Although they adopted many Chinese customs and subscribed to Buddhism, the Qidan maintained a distinct culture, especially in spiritual beliefs and funerary practices. Golden death masks are the most striking of the Liao funerary customs, which included adorning the corpse in body nets of silver, openwork gilt crowns, and boots of gold and silver. Although this mask reveals the general ethnic features of the Qidan, the almond-shaped face, prominent chin, and fine mouth, as well as the minutely scored eyebrows, moustache, and goatee are specific characteristics that support the idea that the majority of Liao funerary masks are portraits of the deceased. *Steven Owyoung; photograph by Lynton Gardiner*

22 Mummy Mask, c. 1325–1224 b.c.

Egypt; plaster, linen, glass, gold, wood, pigments, bitumen; h: 20½ inches (52 cm); The Saint Louis Art Museum, Friends Fund and funds given by Mr. and Mrs. Christian B. Peper, Mrs. Drew Philpott, the Longmire Fund of the Saint Louis Community, the Helen and Arthur Baer Charitable Foundation, an anonymous donor, Gary Wolff, Marge Getty, by exchange, Florence Heiman in memory of her husband, Theodore Heiman, Ellen D. Thompson, by exchange, Dr. and Mrs. G.R. Hansen, Sid Goldstein in memory of Donna and Earl Jacobs, Friends Fund, by exchange, and Museum Purchase, by exchange

Ancient Egyptians took great care to prepare the deceased for an afterlife similar to the life that had been enjoyed on earth. Tombs built to last for eternity were filled with ample grave goods. As the repository for the soul of the deceased, the body needed to remain intact. Embalming and wrapping the body was a long and ordered process. Protective amulets were placed within the linen bindings, and a mask often covered the wrapped mummy. This mask, possibly from a noblewoman at the court of the great king Rameses II, contains glass inlaid eyes, nipples, and a floral diadem on her fashionably braided wig. Made of bitumen or pitch, the wig is modeled over the cartonnage. The face is covered in gold foil; the lips were probably formed of a thicker gold that is now lost. Both the scene carved on the arms of the deceased and the wooden amulets held in her hands confirm that she has joined the god of the underworld, Osiris, and will be protected. *Sidney Goldstein; photograph by David Ulmer*

23 False Head with Wooden Mask, end of Middle Horizon/late Intermediate period (c. 900–1200)

Pachacamac, Central Coast Peru; wood, cinnabar, shell, unspun cotton, cushion filled with leaves, textiles, plant material, resin; h: 10⅝ inches (27 cm); Staatliche Museen zu Berlin, Preussischer Kulturbesitz, Museum für Völkerkunde

In Pre-Columbian times, the upper-class inhabitants of the Andes buried their dead richly dressed, and the faces of the mummies were often covered with masks made of wood or precious metal. False heads might be attached to burial bundles, which were wrapped with layers of cloth to protect the deceased during their journey through the afterlife. This mummy mask still retains some of the pigment on the wood. Several bands cover the upper part of the head; one of these, on the forehead, is a sling for throwing stones. Two pieces of cloth (one on each side, hanging from the headband) complete the mask; the face is now exposed, but the cloth probably covered the face in the grave. *Ted J. J. Leyenaar; photograph by Lynton Gardiner*

24 Funerary Mask, Chalcolithic period (5000–3000 b.c.)

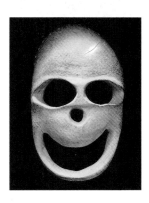

Middle East; stone; h: 6½ inches (16.5 cm); Collection of Mr. and Mrs. Michael Steinhardt

This oval mask resembles a human skull. Its forehead is high and slightly sloping, and the eye sockets are shaped like those of a real skull. Human skulls and masks made of various materials (asphalt, plaster, paint), with encrusted seashells for eyes and displaying individual features of the deceased have been found in Jericho, Israel, and Syria. Most of the molded skulls and stone masks have been found in dwellings, some of them in niches in houses. The skulls and masks were probably used in religious ceremonies and rites connected to the ancestor cult or to the cult of mythological family heroes. After a certain period of use— perhaps when they were assumed to have lost their magic power—these were buried under the floors of the houses. *Maya Avramova; photograph by Lynton Gardiner*

25 Xipe Totec Figure, 1400–1500

Aztec people, Mexico; stone, pigment; h: 23¼ inches (59.1 cm); The Art Institute of Chicago, as a Gift from Mr. and Mrs. Samuel A. Marx

In the second month of the Aztec year, which was called *tlacaxipehualiztli* ("flaying of men"), the return of spring was celebrated. At this time a young man was chosen to be sacrificed to the fertility god Xipe Totec, which means "Our Lord the Flayed One." After the chosen young man was skinned, the high priest of Xipe Totec was dressed with his skin, symbolizing the return of the spring season. The cut through which the heart was torn from the body is clearly visible on this statue—a cord would have been sewn through the holes of the skin, which would be visible in the back of this Xipe Totec figure. Under the skin of the sacrificed young man, the face of the high priest is visible. The Aztecs sacrificed to their gods what they considered the most precious gift possessed by humankind—life itself—in a gift that was particularly appropriate for Xipe Totec, the god of fertility. *Ted J. J. Leyenaar; photograph by Robert Hashimoto*

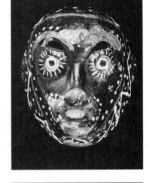

26, 27 Palo Volador Monkey Masks, 20th century

Mayan people, Guatemala; wood, pigment, hair; h: each 7⅛ inches (17.9 cm); Collection of Alfredo MacKenney

The Palo Volador, or Flying Pole, masquerade, which dates back to before European contact and colonization, is widespread among native peoples of Mexico and Guatemala. These two monkey masks were once worn in the Guatemalan version of the masquerade. Dressed in pants, jackets, and masks, two men descend from the top of a tall pole by means of ropes tethered to a rotating wood frame platform. The unwinding ropes form wider and wider circles as the maskers rotate to the ground. This ritual is performed for the spirits in hopes that they will bring the rains for the next growing season. Reflecting a shamanic cosmology, the four-sided wood platform symbolizes the four cardinal points, while the pole represents the sacred tree, or *axis mundi*, which unites this world with the spiritual one. As they descend from the sky, the masked characters bring the renewing spirit of the rainy season. *Jorge and Luis Luján-Muñoz; photographs by Lynton Gardiner*

28 Mask, c. 1820

Brazil; bark cloth, bitumen; h: 21⅝ inches (55 cm); Staatliches Museum für Völkerkunde, Munich

In the northwest Amazon region, masks appear at different social occasions and religious celebrations. They are worn exclusively by men, and most of them represent animals, natural phenomena, and occasionally useful plants. By wearing these masks, the men present their workplace, which is the wilderness, to the village women. This mask is made of bark cloth and painted in black and yellowish brown. With the help of a bent twig and careful darts, the mask keeps its original form. On top of the mask, the inner bark has been cut or torn to create tousled hair. *Helmut Schindler; photograph by Lynton Gardiner*

29 Tago Mask, 20th century

Siassi people, Papua New Guinea; palm bast, pith, bamboo, wood, fiber, tortoise shell, pigment; h: 24¾ inches (62.5 cm); The Saint Louis Art Museum, Gift of Morton D. May

The Tami Island of northeastern Papua New Guinea is central to a strategic trade route. Located between important coastal societies and surrounding islands, the Tami people are middlemen in the trade of raw materials essential to the manufacture of ceremonial objects. This Tago mask, which alludes to the trade relationship between the Tami and their neighbors, represents the ghost of an important ancestor. The mask probably originated in East New Britain, and the red and black paints used to decorate it come from the Siassi Islands. The Tago ceremony is held every 10 to 12 years. Two major dances celebrate the arrival and departure of the Tago ghosts. The yearlong series of ceremonies serves as a reminder of each clan's ancestral connections. *Jacquelyn Lewis-Harris; photograph by David Ulmer*

30 SNAKE MASK, 19th century

Bwa people, Burkina Faso; wood, pigment; h: 180 inches (457.2 cm); Collection of Thomas G. B. Wheelock

The Bwa people of Burkina Faso live in a spiritually charged environment where the borders between the natural and spirit worlds are fluid. This snake mask would have been danced at harvest and funerary rites to celebrate fertility and ancestral force. Transformed by a full raffia costume, the masquerader performs to the delight of fellow villagers. The sacred snake, usually a python, represents one of the creators of human beings. His sensuous, wavy motion also symbolizes lightning and its associative elements—fire, rain, and river water. The mouth of the snake is unusual in its extended length and for this reason it may also make reference to the beak of a bird, another animal popular in Bwa imagery. *John W. Nunley; photograph by Lynton Gardiner*

31 MONKEY MASK, 20th century

Winiama people, Burkina Faso; wood, pigment; h: 10 inches (25.4 cm); Collection of Thomas G. B. Wheelock

Monkeys physically and socially resemble humans, blurring the distinction between people and animals, the cultural world and the natural world. During harvest and funerary festivals performed in the African country of Burkina Faso, masqueraders in raffia primate costumes entertain villagers and invited guests. Mocking individual and stereotypical behaviors, the monkey character makes fun of the human condition. The masker also mimics sexual behavior, much to the amusement of the audience. The meaning of the striations that extend down from the eyes to the sides of the mouth is unclear, although they might represent the markings of a particular species of monkey. *John W. Nunley; photograph by Lynton Gardiner*

32 BLACK MONKEY MASK, 20th century

Dogon people, Mali; wood, pigment; h: 15 inches (38.1 cm); The Metropolitan Museum of Art, Gift of Lester Wunderman

Like all Dogon masks, the black monkey mask is worn at the Dama ceremony, which honors a deceased elder by facilitating the passage of his soul out of the village and enhancing the prestige of his family. The mask is also used in renewal rites known as Sigi, which celebrate the new generation of Dogon people and ensure the fertility of next year's crops. The Dama alludes to Dogon myths concerning the origin of death and the role of masks in counteracting its devastating impact. It can be seen as a public affirmation of the return to order after the disruption caused by death. Long, shaggy, black fibers hang from the black monkey mask to the dancer's knees and cover the short trousers worn by the masquerader. The wearer acts out the black monkey's lewd and antisocial behavior by grabbing his genitals and sometimes sitting conspicuously apart from other masked dancers, thus demonstrating the opposite of Dogon ideal human behavior. *Kate Ezra; photograph courtesy The Metropolitan Museum of Art*

33 MASK OF SADIMBE, 20th century

Dogon people, Mali; wood, pigment, encrustation; h: 43⅝ inches (110.8 cm); The Metropolitan Museum of Art, The Michael C. Rockefeller Collection, Purchase, Nelson A. Rockefeller Gift

Sadimbe is the only Dogon wood mask to represent the female character Yasigine. As the sole woman in each village admitted into the men's Awa society, Yasigine oversees funerals, commemorative Dama ceremonies, and the preparation of the masks and fibers worn in them. Although Yasigine does not wear a mask, she assists Awa members during the Dama and prepares the millet beer and sesame oil they use in rituals. Usually only one Sadimbe masquerader performs at the Dama or the renewal rites of Sigi; this is in contrast to other masks, like the Kanaga, which appear in great numbers. The Sadimbe masquerader dances alongside performers wearing fiber masks that represent women. His costume of fiber bodice, overskirts, and armbands resembles that of other Dogon masked dancers. The Sadimbe mask reminds the Dogon that it was a female, Sadimbe, who originally stole the masks from the indigenous people of the area and began to terrorize the men of her village with them. The men soon took the masks from Sadimbe, and their use became the prerogative of men. *Kate Ezra; photograph courtesy The Metropolitan Museum of Art*

34 TINGETANGE STILT MASQUERADER MASK, 20th century

Dogon people, Mali; mask and costume: wood, fiber, pigment, cowrie shell;
overall costume h: 109¼ inches (277.5 cm); Musée de la Civilisation, Quebec

The stilt masquerader appears early at a Dama commemorative ceremony and the rite of Sigi,
because his strenuous dance is too risky to perform when he is tired. As the ceremony progresses,
the dancer may remove his stilts and dance alongside other men wearing fiber masks representing
women. The stilt dancer's mask is similar to other Dogon female fiber masks, featuring a high-
crested hairstyle and the lavish use of cowries and beads. The stilt dancer wears the black, red,
and yellow fiber skirts and armbands that are typically worn by Dogon masqueraders. His
tight-fitting, brassiere-like bodice often incorporates false breasts made of halved baobab
fruits. The Dogon stilt masquerade character is identified both as a woman and as a waterbird.
Kate Ezra; photograph by Jacques Lessard

35 KANAGA MASK, 20th century

Dogon people, Mali; wood, pigment, fiber; h: 36 inches (91.4 cm); Museum Rietberg Zürich

The Kanaga is one of the most popular of the more than 70 Dogon mask types. With its
superstructure in the form of a double-barred cross, the Kanaga mask represents a type of
bird, an image of God with outstretched arms and legs, and the organization of the cosmos
into upper and lower zones. Like all Dogon masks, it is worn during the Dama ceremony
commemorating a deceased male elder, when dozens of men wearing Kanaga masks perform
together. This character also appears in Sigi festivals, which occur approximately every 60 years
for renewal of agriculture and human fertility. A fiber ruff and hood are attached to the mask,
and the dancer also wears a fiber bodice, overskirts, and armbands. The Kanaga dance is
strenuous and acrobatic: masqueraders bend at the waist and rapidly circle their upper bodies
so that the tip of the mask strikes the earth. *Kate Ezra; photograph by Wettstein and Kauf*

36 MAMUTHONE MASK, 1998

Giannino Puggiani, Mamoiada, Sardinia, Italy; wood, pigment; cloth; h: 11½ inches (29.2 cm);
Commissioned by The Saint Louis Art Museum

The Mamuthones of Mamoiada are the most famous masqueraders on the Italian isle of Sardinia.
Their appearance on January 17 marks the beginning of the Carnival of Mamoiada. On that day the
people of the village light fires and wait for the visit of the Mamuthones. Although the Mamuthone
characters themselves are mute, they have a sinister way of scaring whomever they come upon
with their racket of cowbells. The Mamuthones come from the infernal netherworld when the end of
the winter season and a pause in the agrarian cycle allow for the miracle of spring. The peasants and
the shepherds await, receive, and treat these alien beings well, offering them wine and sweets. The
spirits, thus appeased and friendly, will return to their subterranean world and protect the new agricultural year. *Paolo Piquereddu; photograph by Lynton Gardiner*

37 BOE MASK, 1998

Sebastiano Brasu, Ottana, Sardinia, Italy; wood, pigment; h: 19¾ inches (50.2 cm);
Commissioned by The Saint Louis Art Museum

This Boe mask, which represents an ox, and the Merdule, representing a rough and deformed
countryman, are the principle characters of Carnival in Ottana, Sardinia. They perform pantomimes
in which the Merdules try to control the Boes by holding them with ropes, even goading and beating
them with sticks if necessary. The movements are exaggerated and clumsy: the grotesque Merdule
shouts, grabs, and threatens, while the Boes throw themselves to the ground and beg for drinks and
candies. The men of Ottana stage an ironic and grotesque portrayal of their status as both the
owners of and slaves to their animals, because they must constantly tend to them at the expense
of other work. By mocking their own situation during Carnival, the farmers gain the strength to
face another year of toil. *Paolo Piquereddu; photograph by David Ulmer*

38 KUKOR MASK, 20th century

Sliven County, Bulgaria; wool, cord, beads, mirrors; h: 16⅞ inches (43 cm);
Bulgarian National Ethnographic Museum, Sofia

This mask's elaborate beaded embroidery, rosettes, and meandering patterns of beads are associated with female fertility and water. The elongated nose suggests a phallus, while the wavy lines that extend from the base to the tip of the nose symbolize the mythical serpent. As the procession of maskers travels through the villages, the highly reflective surfaces of the headdresses heighten the dramatic performance. The prominent mirror placed at the center of the mask is intended to ward off any evil spirits by reflecting the light of the sun. When the light reflected from the mirror projects onto onlookers, it gives them fertility and protects them from the evil eye.
Roumiana Danova and Zhivka Stamenova; photograph by Ivo Hadjimishev

39 KUKOR MASK, 20th century

Pavel Banja, Bulgaria; goatskin, wool, goat hair, wood, cloth doll; h: 59 inches (150 cm);
Bulgarian National Ethnographic Museum, Sofia

This headdress is part of a costume that consists of woolen trousers and a sleeveless jacket without a shirt. Young men dressed in costumes such as this make up the bands of kukors who visit several houses of the village, performing for the master of each household. The masqueraders offer their music, dance, and ritual blessings in exchange for food, leaving each household protected for the next year. A "bride" and "groom," both played by male masqueraders, symbolize the promise of fertility for the next generation. Sexual scenes are featured in the masquerade as well. Each kukor uses a sword to "strike" victims who represent the Turks, rulers of Bulgaria from the 13th century through 1878. *Roumiana Danova and Zhivka Stamenova; photograph by Ivo Hadjimishev*

40 SOUVRAKARI MASK, 20th century

Bonsko, Bulgaria; mask and costume: fur, leather, animal parts, wood; overall costume h: 108 inches (274.3 cm);
Commissioned by The Saint Louis Art Museum

This mask, part of the costume for the Bulgarian New Year (also known as Souvrakari), comes from the mountain village of Bonsko, south of the Bulgarian capital of Sofia. Groups of young men wearing these masks dance from house to house on New Year's Day, bringing good luck and health to the occupants. In return, the dancers are given homemade wine, brandy, breads, sausages, and cheese. The bells attached to the costumes sound in unison as the young men jump, skip, and parade through the streets. Beginning at the age of 8, boys join in these renewal ceremonies as an initiation into manhood. Black goatskin versions of this costume are considered to have the most spiritual power. This was once the costume of one of the leading dance groups in Bonsko.
John W. Nunley; photograph by David Ulmer

41 KUKOR MASK, 20th century

Ymbol, Bulgaria; wool, wood, bells, thread; h: 35⅜ inches (90 cm);
Bulgarian National Ethnographic Museum, Sofia

This Kukeri mask was used in the celebration of Carnival to ensure human and agricultural fertility. Its character represents both male and female fertility, as is symbolically conveyed by the red and white cross motifs attached to the face of the mask. The color red represents the sun, masculinity, and the regenerative power of male blood; white represents the female and her element, water. The stylized horns have evolved from the earlier usage of actual goat horns. Throughout the Mediterranean world, the goat is celebrated for its fertility, and its blood regenerates society and nature through its role in sacrifice. The stylized rendering of the mouth, eyes, and nose may have been influenced by icons and frescoes seen in Orthodox Christian churches throughout much of Bulgaria. Christian and pre-Christian notions of nature and humanity are blended in this Carnival mask. *Roumiana Danova and Zhivka Stamenova; photograph by Ivo Hadjimishev*

42 UGLY CHLAUS MASK, 20th century

Switzerland; mask and costume: vegetal matter, papier-mâché, pigment, brass, leather;
overall costume h: 72 inches (182.9 cm); Museum für Appenzeller Brauchtum, Urnäsch, Switzerland

Many agricultural societies perform masked fertility rituals for the New Year's holiday, celebrating
the death of the old year and the birth of the new. In Urnäsch, Switzerland, the Silvesterklausen (also
called Chlause) celebration occurs both on New Year's Eve and on January 13 (the date of New Year's
Eve before the Julian calendar). The original celebration was a peasant-based custom whose only
character was the Ugly, a demon who represented darkness and death. Its unsophisticated costume
was covered with hay, straw, leaves, and bells, and the mask's monstrous expression, fangs, and large,
bulging eyes were intended to scare away evil spirits from the village before the new year. In earlier
times the custom was associated with poverty and begging, and people were so frightened of the
Chlaus that the Church tried to eradicate the ritual. *Cara McCarty; photograph by Lynton Gardiner*

43 PRETTY-UGLY CHLAUS MASK, 20th century

Switzerland; mask and costume: evergreen tree parts, brass, leather; overall costume h: 72 inches (182.9 cm);
Museum für Appenzeller Brauchtum, Urnäsch, Switzerland

In most of the alpine regions of Europe good and evil are usually represented as two distinct
characters. However, in Urnäsch during the 1960s, the Pretty-Ugly Chlaus was created, representing a
mixture of the good and the bad. Resembling trees, the characters' elaborate costumes are covered
with vegetal matter, evergreen decorations, moss, animal parts, bells, and snail shells that symbolize
fertility and new growth. Their leaf- or pinecone-studded masks are capped with leafy sprigs or headdresses that sometimes depict scenes of daily life. Like the other characters, these walking "shrines"
do not operate in contained architectural spaces, but walk miles through the snow in groups that
visit homes, commercial establishments, and isolated farmhouses, where they are welcomed with
drinks and money. They bid farewell to the old year and wish their hosts happiness and bountiful
crops in the new year. *Cara McCarty; photograph by Lynton Gardiner*

44 YOUNG MAN CHLAUS MASK, 20th century

Switzerland; mask and costume: wood, pigment, textile, brass, leather, walking stick, socks;
overall costume h: 84 inches (213.4 cm); Museum für Appenzeller Brauchtum, Urnäsch, Switzerland

Early in this century, the Church instituted the notion of the "good" Chlaus, represented by the
appealing characters of the Handsome Young Man and the Beautiful Young Maiden. These
benevolent characters symbolize prosperity, fertility, and new life, and help assure healthy crops
in the coming year. Considerable effort and expense is lavished on these two costumes. The Young
Man is dressed in velvet pants, jacket, white knit socks, hiking boots, and carries a walking stick.
A harness hangs over the chest and back with two enormous cowbells that are shaken to both
inform people of the Chlaus's arrival and chase away evil spirits. These masks' idealistic expressions
and pinkish skin symbolize youth and renewal, while their ornate headdresses in the shape of
tiered wedding cakes depict detailed scenes of fertility and nostalgia. *Cara McCarty; photograph
by Lynton Gardiner*

45 YOUNG MAIDEN CHLAUS MASK, 20th century

Switzerland; mask and costume: wood, pigment, textile, brass, leather, gloves; overall costume h: 96 inches
(243.8 cm); Museum für Appenzeller Brauchtum, Urnäsch, Switzerland

The Young Man is accompanied by an idealized Young Maiden, who is played by a man
wearing a brightly colored velvet skirt, vest, white blouse, gloves, apron, and hiking boots.
The Young Maiden characters masquerade by mimicking stereotypical feminine movements, and
each wears a harness of 13 small bells. The masks are distinguished by their pink-colored delicate
features, decorated with makeup and a flower in the corner of their mouths. Their heads are
crowned with fanciful headdresses that portray elaborately carved and painted scenes of everyday
village life such as the harvest, woodcutting, and weaving. The motifs on these headdresses,
coupled with yodeling performances and the noise of bells, underscore Urnäsch's history as
a dairy farming community. *Cara McCarty; photograph by Lynton Gardiner*

46 Namahage New Year's Mask, 20th century

Japan; wood, pigment; h: 23⅝ inches (59.8 cm); National Museum of Ethnology, Osaka

According to the traditional lunar calendar of Japan, the first full moon of the year marks New Year's Day; it generally corresponds to the 14th or 15th of January in the solar calendar. The date is called Koshogatsu (Small New Year) in contrast to the Ohshohgatsu (Big New Year), held on the first of January. The theme of gods dressed in mystifying disguises and visiting houses at the Small New Year is found in various parts of Japan. The Namahage rite in Akita Prefecture is the best-known practice of the Small New Year celebrations. Groups of two to five young men disguise themselves as Namahage with fierce masks and straw coats. Made of bark, paper, or wood, the masks are either red or blue in color. The masqueraders visit each village house, violently admonish the children, and bless the family. The head of the family entertains Namahage with sake (rice wine) and food. Namahage are said to be gods who bring good fortune, and by extending hospitality to the gods, people hope to ensure prosperity in the coming year. *Kenji Yoshida; photograph courtesy National Museum of Ethnology, Osaka*

47 New Year's Lion Mask, 20th century

China; papier-mâché, pigment, cloth, hair; h: 24 inches (61 cm); The Field Museum, Chicago

The Lion Dance, commonly performed in northern China, is connected to the annual New Year celebration of the Feast of Lanterns. The dance is executed by three skilled acrobats, two of whom wear the Lion mask and cloth body, while one holds a brightly colored embroidered ball. The Lion is led through the neighborhood, stopping at houses and shops to receive small gifts of money. Because the lion is not indigenous to China, it is believed that the Lion Dance was brought from western Asia during the Tang dynasty (618–907). The historical antecedents to this dance are all related to ritual cleansing for the new year. For example, in the Han dynasty (206 B.C.–A.D. 220), the new year was celebrated at the imperial court with a performance by an exorcist and twelve eunuchs. Dressed in fur, feathers, and horns, they were led by officials in animal masks who danced and shouted, cleansing the royal halls of pestilence and evil spirits. *Steven Owyoung; photograph by John Weinstein*

48 Mask of a Jew Devil, 1991

Mestizo people, San Bartolo Aguacaliente, Guanajuato, Mexico; goat horns, wood, pigment; h: 20¼ inches (51.4 cm); Museo Ruth Lechuga de Arte Popular, Mexico City

In the creation of this unique mask the mask maker made use of the shape of the wood and its branches. On Holy Thursday a number of maskers portray "Jew Devils." Within this group, one has female features and another is a skeleton, while the rest have stylized human characteristics. All of these masks feature animal horns and are therefore called *cuernudos,* "the ones with horns." During the afternoon of Holy Thursday they fight mock battles among themselves. Early the next morning all wickedness has been extinguished, and the maskers escort a procession in which the whole population takes part with songs, candles, and an enormous display of flowers. *Ruth D. Lechuga; photograph by Lynton Gardiner*

49 Goat Carnival Mask, c. 1965

Otomí people, El Nante, Hidalgo, Mexico; wood, goat horns, goat hair, leather; h: 20 inches (50.8 cm); Museo Ruth Lechuga de Arte Popular, Mexico City

According to the 17th-century chronicler Fray Bernardino de Sahagún, the Aztec New Year began on the second of February. This coincides approximately with the European Carnival, which was introduced to Mexico shortly after conquest. The synthesis of pre-Hispanic traditions and European customs resulted in days of rejoicing and uninhibited gaiety before entering the fasting and introspection of Lent. This mask, more in keeping with the European tradition, is worn by small-town revelers who dance in the streets. For this occasion a variety of masks are worn, most of which represent animals or human skeletons. *Ruth D. Lechuga; photograph by Lynton Gardiner*

50 DAYS OF THE DEAD MASK, 20th century

Nahuatl people, Humotitlán, Hidalgo, Mexico; wood, pigment; h: 8 inches (20.3 cm);
Museo Ruth Lechuga de Arte Popular, Mexico City

This mask is worn during the Days of the Dead ceremonies (called Xantolo in the Nahuatl language group), when groups of masqueraders dance in the town's streets. The masks represent many different characters, including Pre-Columbian deities. This mask looks very much like Xipe Totec, a god of the Aztecs. Only the iconographic expression of Xipe Totec has been preserved, and it is now solely associated with the Xantolo dancer. On the Days of the Dead the masqueraders perform in honor of the deceased, who come to visit their relatives and renew the spirit of the community.
Ruth D. Lechuga; photograph by Lynton Gardiner

51 JEW MASK, 1975

Cora people, Jesús María, Nayarit, Mexico; papier-mâché, pigment, teeth, foil, cloth; h: 10 inches (25.4 cm);
Museo Ruth Lechuga de Arte Popular, Mexico City

Holy Week ceremonies in Mexico sometimes include initiation rites for young men. Among the Cora people, male youths take part in the masquerade of *judea*, in which they play "Jews." On the Wednesday night of Holy Week they all meet at a big plaza and form a circle. Each one is called separately by his captain, moves to the center, then drops his trousers and performs a mock sex act. This ritual takes place at night, with only the moon illuminating the bizarre scene. Each youth makes his own mask. First he models a mold out of raw clay, over which he glues layers of paper until it acquires the desired thickness. The clay is then removed and finishing touches are added. On Wednesday the masks are painted white, on Thursday black lines are added, and on Friday the masks are painted with many colors. *Ruth D. Lechuga; photograph by Lynton Gardiner*

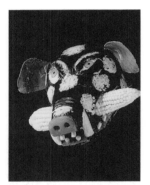

52 PIG CARNIVAL MASK, c. 1965

Zoque people, Ocozocuautla, Chiapas, Mexico; wood, pigment, corn; h: 9½ inches (24.1 cm);
Museo Ruth Lechuga de Arte Popular, Mexico City

This mask is worn on the back of a dancer who wears a small human mask over his face. The corncob worn across the snout may suggest the beginning of the Aztec Year, a time when fields are prepared for planting. During Carnival in Chiapas, the Pig mask may find itself in the company of jaguar, monkey, and horse masks. It is notable that so many Carnival masks represent animals, whether they are native to the Americas or were introduced by the Spaniards after conquest.
Ruth D. Lechuga; photograph by Lynton Gardiner

53 FACE MASK, c. 1965

Zoque people, Ocozocuautla, Chiapas, Mexico; wood, pigment; h: 6¼ inches (15.9 cm);
Museo Ruth Lechuga de Arte Popular, Mexico City

Worn over the face as a companion to the Pig mask (mask 52), this mask can also be a character by himself, in which case it is called Chori. During Carnival there are entire groups of Choris, who are the merrymakers of Carnival: they run through the streets, singing and making jokes, expressing the excitement and fun of Carnival. *Ruth D. Lechuga; photograph by Lynton Gardiner*

54 COJÓ CARNIVAL MASK, 20th century

Mayan people, Tenosique, Tabasco, Mexico; wood, pigment; h: 8 inches (20.3 cm);
Museo Ruth Lechuga de Arte Popular, Mexico City

The dance called Correr el Ponchó includes hundreds of Cojó masks, in addition to jaguars (*tigres*) and women (called *pochoveras*). The Cojó masks are all shaped similarly, but their decoration varies. This Cojó mask has a swordfish painted over the face. The Cojó masquerader wears a hat adorned with flowers; around his waist and knees he puts rows of fresh, green leaves covered with rows of dry leaves. As he dances, he loses the dry leaves, until only the green ones are left. This symbolizes the coming of spring, when the earth's new plants break through the old, dead foliage. The origins of this practice are found in the Aztec ritual performed in the second month of the Aztec calendar, dedicated to the god Xipe Totec, when a priest wore the skin of a sacrificial victim. *Ruth D. Lechuga; photograph by Lynton Gardiner*

55 Pitchy Patchy Mask, 1990
Audrey Mantock, Don Bucknor, and Winston Cole, Jamaica; mask and costume: cotton,
metallic and synthetic fabric, wire-screen mask, straw; overall costume h: 72¼ inches (183.6 cm);
The Saint Louis Art Museum, Friends Fund

Although little is known of the origins of the Pitchy Patchy character, his costume of multilayered
strips of cloth is probably derived from both English mumming dress and African prototypes that
were made of strips of flora instead of cloth. This masker performs with a Jonkonnu masked ensemble on the English holiday of Boxing Day, the day after Christmas. On this day the poor received
"boxes" of food, clothing, and other supplies from their wealthier compatriots. In the plantation era
of the late 17th through the early 19th century, Jonkonnu groups performed at the estate houses of
the master and his family on the plantation. *John W. Nunley; photograph by David Ulmer*

56 Lion Mask, 1980s
Haiti; papier-mâché, pigment, fiber; h: 52 inches (132.2 cm);
UCLA Fowler Museum of Cultural History, Museum Purchase, Manus Fund

57 Devil Mask, 1980s
Haiti; papier-mâché, pigment, rubber; h: 32⅝ inches (83 cm);
UCLA Fowler Museum of Cultural History, Museum Purchase, Manus Fund

58 Dog Mask, 1980s
Haiti; papier-mâché, pigment; h: 11½ inches (29.2 cm);
UCLA Fowler Museum of Cultural History, Museum Purchase, Manus Fund

Papier-mâché animal masks are worn in celebration of the pre-Lenten Carnival of urban Haiti.
French planters introduced the festival and its religious components to the island in the 18th
century. African slaves who worked the cane fields and sugar factories added their music, dance,
and oral traditions to make Carnival a richly festive creole experience. Local politicians, world
leaders, fantastic creatures, celebrities, devils, and animals such as lions and dogs are frequently
represented in masks. The devil mask shown here possibly makes reference to the Yoruba war
god Ogun. The masqueraders wear colorful costumes while dancing in such urban centers as
Port-au-Prince. In today's loosely structured Carnival celebration, participants eat, drink local
rums, and dance in the streets on the Monday and Tuesday prior to the lean days of Lent.
John W. Nunley; photographs by Don Cole

59 Wild Indian Mask, 1980s
Audrey Mantock, Don Bucknor, and Winston Cole, Jamaica; mask and costume: cotton fabric, wires,
feathers, mirrors, Christmas ornaments, masking tape, playing cards, cardboard, tinsel, foil, string,
wire-screen mask; overall costume h: 72 inches (182.9 cm); The Saint Louis Art Museum

Slaves, free Africans, and their descendants were impressed by the dress of Native Americans and
their ancestors as they were portrayed in Wild West shows and publications known as "penny
dreadfuls." American Indian styles of dress and accoutrements were thus incorporated into
Jonkonnu masquerades in the early 20th century. With bow or hatchet in hand and wearing
feathered headdresses, "Wild Indian" masqueraders make their appearance in competitive
performances, each attempting to outdance and outdress the other. Today's Wild Indians, who
perform on national holidays, in the streets, and on stage, symbolize the plantocracy of the past and
some of the historical roots of Jamaican culture. *John W. Nunley; photograph by David Ulmer*

60 Amerindian Mask, 20th century
Violet Leader and Icilma Leader, Saint Kitts; mask and costume: cotton fabric, mirror, ribbon,
cardboard, feathers, wire-screen mask, hair, pigment; overall costume h: 72 inches (182.9 cm);
The Saint Louis Art Museum, Gift of Richard Gaugert

The celebration of masquerade in Saint Kitts–Nevis begins on Boxing Day (December 26) and
continues through New Year's Day. Troupes of six to twelve performers execute a sequence of six
dances accompanied by the African "Big Drum," a kettle or snare drum, and fife. Like other
Caribbean Jonkonnu Indian costumes, this costume includes a feathered headdress and a tomahawk.
Typical of Saint Kitts–Nevis, the character is decorated in a style that dates from the early 20th
century, with ribbons, scarves, mirrors, apron, and a cape. Contemporary maskers share
their performances with tourists, primarily from Europe and North America, who visit the
islands during the warm holiday season. *John W. Nunley; photograph by David Ulmer*

61 JOHN CANOE MASK, 20th century

Fabian Cayetano, Belize; mask and costume: cotton, ribbons, cardboard, crepe paper, feathers, shells, wire-screen mask; overall costume h: 84 inches (213.4 cm); The Saint Louis Art Museum

The Black Caribs, known as Garifuna, who migrated from the West Indies to the Central American country of Belize, brought a masquerade celebration known as John Canoe. Groups of maskers celebrate Christmas Day and Boxing Day by performing a dance from house to house. The all-male ensemble of maskers is accompanied by a female chorus. In return for the performance and the good luck that the maskers bring to each house, the master of the residence provides the group with food and drink. The masquerader's wire-screen mask is worn with a paramilitary costume consisting of knee-length breeches with knee rattles, a long-sleeved white jacket, crossed bandoliers, and a fancy headdress. This style of costume and painted wire-screen mask are derived from the costumes of European morris dancers, introduced from Europe into Latin America and the Caribbean. *John W. Nunley; photograph by David Ulmer*

62 PIERROT GRENADE MASK, 1990

Kelvin Davis, Trinidad; mask and costume: cotton, metallic, and synthetic fabric, wire-screen mask, rope, patent leather; overall costume h: 72 inches (182.9 cm); The Saint Louis Art Museum, Friends Fund

Pierrot Grenade first appeared in Trinidadian Carnival in the late 19th century. The wire-screen mask is accompanied by a full costume that includes shoes, lappets of cloth forming a highly textured, "pitchy-patchy" robe, gloves, and a heart-shaped chest ornament decorated with mirrors. The use of reflecting surfaces on the body recalls the same artistic convention used by Central African artists in the creation of figural sculptures called Nkisi. The mirrors offer a way of passage into the spirit world. Pierrot Grenades often appear in verbal bouts to outdo one another in improvised speech. They also threaten each other with whips and swords as they prance and twirl around, advancing rapidly forward and backward. During the 1950s Pierrot Grenade almost disappeared from Trinidadian Carnival, yet in recent years the character has reemerged in old-time masquerade events sponsored by the government. *John W. Nunley; photograph by David Ulmer*

63 MOCO JUMBIE STILT MASQUERADER MASK, 1980s

Virgin Islands; mask and costume: burlap, paillettes, sequins, feathers, fringe, shell, ribbon, stilts; overall costume h: 72 inches (182.9 cm); The Saint Louis Art Museum

Moco Jumbie masks and costumes appear in a variety of festivals throughout the West Indies. This particular mask and costume were made and performed by John McClaverty of St. Thomas, one of the islands in the United States Virgin Islands. The Moco Jumbie character was introduced to the West Indies by slaves who were born in West Africa. The term *jumbie* is derived from an African source, most likely from a Mande word meaning "spirit." The Jumbie crosses from the spirit world to this one, bringing good luck. In recent years the character has experienced a re-Africanization. The style of headdress in this costume is derived from the Tusian peoples of Côte d'Ivoire, and the dark cloth imitates the natural raffia used in African masquerade costumes. Thus, the artist has purposely included authentic African designs and materials to express his African heritage. *John W. Nunley; photograph by David Ulmer*

64 IREME ABAKUÁ MASK, 1980s

Santiago de Cuba, Cuba; mask and costume: cotton fabric, straw; overall costume h: 72 inches (182.9 cm); The Saint Louis Art Museum

The Abakuá society was a mutual aid association originally established by enslaved Africans from the Cross River area in Nigeria and Cameroon. The Ireme is an Abakuá spiritual being represented by costume masqueraders and doll-like figures. Originally the Abakuá society and the Ireme could be found only in the area around Havana and Matanzas. Today, however, Carnival in Santiago de Cuba incorporates aspects of the festival from all over the country. The headdresses are distinguished by their conical shape, dramatic eyes, and the fringe attached to various parts of the costume. The costumes might have derived from the Spanish brotherhood masquerade groups who walked in procession through the streets in Spain during Holy Week, but today's Abakuá groups perform in folklore presentations to reaffirm Cuban cultural identity. *John W. Nunley; photograph by David Ulmer*

65 LADY OLINDA MASK, 20th century

Sílvio Botelho, Olinda, Recife, Brazil; mask and costume: wood, textile, papier-mâché; overall costume h: 120 inches (304.8 cm); Jackalope, Inc., Santa Fe, New Mexico

Giant puppets are a major Carnival feature in the town of Olinda in northern Brazil, where dozens of these spectacular figures can be seen parading and dancing along the cobblestoned streets. The puppet is constructed of a large papier-mâché head and an immense torso attached to a frame worn on the shoulders of the masker, known as the *alma* (soul), who will dance and spin, giving life to the giant. A flowing skirt or pantaloons completely hides the dancer underneath, who has only a small peephole. Most of these 12- to 15-foot tall giants represent historical, comical, or satirical figures important to the people of Olinda. Recently, a number of political candidates commissioned "giants" of themselves to use in their campaigns. *Katarina Real-Cate, photograph by Ian Logan*

CHAPTER 4: MEN AS WOMEN

66 FEMALE SPIRIT MASK

Punu people, Gabon; wood, pigment; h: 11⅞ inches (30 cm); Musée Dapper, Paris

Female spirit masks are found in central and western Gabon. Masqueraders dressed in costumes of raffia, cotton cloth, and animal skins perform on high stilts, displaying terrific acrobatic and athletic skills and impressing audiences and guests from out of town. In the past these masqueraders performed at funerary rites, but nowadays they appear at various public holidays and national events. The masks represent an idealization of female beauty. The heart-shaped face, nearly closed eyes, full lips, and finely formed nose represent a woman who exudes calm and control. The double sagittal-crested coiffure with side braids was the typical Punu woman's hairstyle in the early 20th century. *John W. Nunley; photograph by Hughes Dubois, courtesy Archives Musée Dapper*

67 MAIDEN CARNIVAL MASK, 20th century

Nahuatl people, Tepeyanco, Tlaxcala, Mexico; wood, pigment, glass eyes; h: 9 inches (22.9 cm); Museo Ruth Lechuga de Arte Popular, Mexico City

In most Mexican dances men take the roles of women, but this was not true in pre-Hispanic times. The custom was probably introduced by Spanish missionaries. In 16th-century Europe, young men acted as women because it was not considered decent for a woman to participate in public displays. In many towns in the state of Tlaxcala, men dressed as men and men dressed as women dance in pairs. The men represent 18th- or 19th-century landowners who always wear the same costume, whereas the women's outfits often change. Within the last thirty years, women have gradually reclaimed their roles in dance, although they still do not wear masks. The last town to make this change has been Tepeyanco. Masks for men masquerading as women have now become scarce and are only produced on request. The dance itself has many meanings, the most important of which is to call forth the rain. *Ruth D. Lechuga; photograph by Lynton Gardiner*

68 MARINGUILLA MASK, 1987

Antonio Saldaña and Maclovia Anguiano, Michoacán, Nuevo San Juan, Mexico; carved wood, pigment, glass eyes, hair, string, hairpiece, leather; overall costume h: 72 inches (182.9 cm); International Folk Art Foundation Collections in the Museum of International Folk Art, a unit of the Museum of New Mexico, Santa Fe

Each winter in the highland villages of Michoacán, Mexico, the Tarascan, or Purepecha, Indians perform a series of dances to honor the birth and infancy of Christ. Many of the dancers' masks portray wealthy Europeans who lived in this region during the colonial era; their features and personalities were adopted by the masqueraders to symbolize prestige and authority within the indigenous communities. One of these masked characters is the Maringuilla, or "Little Mary," who dances arm in arm with an older "Hacienda Owner," called Viejo. Much of the performance takes on humorous overtones as the man masquerading as Maringuilla exaggerates the feminine aspects of his role. This is underscored by the delicate features of the young girl's mask: her long eyelashes, rosy cheeks, and sweet red lips. *Barbara Mauldin; photograph by Ian Logan*

69 MAIDEN'S MASK, 20th century

Igbo people, Nigeria; wood, pigment, beads, buttons, wire bells; h: 23 inches (58.4 cm);
Collection of Geraldine and Morton Dimondstein

Entitled Igbogbo Mmuo ("Spirit of a Young Girl"), this mask originated in the heartland of Igbo country in southeastern Nigeria. Young men wear such masks and costumes during harvest festivals for the new year. Masquerading as girls, mothers, and elder women, the young men honor the female fertility spirit of the earth known as Ani. By acting out female roles, the men also communicate to women their idealized view of feminine behavior. The costume paired with this mask is elaborately decorated in brightly colored patterns that include rosettes, stripes, and triangles. The mirrors above the breasts may have the ritual function of serving as the doorway to the spirit world of fertility. Facial patterns and the elaborate hairstyle represent female beauty, while the painted white skin indicates spirituality. *John W. Nunley; photograph by Ian Logan*

70 YAGULE MASK, 20th century

Dogon people, Mali; wood, cowrie shells, fiber, baobab fruit, pigment; h: 13 inches (33 cm);
UCLA Fowler Museum of Cultural History, Gift of Dr. Stanley Geller

Dogon masks that represent humans are usually made of fibers rather than carved wood. Most fiber masks represent women of the Bamana, Fulani, and Samana peoples who live near the Dogon, but some, such as Yagule, represent Dogon women. Like other female masks, Yagule features an elaborate high-crested hairstyle ornamented with beads or cowries; long, twisted fiber strands hang at the sides. Yagule differs from other female masks in that the panel covering the face entirely encloses the wearer's chin and is completely covered with cowrie shells. Like other Dogon masqueraders, dancers wearing fiber masks that represent women wear skirts of long, curly, black fibers and straight red and yellow fibers, with fiber ruffs around the elbows and wrists; their brassiere-like bodices are fitted with false breasts made of baobab fruits. *Kate Ezra; photograph by Don Cole*

71 MAMMY WATA MASK, 20th century

Guro people, Côte d'Ivoire; wood, paint; h: 21½ inches (54.6 cm); National Museum of African Art, Smithsonian Institution, Bequest of Eliot Elisofon

The Guro people of central Côte d'Ivoire have a variety of masks to honor ancestors and spirits as well as entertainment masks for more profane matters. This mask honors the water spirit known widely by her Pidgin English name Mammy Wata, or "Mother-Water." She is generally regarded as a "foreigner," while at the same time she embodies elements of indigenous African beliefs in water spirits. She is seen as a beautiful, seductive being who can bring great wealth to those she favors and poverty, impotence, insanity, or death to those she does not. In this mask a Guro artist has taken, interpreted, and re-presented an imported image that has a fascinating history. It is based upon a popular German poster of a female snake charmer. First printed circa 1885, the poster reached Africa soon after, and by 1901 the image had already appeared in a carved, water-spirit headdress in the Niger River Delta of Nigeria. In 1955 the poster was reprinted in India and sold widely throughout West Africa, where it spawned a flowering of Mammy Wata images in many different places. *Henry John Drewal; photograph by Franko Khoury*

72 MAKIPO MASK, 20th century

Makonde people, Kenya; wood, pigment; h: 7 inches (17.8 cm); Linden-Museum, Stuttgart, Staatliches Museum für Völkerkunde

In the Makonde tradition this female mask might have been joined by a "Belly Mask" to represent a pregnant woman. Such masks would have been complemented by costumes of cloth, feathers, and vegetal material and would have been danced in the Makipo initiation society for young men and women. Returning from their separate bush schools after a period of seclusion, the initiates and maskers join in celebration. Such masks represent ancestral spirits who teach the young people how to exercise the responsibilities of adulthood. The dense patterns of scarification on the face are typical of Tanzanian Makonde masks. *John W. Nunley; photograph by Anatol Dreyer*

73 Phwō Mask, 19th century

Chokwe people, Angola; wood, pigment, cloth, bone, clay, fiber, raffia; h: 12⅝ inches (32 cm);
Collection of Pearl and Daniel Crowley

Chokwe people celebrate masquerades with itinerant dancers who travel from village to village to perform. The masks and costumes are carried in oblong baskets known as *cipawa*. They often portray elder women, mothers, and maidens, and occasionally an elder male noble who brings prosperity to the host village. This Phwō maiden, or mother mask, bestows fertility upon the audiences for whom she performs. The delicately patterned scarification marks and slightly closed eyes indicate that this female is of noble status; the reed piercing her nose is a sign of beauty. Such masks are made by specialized artists who receive a copper ring from the intended masked performer as a sign of their commission. The ring stands as a symbolic payment for a fiancée. Thus the mask and the dancer enter a symbolic marriage. Upon the death of the dancer, the "marriage" is ended and the carving is ceremonially buried. *John W. Nunley; photograph by Ian Logan*

74 Gelede Mask, 20th century

Yoruba people, Nigeria; wood, patina, traces of indigo; h: 13 inches (33 cm);
The Saint Louis Art Museum, Museum Shop Fund

Gelede masks are danced in order to please the elder females, Ajé, who are thought to control female fertility. Through the agency of the mask, large families are brought into existence for the benefit of all Yoruba society. This Gelede mask is an excellent example of a Yoruba double-face mask. The two faces allow for four eyes, and among many African people, including the Yoruba, it is believed that only persons with four eyes can see and negotiate with witches and elder women; four eyes also represent the ability to see both the visible and invisible realms of existence. The double face symbolizes twins as well, who are thought to bring good luck to the mothers and families that have them. This mask is rendered in a naturalistic style, and the faces are rendered as neither young nor old, but in the prime of life. *John W. Nunley; photograph by David Ulmer*

75 D'mba Mask, 19th or 20th century

Baga people, Guinea Coast; wood, metal; h: 39⅝ inches (100.8 cm); Museum Rietberg Zürich

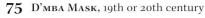

The Baga are a small community of agricultural folk on the coast of the Republic of Guinea. Due to the influence of Islam almost every Baga mask character has disappeared. However, the oldest villagers remember D'mba, who stood for the ideal of a strong, influential woman. The mask itself does not characterize a goddess but displays a woman's beauty, elegance, and cleverness at the height of her power. It is now rare for dancers to wear the big, heavy mask. D'mba mainly appears at weddings in order to show the newlyweds how to achieve happiness and to encourage them to behave correctly within the community. D'mba attends funerals and advises the departed on their way to the next world to protect the villagers. At planting time D'mba incites young farmers to work, and at harvest festivals D'mba thanks spirits for the successful crop. *Lorenz Homberger; photograph courtesy Museum Rietberg Zürich*

76 Old Woman Mask, early 20th century

Switzerland; wood, pigment, cloth; h: 8 inches (20.3 cm); Museum Rietberg Zürich

77 Old Woman Mask, early 20th century

Switzerland; wood, pigment, cloth; h: 7¾ inches (19.7 cm); Museum Rietberg Zürich

78 Ghost Mask, early 20th century

Switzerland; wood, pigment, cloth; h: 8 inches (20.3 cm); Museum Rietberg Zürich

Mask customs in central Switzerland have been documented since the 18th century, and there are indications that as early as the Middle Ages masks were used for Carnival. In central Switzerland, satire was a major part of Carnival. Often, mask faces were meant to caricature social outcasts or eccentrics. Clerical and secular high officials were often ridiculed for their behavior. The three masks pictured here were all made by the same wood-carver, whose hand is recognized in the even-tempered faces consisting of large, flat elements. The eyebrows are the main feature of the face: they rise up like flames on the sleek forehead and are very plastically pronounced. The basic characters were the devil, a ghost, and an old woman, produced for a group to wear together on one occasion. The appearance and the clothing of the three masked characters were not standardized. *Judith Rickenbach; photographs by Rainer Wolfsburger*

79 OLD MAID MASK, c. 1940

Nahuatl people, Tixtla, Guerrero, Mexico; wood, pigment; h: 7½ inches (19.1 cm);
Museo Ruth Lechuga de Arte Popular, Mexico City

The character of the old woman is very common in dances all over Mexico. Among Indians the elderly are greatly respected for their knowledge and experience, both in everyday life as well as in the special ceremonies of their communities. This mask is worn in the Manueles dance, performed by children clad in city clothes, high hats, and the masks of young men. The dance also features a man dressed as an old woman wearing old-fashioned city clothes, a mask, and a wig. Each dancer carries a walking stick, made out of a painted twig, in the shape of a snake. The snake is a symbol of thunderbolts and rain, suggesting that this dance descends from ceremonies for rain.
Ruth D. Lechuga; photograph by Lynton Gardiner

80 DZONOQUA MASK, 1800–1850

Kwakwaka'wakw people, Canada; wood, pigment, hair, raffia, cloth, nails; h: 11½ inches (29.2 cm);
The Saint Louis Art Museum, Gift of Morton D. May

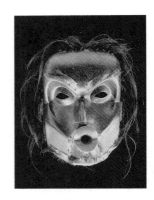

Dzonoqua, the mythic Wild Woman of the Woods, is feared because she kidnaps and eats children. She is also capable of reviving the dead and providing great wealth for a chosen few. This mask depicts Dzonoqua's deeply set eyes and her open mouth ready to issue forth her characteristic "wuu, wuu, wuu" sounds. Her large and pendulous breasts announce her femininity, but her face is bearded. Legend has it that a hunter killed Dzonoqua's son in revenge when she stole his salmon. Another mortal took pity on the monstrous mother and brought her the corpse. After reviving her son, Dzonoqua rewarded the mortal by giving him skins, meat, and a mask of her face that he and his descendants were allowed to wear at ceremonials. Although Dzonoqua dancers mimic the perpetual sleepiness of the Wild Woman of the Woods, a chief will also wear this mask when he presents a special copper, the Kwakwaka'wakw symbol of immense wealth, to his audience.
Aldona Jonaitis; photograph by David Ulmer

81 RANGDA MASK, 20th century

Abian Kepas, Sumerta, Bali, Indonesia; wood, fiber, cotton, leather, mirror, pigment; h: 48 inches (121.9 cm); UCLA Fowler Museum of Cultural History, Gift of Mr. and Mrs. W. Thomas Davis and the Rogers Family Foundation

Rangda is featured in the Balinese story of *Calonarang*, in which a widow takes revenge on Balinese villages by using black magic. She is ultimately an apotropaic figure, used to counter the influences of black magic in the village. Sacred Rangda masks are kept in the temple of the dead, where they are referred to as Ratu Dalam, meaning the "monarch of the temple." Morally ambiguous, Rangdas can also be used to represent the emanation of power from a god, goddess, or even a demon who appears in Balinese theater. They are sometimes pitted against the lionlike Barong Ket in ceremonies and performances that are designed to display the power of both. In sacred performances, the actor-priest "playing" Rangda becomes possessed, inspiring delirium and the urge for self-destruction among the Barong's followers. This has inspired the popular "Barong and Keris" shows performed regularly for tourists. *John Emigh; photograph by Don Cole*

CHAPTER 5: THEATER

82 FAUST II MASK, 1983

Wolfgang Utzt, Germany; leather; h: 14½ inches (36.8 cm); Collection of Wolfgang Utzt

Theater designer Wolfgang Utzt is known for the imaginative and powerful masks he has created for the contemporary German stage. This full-face leather mask, which looks almost like a close-fitting second layer of skin, is unusual in that it extends beyond the face to the bottom of the neck. This mask, first used in the production of *Faust II* directed by Friedo Solter, wears a wrinkled, woeful expression that is evocative of Greek tragic masks. *Lesley K. Ferris; photograph by David Ulmer*

83 Big Horned Demon Mask from Domestic Resurrection Circus, 1990

Peter Schumann, United States; pâpier-maché, burlap, hay, wood, pigment; h: 45 inches (114.3 cm);
Bread and Puppet Theater

Founded in New York City in 1961 by Peter Schumann, Bread and Puppet Theater was created in part as a reaction against the West's emphasis on literary theater and the effects of modern life and its materialization. Schumann and his company members use a variety of inventive masks and puppets to create a visual, nonverbal theater that examines contemporary issues. Since its inception the company has become well known for disturbing visual images that combine religious iconography and political commentary. In 1974 the company moved to Glover, Vermont, where they have continued to produce work for summer festivals in Glover as well as for specific commissions and revivals. A recurring project is the Domestic Resurrection Circus, an outdoor extravaganza with a carnival-like atmosphere presented each summer, which includes as many as 100 various masked figures and giant puppets. *Lesley K. Ferris; photograph by David Ulmer*

84 Scar's Mask, 1997

Julie Taymor and Michael Curry, United States; carbon graphite and pigment; h: 24½ inches (62.2 cm);
Walt Disney Theatrical Productions

Julie Taymor is known for her singular style as a director and designer of striking masks and puppets. In the Broadway production of *The Lion King,* she uses masking to emphasize the duality of human/animal. This mask for Scar, the evil brother of the good king Mufasa, is attached to a harness and worn as a headdress above the actor's face. Thus the face of the actor and the mask are seen simultaneously by the audience. In Taymor's mask-making process she first carves the mask in clay, then brushes liquid silicone over the clay mold to create a thick rubber shell; this shell in turn becomes the imprint for the final mask, which is made from carbon graphite, a strong but lightweight material. *Lesley K. Ferris; photograph by Lynton Gardiner, © Disney*

85 The Abstract Mask, 1999 reconstruction of the 1922 original

Oskar Schlemmer, Germany; papier-mâché, plaster, pigment; h: 20½ inches (52 cm); Theatre Estate Oskar
Schlemmer (Bühnen Archiv), courtesy C. Raman Schlemmer, Oggebbio, Italy

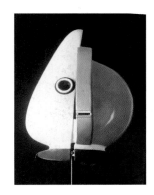

Oskar Schlemmer was a German sculptor, painter, and designer who created masks and costumes using geometric shapes that represented the various body parts. He wrote in 1922, "Life has become so mechanized, thanks to machines and a technology which our senses cannot possibly ignore, that we are intensely aware of man as a machine and the body as a mechanism." Schlemmer saw the body as a means to creating "moving architecture" in the theater. Like many theater designers of the early 20th century, he sought to unite the human figure with the three-dimensionality of stage space. Schlemmer, head of the Bauhaus theater workshop from 1923 to 1929, designed a series of dance pieces using his mask designs. When he began working on his ground-breaking *Triadic Ballet* (1922), Cubists, Futurists, and Dadaists had already begun to break down the body into abstract forms. "Der Abstrakte" ("The Abstract") is a mask from the third and final section of *The Triadic Ballet,* in which three performers are clothed in black against a stage draped in black curtains. *Lesley K. Ferris; photograph courtesy Photo Archive C. Raman Schlemmer*

86 Darth Vader's Mask, 1980s reproduction of 1977 original

Don Post Studios, United States; fiberglass, metal; h: 14¼ inches (36.2 cm); Don Post Studios

Cinematic masks are worn predominantly by villains, monsters, or superheroes. The most celebrated film mask in recent years was worn by Darth Vader in George Lucas's spectacular space epic *Star Wars.* As one of this century's most infamous villains, his impenetrable black mask and costume epitomize evil, despair, and an unrelenting quest for power. They imprison Vader's goodness, which has been seduced and corrupted by the dark side. As part of his life-supporting body armor, the mask contained the breathing apparatus necessary for him to survive. With the climactic removal of Darth Vader's mask in *Return of the Jedi,* we learn of his scarred human face, a symbol of his corruption. *Cara McCarty; photograph by David Ulmer*

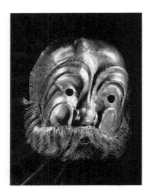

87 Harlequin Commedia dell'Arte Mask, 18th century

Italy; leather, hair; h: 6⅞ inches (17.5 cm); Bibliothèque nationale de France. Bibliothèque-Musée de l'Opéra

Harlequin (in Italian, Arlecchino) is one of the most well known commedia characters. A servant figure who first appeared as a clownish simpleton, Harlequin regularly teamed up with the scheming and crafty Brighella. Known as the "prince of numskulls," Harlequin had occasional flashes of wit as he tried to trick his master in numerous scenarios. Extremely agile, at times acrobatic, he wore a black half mask with small beady eyes, the forehead wrinkled with a wart, an arched bushy eyebrow, and a short beard made with stiff bristles. Unlike the full-face masks of Greek theater, the half masks of the commedia actors provided a clear definition of character while allowing facial mobility for the mouth and chin to express a whole range of emotions. Harlequin's costume began as a series of irregularly placed colorful patches, but over time the patches became triangles or lozenges; as the costume changed, the mask lost its facial hair. *Lesley K. Ferris; photograph by Lynton Gardiner*

88 Foolish Devil's Mask, 1650-1700

Belgium; iron, pigment; h: 21¾ inches (55 cm); Gent, Oudheidkundig Museum van de Bijloke, Belgium

In medieval church pageants the devil character was often depicted with bodily distortion. The devil was usually exposed as a fool in order to highlight the superiority of the divine. When the Church outlawed masking in the 16th century, the tradition of depicting the battle between good and evil with caricatured masks continued in Carnival theater and public punishment rites. "Sin" was located directly upon the sinner's body in the form of a "mask of shame." The protruding tongue on this mask refers to a "sharp tongue," or the propensity to gossip. Its round eyeglasses, which appear in many Renaissance devil depictions, probably signify greed. The iron disks on either side of the head would produce a jangling sound when set in motion. These visual and aural characteristics were all intended to call attention to the base and comic elements of the person behind the mask. *Meghan Barnes; photograph courtesy Gent, Oudheidkundig Museum van de Bijloke*

89 Decorative Mask, 2nd century

Roman Empire; terra-cotta, pigment; h: 11¼ inches (28.5 cm); Römisch-Germanisches Museum der Stadt Köln

This terra-cotta mask, which was excavated south of Cologne, Germany, does not belong to the traditional tragic or comic genres of theater masks. Although little is known about theater performances in the northwest region of the Roman Empire, the mask's bald head, enormous crooked nose, large eyes, and open V-shaped mouth with teeth are features characteristic of masks specific to that area. Roman actors wore masks of either wood or plaster. This mask would not have been worn because of its great weight. Instead, it was most likely used as a decorative architectural element in the garden court of a private residence or in a sanctuary or other public building. *Hannelore Rose; photograph by Lynton Gardiner*

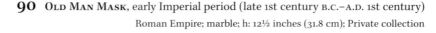

90 Old Man Mask, early Imperial period (late 1st century B.C.–A.D. 1st century)

Roman Empire; marble; h: 12½ inches (31.8 cm); Private collection

This carved marble mask from the environs of Pompeii is an evocation of a New Comedy character from the earlier Hellenistic era, the "Old Man." The Old Man is recognized by his exaggerated expression, overhanging W-shaped brow, broad nose with flaring nostrils, and large, heart-shaped mouth. This mask is stylistically similar to the colossal masks affixed to the keystones of the facade of the Theater of Marcellus commissioned by Augustus around 13 B.C. in Rome. Primarily used as an architectural decoration, the mask would have been suspended from an iron ring that pierced its top. Wealthy patrons of the arts hung such masks in their villas or gardens to honor the god Dionysus in their pursuit of pleasure, felicity, and leisure. This practice imitated the decorations of Dionysus's theater in Athens, where masks were hung in dedication around his temple after performances. *Lesley K. Ferris; photograph by Lynton Gardiner*

91 DEVIL MORALITY PLAY MASK, 19th century

Tirolean region, Austria; wood, pigment; h: 23⅝ inches (60 cm); Tiroler Volkskunstmuseum, Innsbruck

92 SKELETON MORALITY PLAY MASK, 18th century

Tirolean region, Austria; wood, pigment; h: 9⅝ inches (24.5 cm); Tiroler Volkskunstmuseum, Innsbruck

93 PRIEST MORALITY PLAY MASK, 18th century

Tirolean region, Austria; wood, pigment; h: 12⅝ inches (32 cm); Tiroler Volkskunstmuseum, Innsbruck

The Nicholas Plays were first created by the Church for its members-in-training. In the big plays common in northern Tirol, scenes are performed in different locations. Characters include the herald, who explains the scenes, shepherds, peasants, soldiers, foresters, and the devil, who is usually dressed as a huntsman. The patience of the children in the audience is put to a severe test because Saint Nicholas does not actually appear until the very end of the play. His appearance is meant to test the children's religious knowledge and to reward as well as punish them. The Nicholas Plays portray the opposition of good and evil in the battle for the human soul. This battle is often articulated through a monologue by the devil, called the "devil's sermon," in which the devil illustrates how people can lead their lives comfortably and licentiously. Among the most impressive scenes is the Young Man scene: a young man in the full flush of youth, living a zestful life, is confronted by Death. At first the young man does not recognize Death as he approaches him, even making fun of his scrawny figure. He doesn't listen to the remonstrations of Death that he should turn to God now, for the very next day he will be dead. Death puts an end to the many-stanzaed exchange between himself and the youth by shooting the youth with an arrow. The veneration of Saint Nicholas as an adviser during death can be dated to the 17th century. *Herlinde Menardi; photographs by Lynton Gardiner*

94 PEDRO PORTOCARRERO MASK, end of 19th century

Mayan people, Guatemala; wood, pigment; h: 8¼ inches (21 cm); Collection of Alfredo MacKenney

95 MALINCHE MASK, 20th century

Mayan people, Guatemala; wood, pigment; h: 7½ inches (19 cm); Collection of Alfredo MacKenney

96 TECUN UMAN ALIVE MASK, 20th century

Mayan people, Guatemala; wood, pigment; h: 7⅞ inches (20 cm); Collection of Alfredo MacKenney

97 TECUN UMAN DEAD MASK, 20th century

Mayan people, Guatemala; wood, pigment; h: 7⅝ inches (19.5 cm); Collection of Alfredo MacKenney

These four Mayan masks were once part of a larger suite of characters that performed the Baile de la Conquista ("The Dance of the Conquest"). This theatrical performance was often scripted and presented in village plazas. Spanish missionaries first introduced the masquerade, which reenacts the Christian Spanish conquest of the Islamic Moors who occupied Spain for at least five centuries. On one level the masquerade thus reinforces the power of Christianity over "paganism." More importantly, the reenactment depicts the Spanish general Pedro Alvarado and his men who were dispatched by Hernán Cortés from the Aztec capital of Tenochtitlan to conquer the Maya, led by the great chief Tecun Uman. The battle took place in 1524 in what is today Guatemala. Tecun Uman fought bravely alongside his men, but they were defeated. His spiritual essence is noted in the mask Tecun Uman Alive by the two sacred quetzal birds flanking his forehead. The Tecun Uman Dead Mask depicts the ruler, without the birds, at the moment of his death. Legend has it that upon his death the sacred birds ascended to the realm of the gods, taking the spirit of the warrior chief with them; he lives on there, protecting his people to this day. Although this theater production tells the tale of the defeat of the early Maya, today it is performed to celebrate the Mayan spirit, which has survived and thrives culturally. Further enriching this play is the Malinche Mask, which represents the Native American woman Malinche who helped Cortés defeat the Aztecs in 1521. This story of the betrayal of her people is well known to the play's audiences. The beautiful Malinche had a son with Cortés, whom she named Don Martin, thus bringing into the world the first Mestizo, and creole culture was born. This masked theater play is very popular among the Maya, as it reconstructs the past while presenting the evolving, complex identity of Native and European origins in the context of popular culture. *Jorge and Luis Luján-Muñoz; photographs by Lynton Gardiner*

98 TIGRE MASK, C. 1975

Mixtec people, Jicayan, Oaxaca, Mexico; wood, pigment, mirrors, horsehair;
h: 12¾ inches (32.4 cm); Museo Ruth Lechuga de Arte Popular, Mexico City

During Carnival all over the Mixtec coast of Oaxaca, groups appear and enact little scenes. In the
Tigre act a masquerader costumed as the Tigre (a jaguar) kills a sheep, who is played by a masked
boy. Masqueraders dressed as farmers act in mime as they discover that one sheep is missing.
After thinking hard, they come to the conclusion that the Tigre is to blame, and they send out
the masquerader Dog to find the dangerous animal. The Tigre hides in different places and then
climbs a tree, where the Dog finds him. The Tigre is then killed and taken away. *Ruth D. Lechuga;
photograph by Lynton Gardiner*

99 NULAMAL MASK, 1897

Kwakwaka'wakw people, Canada; wood, pigment; h: 11 inches (27.8 cm); Royal British Columbia Museum

Beings who enforce rules of behavior appear in ceremonies around the world and often display
clownlike or vulgar behavior. Among the Kwakwaka'wakw, it is the Nulamal, or "fool dancer," who
keeps the crowds orderly during the Winter Ceremonial. Reckless, mean-spirited, and dirty, the fool
dancer obtains his special power from supernatural creatures, who live on a floating village and have
enormous runny noses. An ancestor who originally encountered these beings returned home with a
perpetually runny nose and began to act irrationally, eating his own mucus. Slowly, like the Man-
eater, he was later subdued. Only those individuals with the inherited right can wear this mask, and,
as in the Hamatsa ritual described below, they are initiated in a ceremony during which they reenact
the initial encounter. *Aldona Jonaitis; photograph courtesy Royal British Columbia Museum*

100 CROOKED BEAK MASK, late 19th century

Kwakwaka'wakw people, Canada; cedar bark shreds, cord, pigment; h: 18¼ inches (46.4 cm);
Collection of Ralph T. Coe

The Kwakwaka'wakw hold elaborate winter masquerades and performances, the most prestigious
of which is the Hamatsa, or cannibal dance. The privilege of performing this dance is based on the
legend of several young men who traveled to the North End of the World to visit Man-eater, a malevolent supernatural whose body was covered with blood-rimmed mouths. On their way the young
men encountered a woman who advised them to dig a hole in the corner of the monster's house, fill
it with hot stones, and then wait in another corner. The monster entered, ran around the room four
times, glancing upward rather than looking where he was going, and fell into the pit to his death.
The woman taught the young hunters the songs of the cannibal spirit, and they returned home with
masks and other ritual regalia. This mask depicts one of the monster's bird attendants. When the
Hamatsa bird dancers enter a house, their bodies are hidden by shredded red cedar bark, their masks
positioned with beaks angled skyward at a 45-degree angle. Dancers, usually four in number, arrive
one at a time, each depicting a different bird attendant of the Man-eater. The dancers step in a
springy walk, making high-pitched sounds, cocking their heads, and pulling hidden strings that
snap the beaks open and shut with a clapping noise. *Aldona Jonaitis; photograph by David Ulmer*

101 TRANSFORMATION MASK, late 19th century

Kwakwaka'wakw people, Canada; wood, pigment; h: 16 inches (40.6 cm); Portland Art Museum,
Axel Rasmussen Collection, purchased with Indian Collection Subscription Fund

The most extraordinary Northwest Coast mask is the Kwakwaka'wakw transformation mask,
which depicts different manifestations of the same being. During a ceremonial appearance, the
dancer wearing the mask turns his back to the audience and pulls a number of strings to snap open
the mask. The dancer then turns around to reveal the anthropomorphic shaman's face within. Often
the rhythm of drums changes to a fast staccato when the dancer "transforms," and then resumes a
slower, more elegant beat as he dances around the house. Such masks usually relate to a family
legend about a spiritual being that presented itself in various forms to an ancestor, providing him
and his family with wealth and the right to wear a mask representing the supernatural being. The
prerogative to perform the legends associated with such masks is a source of great pride for a family.
Aldona Jonaitis; photograph courtesy Portland Art Museum

102 Kolam Mask of the First Queen, late 19th century

Sri Lanka; wood, pigment; h: 17⅝ inches (44 cm); Staatliche Museen zu Berlin, Preussischer Kulturbesitz, Museum für Völkerkunde

Kolam is a form of masked entertainment that was popular in the southern part of Sri Lanka during the 19th and early 20th centuries. The mythic origin of Kolam involves a pregnant queen who developed a great craving for masked dances. The mythical queen and her court are mirrored in production by a royal family who presides over the stories of village life and popular lore that make up the Kolam repertoire of men, animals, demons, and gods. The masks of the King and Queen are so large and elaborate that the leader of the Kolam troupe has to guide the male performers wearing the masks. *John Emigh; photograph by Lynton Gardiner*

103 Krishnattam Mask of Vividan, 1999

Guruvayur, Kerala, India; wood, pigment, deer hair, cloth, foil, wax; h: 26⅞ inches (67 cm); C. Raman Schlemmer, The Malabar Collection

Near the end of the 16th century, the Zamorin king Manavedan devised a unique blend of dance, song, acting, narrative, and devotional offering that has survived as the Krishnattam dance-theater of the Guruvayur Temple in Kerala, India. The repertoire is based on retellings of the *Bhagavata Purana,* and its 8 plays recount the exploits of Krishna, an avatar of the god Vishnu, and his brother, Balarama. Large, elegant masks are used to represent animals and demons. One of the plays enacts the defeat of Vividan, a demon who has taken the form of a great black ape. Vividan steals Balarama's weapons and taunts him. A terrific fight ensues, and when Vividan is defeated it is said that "the crest of the mountain is splintered into a hundred pieces by his weight." Commissioning a Krishnattam play is thought to bestow merit. *John Emigh; photograph by David Ulmer*

104 Pyolsandae Mask of the Old Monk, 20th century

Yangju, South Korea; gourd, paper, cloth, pine bark, pigment; h: 10 inches (25.5 cm); American Museum of Natural History, New York

105 Pyolsandae Mask of a Dancing Girl, 20th century

Yangju, South Korea; paper, gourd, cloth, pine bark, pigment; h: 9⅞ inches (25 cm); American Museum of Natural History, New York

In the masked dance of Pyolsandae, as performed in the town of Yangju, the character of the Old Monk (Nojang) represents a religious leader who has devoted his life to studying and preaching Buddhism. One day in the village he sees two Dancing Girls and feels great lust. A Dancing Girl (Somu) was a female member of a traveling drama company who also indulged in prostitution. As the dance progresses, the Old Monk's desire for the Dancing Girls becomes more aggressive. He throws away his staff and string of beads and attempts to seduce the Dancing Girls. He buys one of them a pair of shoes, which represents the consummation of his desire. The scene between them is witnessed by the character Prodigal (Ch'uibari), who becomes not only morally outraged but extremely jealous. Prodigal is a bachelor who, without an aim in life or any particular skill, became a monk but is unable to give up his desire for drink, physical pleasure, and money. Prodigal fights the Old Monk, his teacher, to win the Dancing Girl, then belittles and chastises the Old Monk. Unrepentant, the Old Monk runs off with another Dancing Girl. *Alyssa Kim; photographs by Lynton Gardiner*

106 Chho Mask of Kirata, c. 1980

Chorida, Purulia District, West Bengal, India; papier-mâché, pigment, peacock feathers, feathers, wool, mixed media; h: 34⅝ inches (88 cm); National Museum of Ethnology, Osaka

The masks used in the vigorous and popularly supported Chho dance-theater of Purulia District, West Bengal, India, are particularly bold and striking. The masks depict characters from Hindu epics and Puranic mythology. Competing teams of dancers within the rural villages of Purulia wear the masks in performances that combine devotional narratives and acrobatic prowess. In an episode taken from the epic *Mahabharata,* the hero Arjuna is tested by the god Shiva, who is disguised as the "tribal" hunter, Kirata. For the first time, Arjuna finds himself inferior to a rival combatant, and he humbles himself before the mysterious hunter. Thus honored, Shiva reveals his ruse and awards Arjuna a powerful weapon with which he can defeat his rivals. The population of Purulia identifies strongly with the figure of Kirata and celebrates its own vitality and strength through the attention lavished on this mask. *John Emigh; photograph courtesy National Museum of Ethnology, Osaka*

107 KHON MASK OF TOSAKANTH, 19th century

Thailand; papier-mâché, leather, wood, mother-of-pearl, mirrors; h: 27¾ inches (70.5 cm); Staatliche Museen zu Berlin, Preussischer Kulturbesitz, Museum für Völkerkunde

Tosakanth, also known as Ravana, is the demonic adversary of the hero Rama in the Thai tradition of the *Ramayana*. The epic story of Rama and his quest to recover his stolen bride, Sita, from the ten-headed demon king, came to Thailand directly from India and also by way of Indonesia and Cambodia. Over succeeding centuries, the narrative has proved to be a flexible and resilient vehicle both for the refinement of art and for the contemplation of moral and religious principles. Thai and Cambodian artists ingeniously solved the problem of representing Tosakanth's ten heads, while leaving the dancer with the mobility needed for vigorous dancing, by stacking the heads high on an elaborately ornamented helmet mask. The result is to give the potentially grotesque ten-headed demon King an ironic elegance and grandeur—qualities that in turn enhance the moral complexity and aesthetic beauty of the Khon dance dramas. *John Emigh; photograph by Lynton Gardiner*

108 WAYANG WONG MASK OF JATAYU, early 20th century

Bali, Indonesia; wood, pigment, leather, glasslike fragments; h: 16½ inches (41.9 cm); Royal Tropical Institute, Tropenmuseum, Amsterdam

The Balinese tradition of Wayang Wong theatricalizes events from the Hindu *Ramayana*. The striking animal and demonic masks within this tradition are characterized by bared teeth and fangs, bulging eyes, and gilded filigree leather decorations extending from the ears. The imaginative exaggeration of these features gives prominence to raw sensation. Although all of these fantastic creatures exude great energy, some are positive and others negative. Like the shaman, Rama needs help from the world of animal forces in order to counter destructive powers. The mythical Garuda bird, Jatayu, tries valiantly to stop Ravana's kidnapping of Rama's wife, Sita, and manages to tell Rama of her capture before dying in his arms. *John Emigh; photograph courtesy Royal Tropical Institute, Tropenmuseum, Amsterdam*

109 TELEK MASK, early 20th century

Bali, Indonesia; gilt wood, pigment; h: 6⅜ inches (16 cm); Royal Tropical Institute, Tropenmuseum, Amsterdam

Balinese masks of human faces depict a continuum of approaches to living, from the very refined to the coarse and crude. Telek masks are of mysterious origin and are closely related to sacred ritual masks still worn by young girls in the village of Ketewel. Indeterminate in gender and in expression, the masks depict graceful semihuman characters that sometimes accompany the Barong Ket in his theatrical confrontations with Rangda. Early versions of these masks may have provided a prototype for those used in Balinese dance drama for the most refined of characters, from the hero Rama in Balinese Wayang Wong to the elegant Kings (Dalem) of Balinese Topeng. Theater director Peter Brook said of one such mask that it was "an image of a man without a mask . . . an outer casing that is a complete and sensitive reflection of the inner life." *John Emigh; photograph courtesy Royal Tropical Institute, Tropenmuseum, Amsterdam*

110 TOPENG BABAKAN MASK OF PANJI, early 20th century

Cirebon region, West Java, Indonesia; wood, pigment; h: 6⅝ inches (17 cm); Royal Tropical Institute, Tropenmuseum, Amsterdam

The Topeng Babakan tradition of the Cirebon region of West Java depicts characters and stories centered around the legendary Javanese Hindu Prince Panji and his love, Candra Kirana. Panji is the most *halus,* or refined, of the characters, the ideal male. Solo dances and dramatized incidents alternate, and men and women may perform any of the roles within this tradition. Dancing begins without a mask, and the mask is placed on the face only once the spirit of the character has been established, making the creation of character a visible process. Cirebon was an early center of Islamic influence in Java, and masks from this region are characterized by a greater abstraction of the human face than in the comparable genres in Bali and are notable for their elegant simplicity. *John Emigh; photograph courtesy Royal Tropical Institute, Tropenmuseum, Amsterdam*

111 COMIC TOPENG MASK, early 20th century

Lombok, Indonesia; wood, pigment; h: 7½ inches (19 cm); Royal Tropical Institute, Tropenmuseum, Amsterdam

The refined princes and strong warriors of the Topeng plays performed in Bali and in villages on the western side of neighboring Lombok island are juxtaposed to antic clownlike characters in the course of improvised performances. Foolish ministers, village eccentrics, and caustic commentators add new perspectives to the evolving dramas and entertain with their parodic dances, satiric humor, and general buffoonery. The masks have grotesque and frequently malformed features. The idea is not to negate the grace and power of the heroes, but to fill out the living tapestry of human behavioral patterns that constitutes the full performance and to incorporate the fullest possible range of thoughts and attitudes, all held in balance by the performer or the company of performers.
John Emigh; photograph courtesy Royal Tropical Institute, Tropenmuseum, Amsterdam

112 NOH MASK OF A YOUNG GIRL, Edo period (1615–1868), 19th century

Japan; wood, pigment; h: 7⅝ inches (19.4 cm); Private collection

113 NOH MASK OF A YOUNG NOBLEMAN, Edo period (1615–1868), 19th century

Japan; wood, pigment; h: 8 inches (20.3 cm); Private collection

Some Noh masks depict generic character types and can be used in many plays within the repertoire. The mask of a young nobleman (Chūjō) is used to portray young aristocratic warriors, such as the ghost of the warrior Kiyotsune, who appears to his widow, to whom he tells the story of his drowning and the downfall of the Heike clan before he gains release from the torment of remembrance. The deep furrow between the eyes of the Chūjō mask casts a shadow of sadness on its face. The mask of a young girl (Waka-onna) is one of several used to depict young women in the central "wig" plays that are considered the greatest test of the Noh actor. Its gentle smile and open features suggest innocence and vulnerability. As the head is presented at different angles to the audience, the expression subtly shifts. *John Emigh; photographs courtesy The Metropolitan Museum of Art*

114 KYŌGEN MASK OF THE GOD DAIKOKU, Edo period (1615-1868), c. 1800

Japan; wood, pigment; h: 6¾ inches (17.1 cm); Seattle Art Museum, Gift of J. Mayuyama

In traditional performances since the 14th century, comic Kyōgen playlets imbued with the spirit of everyday life and fueled by a love of parodic play are inserted between the starker, more remote dramas of Noh theater. While many of the prosaic characters of Kyōgen are portrayed through facial displays that would be inhibited by masking, demons, ghosts, gods, animals, and old men and women are all frequently represented with the help of whimsical and sometimes grotesque wooden masks. The broad features characteristic of Kyōgen masks may be laughing, befuddled, apoplectic, leering, and sometimes just plain silly. Daikoku is a generous and jolly deity with a bag of treasures in one hand and a hammer to strike new coins in the other. The mask's huge ears and wide face are reminiscent of the Gigaku masks that accompanied the introduction of Buddhism and more general Chinese and central Asian cultural influences in the 7th to 9th centuries.
John Emigh; photograph by Paul Macapia

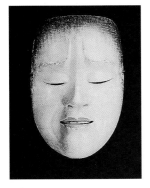

115 NOH MASK OF THE BLIND MONK, Edo period (1615–1868), 19th century

Japan; wood, pigment; h: 7¾ inches (19.8 cm); The Metropolitan Museum of Art, The Howard Mansfield Collection, Gift of Howard Mansfield

The Japanese Noh mask is a form of sculptural art that is fully realized only through the actor's practiced movements on an illuminated stage, accompanied by the transcendent sounds of a chanting chorus, the shrill notes of a flute, and the percussive rhythms of hand-beaten drums. This mask is used in the Noh play *Yoroboshi* (*The Blind Monk*), a tale about a falsely accused youth who is driven blind with grief after he is rejected by his family. Realizing his mistake, his repentant father journeys to the great Shittenō-ji temple in Osaka to pray for his son. The blind boy begs for his bread daily at this same temple, enjoying the few pleasures afforded by his imagination and trusting in the saving mercy of the bodhisattva Kannon, who eventually reunites father and son. *Barbara Ford; photograph courtesy The Metropolitan Museum of Art*

116 SHAMAN'S MASK, C. 1770

Evenki people, Siberia; mask and costume: reindeer skin, fur, cotton, silk, copper, iron, bronze, glass beads, vegetal matter, pigment; overall costume h: 66 inches (167.6 cm); Institut für Ethnologie der Universität Göttingen, Abteilung Völkerkundliche Sammlung

In many societies, warding off evil and danger is the responsibility of shamans and diviners. Shamans use masks and costumes as a kind of armor that helps protect them while negotiating with evil forces of the spirit world. As essential elements in the act of transformation, shamans' costumes are extraordinary assemblages of appendages and power symbols that constitute a complete symbolic system to help the shaman obtain a trance state to mediate with spiritual forces. The copper mask is tied onto the face to illuminate it at night beside the fire, where the magic occurs. This shamanic armor is a visual feast compared with many masks and costumes designed for physical protection. Such masks and costumes are exceedingly rare because most are burned along with the owner at death. *Gundolf Krüger and Cara McCarty; photograph by Lynton Gardiner*

117 ANTI-SORCERER'S MASK, 20th century

Oku, Cameroon; mask and costume: fiber, wood, pigment, leather, shells, feathers, metal, horns, beak of a hornbill, seed pods; overall costume h: 60 inches (152.4 cm); Collection of Charles and Kent Davis

This dark tunic with a hood was worn by the lone masquerader of a society of medicine men and healers in the small kingdom of Oku in the northern part of the Cameroon Grassfields. These societies, called Ngang, specialized in identifying witches and sorcerers and stopping their destructive actions. The specialists of Ngang, good sorcerers themselves, treated the illnesses caused by the antisocial and greedy members of the community. The masquerader wears a fiber garment trimmed with potent objects. Animal horns, the beak of a hornbill, bundles of feathers, teeth, pieces of leather, and encrusted substances allude to the animals into which witches and sorcerers transform themselves to carry out evil deeds. Several wooden power figures, seed pods containing medicines, even a 1930–31 identification tag marked with "Bamenda" (the name of the capital of the province where Oku is located) add to the dangerous quality of the garment. It ultimately protected its wearer from the evil manipulations of the witches and sorcerers and helped him to discover and destroy them. *Christraud Geary; photograph by David Ulmer*

118 MBOLI ANTI-SORCERER'S MASK, late 20th century

Guro people, Côte d'Ivoire; raffia, bone, seed pods, monkey skull, cloth; h: 14¼ inches (36 cm); Royal Museum for Central Africa, Tervuren, Belgium

Found only among the northern Guro, the Mboli mask is a sacred mask. Contrary to profane masks, the Mboli is cared for by a particular household responsible for its maintenance, display, and all sacrifices made to the mask. This mask, which has an impressive accumulation of vegetal and animal elements, finds and neutralizes sorcerers. The dancer is always assisted by a guide who looks after his heavy costume and takes part in the show under the influence of the spiritual force of his protective fetishes. The wearer performs brisk, precise dance steps. Family members in charge of its worship can appeal to the Mboli and request favors, thank the mask for an intervention, or ask its forgiveness. During the sacrifices the mask remains quiet, as if uninhabited by the spirit that animates it when the masker is dancing. *Anne-Marie Bouttiaux; photograph courtesy Royal Museum for Central Africa*

119 KONO SOCIETY MASK, early 20th century

Bamana people, Mali; wood; h: 36 inches (91.4 cm);
Collection of W. and U. Horstmann, Zug, Switzerland

Kono is one of several Bamana men's initiation societies whose goal is to manipulate supernatural powers in order to punish antisocial behavior and promote health, prosperity, and fertility. The Kono mask is a horizontal helmet with a long snout and large ears. It combines features of animals known for their speed, aggression, or intelligence, all qualities that contribute to Kono's ability to act supernaturally on behalf of the community. The entire mask is covered with a thick layer of animal blood and vegetal matter, whose vital force enhances its spiritual power. The mask is worn with a voluminous costume covered with bird feathers, and must not be viewed by women or uninitiated men. *Kate Ezra; photograph by Lynton Gardiner*

120 DEER MASK, 1930s

Eastern Cherokee people, North Carolina, United States; wood, bone; h: 14¼ inches (36.2 cm);
Denver Art Museum, Purchase from F. G. Speck

In earlier times the Cherokee made animal masks for use in prehunting rituals to bring success to the hunters. The hunter would don the mask and a deerskin and take part in a dance that would magically help him locate and kill the animal. Sometimes hunters would wear the masks while hunting and then wear them again for a second dance upon their triumphant return. In the 1930s Will West Long of the Eastern Cherokee carved a number of these masks as replicas of those he had seen when a boy. Although not specifically attributed to him, this is very likely one of Long's carvings. *Dick Conn; photograph by David Ulmer*

121 MBANGU MASK, early 20th century

Pende people, Democratic Republic of Congo; wood, pigment, fiber; h: 10⅝ inches (27 cm);
Royal Museum for Central Africa, Tervuren, Belgium

Mbangu belongs to the category of masks worn during village festivals and rituals. Maskers perform at the end of the boys' initiation seclusion, and they are also increasingly associated with simple entertainment. The masks parody human society and represent different characters who are often recognized only after the audience is able to view their behavior, costume, and dance. This mask's shape reveals that it is Mbangu, victim of sorcerers, ridden by disease and struck by ill fate. The asymmetrical features are a result of facial nerve palsy. The black and white colors are reminiscent of a face half burned from falling straight into the embers. Pockmarks appear on the left eyelid. *Anne-Marie Bouttiaux; photograph by David Ulmer*

122 SHAMAN'S MASK, c. 1875

Eskimo people, North America; wood, paint, feathers; h: 14 inches (35.6 cm);
The Saint Louis Art Museum, Friends Fund

Eskimo masks depict the anthropomorphic and supernatural spirits of the shaman. The form of these masks was determined by the individual, usually the shaman, who encountered the spirits in a vision. The masks allowed the audience a glimpse into the cosmic realm. Masks not only entertained the human community but also engaged and protected the spirits of the game animals during midwinter dances. Such dances were thought to please the animal spirits who agreed to be taken in the next hunting season, ensuring the survival of the community. *Aldona Jonaitis; photograph by Bob Kolbrener*

123 MASK FROM A CAVALRY SPORTS HELMET, late 1st–early 2nd century A.D.

Provincial Roman; bronze; h: 10 inches (25.4 cm); The J. Paul Getty Museum, Los Angeles

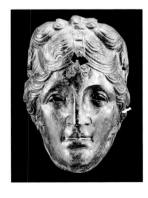

This kind of helmet was worn by elite provincial auxiliary cavalry in a sport combat of cavalry displays, held on special occasions as a demonstration of military power to impress the populace. The sport comprised feats of horsemanship and military technique. The helmet was only one part of a set of splendid bronze and leather armor. The expressionless face, with its statuelike features, probably represents an Amazon. Legendary accounts of battles between Greeks and Amazons were passed down to the Romans, whose sports helmets depict both male and female faces. *Walter J. Karcheski, Jr.; photograph courtesy The J. Paul Getty Museum*

124 TURBAN HELMET, 15th century

Iran; steel and silver inlay; h: 20 inches (50.8 cm); The Walters Art Gallery, Baltimore, Maryland

This helmet's modern name derives from its shape and large proportions, suggesting that a turban was worn as cushioning. The swirling flutes on the surface are suggestive of the spiraling folds of such headwear. Unlike Western headgear, Islamic helmets did not completely encase the head within a steel shell. Instead, a combination of plate and mail provided good protection and ventilation. Masklike aspects are emphasized by the deep mail hood covering all but the wearer's eyes, whose presence only intensifies the helmet's mysteriousness. The face could be revealed by lifting the veil and hooking it at the brow. Universally, headgear is the crowning glory of military garb, and until the 19th century in Islamic cultures it was also the primary indicator of an individual's social status. *Walter J. Karcheski, Jr.; photograph by Lynton Gardiner*

125 FIELD ARMOR IN THE "MAXIMILIAN" STYLE, 1510–25

Wilhelm von Worms the Elder, Nuremberg and Landshut, Germany; steel, cloth, leather; overall costume h: 66 inches (167.6 cm); The Saint Louis Art Museum

Armor's primary function was to serve as battlefield defense. Special attention was always paid to the head, where blows could be lethal. The masklike visor was strong, with curved surfaces to deflect weapons, and pierced with slots necessary for vision and ventilation. In the Middle Ages and the Renaissance, a helmet was only one element of a complete suit of armor. The "Maximilian" style (so named in the 19th century after an early 16th-century emperor) reflected the fashion aesthetic of its wearers, its form imitating male costume of the period. Surface flutes, such as corrugation, added rigidity and deflected weapons from the body, but also suggested garment pleats. The broad-toed foot defenses were themselves metal copies of period shoes. *Walter J. Karcheski, Jr.; photograph by David Ulmer*

126 JOUSTING HELM, 1483–85

Christian Spör, Austria; steel, brass, paint; h: 17¾ inches (45 cm); The Art Institute of Chicago, George F. Harding Collection

This *stechhelm,* known as both a Jousting Helm and a German Joust, was worn during a mock combat, wherein a pair of armored participants on horseback sought to unseat each other by thrusts with strong wooden lances. Originally essential war training for knights, such contests grew so popular among participants and audiences alike that during the 15th century they became exclusively sporting events. The helmet had a single, recessed eyeslot and a solid frontplate to reduce risk of injury. Of course, such extensive protection prevented recognition unless the user wore personalized symbols, such as coats of arms. Since this armor was built purely for sport, it was designed for maximum safety and was extremely heavy and confining. Riders mounted their horses by means of a set of steps. *Walter J. Karcheski, Jr.; photograph courtesy The Art Institute of Chicago*

127 SŌMEN MASK, c. 1680, Edo period (1615–1868)

Myōchin Muneakira, Japan; forged and embossed iron sheet; h: 8⅝ inches (21.9 cm); The Weston Collection

Sōmen masks appeared in the late 15th century, a time of unceasing warfare in Japan. It provided no more protection than earlier masks and was uncomfortable and limited peripheral vision, and thus it was abandoned by the mid-16th century. It was revived in the late 17th century, essentially as a presentation object. Most were composed of three parts and featured a fierce expression. Two-part, and especially single-plate, Sōmen are quite rare, requiring a true technical prowess mastered only by Myōchin Muneakira, who made this Sōmen. The full mask allows for a wider range of representtions, including Shinto and Buddhist deities. This mask may represent a Niō (Buddhist deity). *Robert Burawoy; photograph by David Ulmer*

128 SAMURAI MASK AND HELMET, 1845

Nakayawata Minamoto, Japan; iron, leather, silk, brass; h: 15 inches (38 cm); Barbier-Mueller Collection, Dallas

With the fall of Osaka castle in 1615, Japan's civil wars came to an end. One last military action occurred in 1637-38, to quell an insurrection at Shimabara, before armor fell out of use. Armor resurfaced in the 18th century, but it was exceedingly decorative and had little practicality. In reaction to this decadence, however, armorers revived the more serviceable styles of medieval armor, as exemplified by this austere, black-lacquered mask and accompanying suit. It is signed "Nakayawata Minamoto no Yoshikazu," who was a member of the Iwai school in the employment of the Hachisuka, lords of Tokushima in Awa province, and one of the better armorers of the 19th century.
Robert Burawoy; photograph by Tom Jenkins

129 FIREFIGHTER'S RESPIRATOR, c. 1900

United States; leather, metal, glass; h: 24 inches (61 cm); Collection of Allan Stone Gallery, New York

This protective hood was used by firefighters operating in hazardous atmospheres that required protective respiratory equipment. Very different from the hatlike helmet worn when extinguishing ordinary fires, its enclosed hood design and integrated mask permit the firefighter to work in dense smoke or poisonous gas. Made of rigid leather and fabric, it fits over the head like a sack, tightened with a belt. In times of danger speed is critical, and the hood can be put on or removed quickly. Today comparable hoods are made of durable aluminum and Kevlar and have gold-colored panoramic visors for optimum visibility. As with other firefighter's equipment, this design probably descended from miner's gear. *Cara McCarty; photograph by Lynton Gardiner*

130 COLD WEATHER MASK, c. 1950

Superior Togs Corporation, United States; felt; h: 8½ inches (21.6 cm); The Saint Louis Art Museum

This mask, part of the United States Air Force's uniform, is one of the few masks worn in the 20th century by the military. Made of camouflage flesh-colored felt, it is like a second skin, a soft blanket for the face. Its purpose is to protect the face from cold weather and frostbite. The small eye holes and nose covering, which extends below the mouth, minimize exposed skin. The "one-size-fits-all" design contributes to a sense of anonymity and underscores the general standardization of 20th-century products. Whereas much protective headgear is a "game face" that hides any expression of doubt or fear from the enemy, there is nothing intimidating about this endearing mask.
Cara McCarty; photograph by David Ulmer

131 RESPIRATOR, 1930s

Ohio Rubber Company, Ohio, United States; rubber, glass, metal; h: 9 inches (22.9 cm); Collection of Allan Stone Gallery, New York

Like traditional European armor that revealed important information about its wearer and its culture, modern industrial masks are portraits of our technological society. They speak directly and powerfully of the dangers of our own age, such as gas assaults and toxic fumes. Gas masks are an essential piece of equipment in modern warfare and are worn not only by the military but by civilians as well. Their proboscis and resemblance to insects project a predatory and warlike image. They are devastating affirmations of our aggressive nature and are very real and terrifying reminders of our society's worst fears. They are no less disturbing and mysterious than their predecessors and have become the modern icon associated with some of the most horrific acts of the 20th century.
Cara McCarty; photograph by Lynton Gardiner

132 FIREFIGHTER'S RESPIRATOR, c. 1910

J. Mandet, France; brass, glass, leather; h: 12 inches (30.5 cm); Collection of William Greenspon

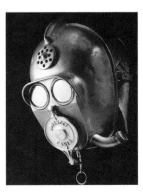

Designed to protect one's eyes and respiratory system, the details on this smoke helmet have been executed with the style and finesse of the best French fashion, still seen in the uniforms of French firefighters today. The use of machine imagery for human features is not inconsequential. This helmet was made at a time when artists were celebrating the ever-expanding and powerful industrial world—the brave new world of the machine. It portrays the wearer as a mechanized individual, symbolically conveying the strength of modern technology necessary to conquer smoke and fire.
Cara McCarty; photograph by Lynton Gardiner

133 HOCKEY GOALTENDER'S MASK, 1964

Ernest C. Higgins, Co., Massachusetts, United States; fiberglass; h: 10½ inches (26.7 cm);
The Museum of Modern Art, New York, Emilio Ambasz Fund

Deep perforations in hockey masks, strategically positioned and shaped to provide ventilation and deflect oncoming pucks, resemble the battle scars one is apt to incur in this physically intense and often violent game. Masks are often painted for team identification. In an arena sport like hockey, masks are very much a part of the spectacle: their sinister appearance ups the ante of confrontation and intimidation. Hockey goalies develop "cage courage" when masked: armored and disguised they feel bigger and protected, confident to play the game more aggressively. Like the demons who guard the facades of buildings, the goalie transcends into a new zone of toughness and defiance when he dons his mask to guard his territory and make his saves, keeping the evil spirit—the puck—from invading his space. *Cara McCarty; photograph by Lynton Gardiner, © The Museum of Modern Art, NY*

134 BULLET-RESISTANT MASK, 1989

American Body Armor and Equipment, Inc., Florida, United States; Kevlar, metal, polyester resin;
h: 11 inches (27.9 cm); The Saint Louis Art Museum, Gift of American Body Armor and Equipment, Inc.

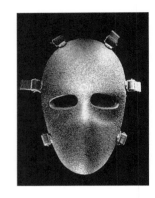

In addition to their protective function, modern industrial masks have the same psychological impact as their predecessors: they intimidate, mystify, and can transform the wearer's behavior. This beautifully contoured, bullet-resistant face shield is one of the more terrifying masks in contemporary Western society. Made of Kevlar, it is part of the armor worn by law enforcement officers during drug raids or when apprehending snipers. The physical protection it provides is enhanced by a strong psychological presence, serving to unnerve and intimidate. Concealing all but the eyes, this impenetrable mask gives the wearer an immediate advantage over the suspect. It enables the police officer to surprise and frighten the suspect into compliance, and ultimately to expedite the arrest. *Cara McCarty; photograph by Lynton Gardiner*

135 MOTOCROSS HELMET, 1985

Arai Helmet, Ltd., Florida, United States; fiberglass, reinforced resin laminate, expanded polystyrene, and nylon-rubber thermoplastic; h: 9¾ inches (24.8 cm); The Saint Louis Art Museum, Gift of Arai Helmet, Ltd.

While many masks are worn for ritual, masquerade, and theater, some are merely for protection. The threat of lawsuits, advances in new materials, and improved health and safety standards account for the recent proliferation of protective headgear. Technology has given us synthetic and composite materials that greatly improve the fit, strength, and shock absorption of headgear in addition to its ability to protect. The durable shell and design of this motocross helmet is necessary armor that shields against windblast, rain, noise, headaches, road debris, and catastrophic head injury. As high-performance gear, its overriding purpose is for riding comfort as it keeps the wearer alive. *Cara McCarty; photograph by David Ulmer*

136 BASEBALL CATCHER'S MASK, 1985

All-Star Sporting Goods, Massachusetts, United States; leather, steel, Velcro;
h: 11⅝ inches (29.5 cm); All-Star Sporting Goods

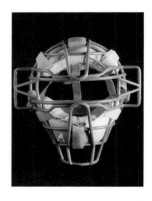

Baseball catcher's masks have changed very little since they were first worn in 1877. Invented by Fred Thayer, captain of Harvard's Baseball Club, their primary purpose is to protect the catcher's face from foul tips and balls traveling at high speeds. Initially developed as a confidence-boosting mask for catchers standing behind the bat, it allowed catchers to get closer to the plate to catch foul balls. The cage design, inspired by fencing masks, allows visibility and ventilation, and leather padding cushions the face against the impact of a speeding ball. Like most sports masks, the catcher's mask was first met with ridicule because protective gear was considered unmanly and cowardly. These wire masks are based on a grid structure that also serves as a target for the pitcher. *Cara McCarty; photograph by David Ulmer*

137 FENCING MASK, 1997

Zivkovic Modern Fencing Equipment, Inc., Massachusetts, United States; stainless steel, Kevlar, plastic; h: 15½ inches (39.4 cm); Zivkovic Modern Fencing Equipment, Inc.

Fencing is a martial sport involving both offensive and defensive combat fought with a sword. As an early form of one-on-one combat, dueling with swords was for a long time part of the basic training method for soldiers. After swordplay became only a sport in the 17th century, the wire mask was invented to protect the face. Relief sculptures dating from 1190 B.C. show that fencing masks were initially worn by the ancient Egyptians. In 1750 the father of the French fencing master La Boëssière reintroduced the mask, which became an essential piece of the fencer's protective equipment. Unlike many masking traditions that are intended to release inhibitions, fencing is based on precision and discipline. The fine wire mesh of fencing masks resembles and probably predates the wire-screen masks traditionally worn during Carnival in Tirol, Austria, that were eventually introduced into the Caribbean and South America for Carnival. *Cara McCarty; photograph by David Ulmer*

138 SPEED-SKIING HELMET, 1981

Fasttrack Enterprises, Ltd., Alberta, Canada; fiberglass, plastic; h: 10½ inches (26.5 cm); The Museum of Modern Art, New York, Mrs. John D. Rockefeller 3rd Purchase Fund

Full-face helmets such as this are worn by speed-skiers, who ski straight down a mountain as quickly as possible, sometimes reaching speeds of 150 miles an hour. Not only does the helmet increase the skier's chance of survival while traveling at high speeds, but it also helps focus the skier's concentration by muffling sound and restricting vision as the skier slices through the wind. The mental demands of such life-threatening competition are strenuous, and participants strive to elevate themselves into a trancelike state of mind. They study Zen, tai chi, and transcendental meditation to hone their concentration and keep their bodies in line against the force of air. An example of high-performance design, this aerodynamic, wing-shaped helmet has been stripped to its essence. *Cara McCarty; photograph by Lynton Gardiner, © The Museum of Modern Art, NY*

139 APOLLO 15 SPACE HELMET, 1971

ILC Industries, Inc., Delaware, United States; mask and suit: textile, aluminum, gold; overall suit h: 78 inches (198.1 cm); National Air and Space Museum, Smithsonian Institution, Washington, D.C.

This helmet, worn by James Irwin during the Apollo 15 lunar space mission, is one of the most poignant examples of modern protective headgear. Unlike the disturbing effect of many masks designed for physical protection, space helmets have an aura of innocence and benevolence. Designed to accommodate the astronaut's physical needs, the entire space suit is a portable life-support system that allows astronauts to survive in an alien environment. As space-age armor, it protects the astronaut from the inhospitable forces of nature, such as assaults from flying meteoroid particles and temperature extremes, and the reflective gold visor protects the face and eyes from solar radiation. Like other masks and costumes, space suits have taken humankind a step further on the journey begun in Paleolithic times when humans first began to explore flight and other identities. *Cara McCarty; photograph by Lynton Gardiner*

NOTES

Chapter 1: Prehistory and Origins

1. Alexander Marshack, "Evolution of the Human Capacity: The Symbolic Evidence," *Yearbook of Physical Anthropology* 32 (1989): 6.
2. Marshack, "Evolution of the Human Capacity," 5.
3. Barbara J. King, *The Information Continuum: Evolution of Social Information Transfer in Monkeys, Apes, and Hominids* (Santa Fe: SAR Press; distributed by the University of Washington Press, 1994), 107.
4. William Irwin Thompson, *The Time Falling Bodies Take to Light: Mythology, Sexuality, and the Origins of Culture* (New York: St. Martin's Press, 1981), 110.
5. Ann Sieveking, *The Cave Artists* (London: Thames and Hudson, 1979), 208–09.
6. Thompson, 109.
7. Jean-Loup Rousselot, personal communication, December 1995.
8. John Nunley, *Moving with the Face of the Devil: Art and Politics in Urban West Africa* (Urbana: University of Illinois Press, 1987), 116.
9. Ruth D. Lechuga, *Mask Arts of Mexico* (London: Thames and Hudson, 1994), 169.
10. Henri Lhote, "The Rock Art of the Maghreb and Sahara." In *The Art of the Stone Age: Forty Thousand Years of Rock Art*, ed. Hans-Georg Bandi et al., trans. Anne E. Keep (New York: Crown Publishers, 1961), 144–45.
11. J. F. Thackeray, "New Directions in the Study of Southern African Rock Art," *African Arts* (January 1993), 74–75.
12. Peter Garlake, *The Hunter's Vision: The Prehistoric Art of Zimbabwe* (Seattle: University of Washinton Press, 1995), 73.
13. Evan M. Maurer, *Visions of the People: A Pictorial History of Plains Indian Life* (Minneapolis: Minneapolis Institute of Art, 1992), 23.
14. J. J. Brody, *Mimbres Painted Pottery* (Santa Fe, New Mexico: School of American Research, 1977), 62.
15. Scott Thybony, *Rock Art of the American Southwest* (Portland, Oregon: Graphic Arts Center, 1994), 90.
16. Andreas Lommel, "The Rock Art of Australia." In *The Art of the Stone Age: Forty Thousand Years of Rock Art*, ed. Hans-Georg Bandi et al., trans. Anne E. Keep (New York: Crown Publishers, 1961), 212.
17. Robert Brooks and Vishnu Wakankar, *Stone Age Painting in India* (New Haven, Connecticut: Yale University Press, 1976), 79-80.
18. Anatolii Ivanovich Martynov, *The Ancient Art of Northern Asia* (Urbana: University of Illinois Press, 1991), 148, 172.
19. Martha Nemes Fried and Morton H. Fried, *Transitions: Four Rituals in Eight Societies* (New York: Norton Press, 1980), 269.
20. Robert Davidson and Ulli Steltzer, *Eagle Transforming: The Art of Robert Davidson* (Seattle: University of Washington Press, 1994), 96.
21. Davidson and Steltzer, 96.
22. Peter T. Furst, "Jaguar Baby or Toad Mother: A New Look at an Old Problem in Olmec Iconography." In *The Olmec and their Neighbors: Essays in Memory of Matthew W. Stirling*, ed. Elizabeth P. Benson, 149–62 (Washington, D.C., and Cambridge: Dunbarton Oaks Research Library and Collections, and Trustees for Harvard University Press, 1981), 158–59.
23. Furst, 150.
24. Morris E. Opler, *Apache Odyssey: A Journey Between Two Worlds* (New York: Irvington Publishers, 1983), 371.
25. Anthony Shelton, "Fictions and Parodies: Masquerade in Mexico and Highland South America." In *Masks and the Art of Expression*, ed. John Mack (New York: Harry N. Abrams, Inc., 1994), 98.

Chapter 2: Rites of Passage

1. Arnold Van Gennep, *Rites of Passage* (London: Routledge and Keegan Paul, 1960), 3.
2. Jan Vansina, "Zairan Masking in Historical Perspective." In *Face of the Spirits: Masks from the Zaire Basin*, ed. Frank Herreman and Constantijn Petridis (Gent, Belgium: Snoeck-Ducaju, 1993), 235.
3. Arlene Wolinski, "Egyptian Masks: The Priest and his Role," *Archaeology* 40/1 (January/February 1987): 23.
4. Victor Witter Turner, *The Ritual Process: Structure and Anti-Structure* (Chicago: Aldine Publishing Company, 1969), 8.
5. Phyllis Plattner, personal communication, 1993.
6. Alice Schlegel and Herbert Barry, "The Evolutionary Significance of Adolescent Initiation Ceremonies," *American Ethnologist* 7/4 (1980): 711.
7. Frederick Lamp, "Cosmos, Cosmetics and the Spirit of Bondo," *African Arts* 18/3 (May 1985): 28.
8. John Nunley, *Moving with the Face of the Devil: Art and Politics in Urban West Africa* (Urbana: University of Illinois Press, 1987), 54.
9. Lamp, "Cosmos," 30.
10. Frederick Lamp, personal communication, October 12, 1995.
11. Lamp, "Cosmos," 43.
12. Kenji Yoshida, "Masks and Secrecy among the Chewa," *African Arts* 26/2 (April 1993): 45.
13. Marie-Louise Bastin, "The Akishi Spirits of the Chokwe." In *Face of the Spirits: Masks from the Zaire Basin*, ed. Frank Herreman and Constantijn Petridis (Gent, Belgium: Snoeck-Ducaju, 1993), 84.
14. Bastin, 85.
15. Iris Hahner-Herzog et al., *African Masks from the Barbier-Mueller Collection, Geneva* (Munich: Prestel-Verlag, 1998), 95.
16. Marilyn Houlberg, personal communication, June 12, 1990.
17. Wolinski, 27–28.
18. Kathleen Berrin, "Unknown Treasures: The Unexpected in Teotihuacan Art." In *Teotihuacan: Art from the City of the Gods*, ed. Kathleen Berrin and Esther Pasztory (New York and San Francisco: Thames and Hudson and Fine Arts Museums of San Francisco, 1993), 184.
19. Berrin, 209.
20. Henri Stierlin, *Art of the Maya: From the Olmecs to the Toltec-Maya* (New York: Rizzoli, 1981), 92.
21. Linda Schele and Mary Ellen Miller, *The Blood of Kings: Dynasty and Ritual in Maya Art* (Fort Worth: Kimbell Art Museum, 1986), 268–69.
22. Elisabeth Cameron, "Ancestors and Living Men Among the Batak." In *The Eloquent Dead: Ancestral Sculpture of Indonesia and Southeast Asia*, ed. Jerome Feldman (Los Angeles: UCLA Fowler Museum of Cultural History, 1985), 85.
23. Emmanuel Kasarherou, *Le Masque Kanak* (Marseille: Editions Parenthèses, 1998), 11.
24. Kasarherou, 48.
25. Yoshida, 40.

Chapter 3: Festivals of Renewal

1. Abdellah Hammoudi, *The Victim and Its Masks: An Essay on Sacrifice and Masquerade in the Maghreb*, trans. Paula Wissing (Chicago: University of Chicago Press, 1993), 60.
2. Joseph Mora, *The Year of the Hopi: Paintings and Photographs* (Washington, D.C: Smithsonian Institution Traveling Exhibition Service, 1979), 19.
3. Edwin Oliver James, *Seasonal Feasts and Festivals* (London: Thames and Hudson, 1961), 45–49.
4. James, 136.
5. Antonio Regalado, personal communication, December 6, 1997.
6. Cesare Poppi, "The Other Within: Masks and Masquerades in Europe." In *Masks: The Art of Expression*, ed. John Mack, 190–215 (London: British Museum), 210.
7. Walter E. A. Van Beek, "Enter the Bush: A Dogon Mask Festival." In *Africa Explores: Twentieth-Century African Art*, ed. Susan

Mullin Vogel (New York: The Center for African Art; Munich: Prestel-Verlag, 1991), 67.

8. Van Beek, 61.

9. Van Beek, 67.

10. Van Beek, 59.

11. Van Beek, 62.

12. John Nunley and Judith Bettelheim, *Caribbean Festival Arts: Each and Every Bit of Difference* (St. Louis and Seattle: The Saint Louis Art Museum and University of Washington Press, 1988), 37.

13. Naphtali Lewis and Meyer Reinhold, eds., *Roman Civilization, Vol. 1: The Republic and the Augustan Age*, 3rd ed. (New York: Columbia University Press, 1990), 515.

14. E. A. Thompson, *The Goths in Spain* (Oxford: Clarendon Press, 1969), 309.

15. Lesley Adkins and Roy A. Adkins, *Handbook to Life in Ancient Rome* (Oxford: Oxford University Press, 1998), 282.

16. Lyubomira Parpulova-Gribble, unpublished manuscript, 1.

17. Kenneth M. Bilby, personal communication, April 11, 1998.

18. Nunley and Bettelheim, 71–83.

Chapter 4: Men as Women

1. John Nunley, *Moving with the Face of the Devil: Art and Politics in Urban West Africa* (Urbana: University of Illinois Press, 1987), 108.

2. Nunley, *Moving*, 116.

3. Ovid, *Pygmalion*, trans. Rolfe Humphries (Bloomington: Indiana University Press, 1955), 242.

4. Ovid, 243.

5. Genesis 2:23, *The Holy Bible. King James Version* (New York: New York Bible Society International), 8–9.

6. Herbert Haag et al. *Great Women of the Bible in Art and Literature* (Grand Rapids, Michigan: Eerdmans, 1994), 19.

7. Vern L. Bullough and Bonne Bullough, *Cross Dressing, Sex and Gender* (Philadelphia: University of Pennsylvania Press, 1990), 27.

8. Lesley Ferris, *Acting Women: Images of Women in Theatre* (New York: New York University Press, 1989), 43.

9. Peggy Phelan, "Crisscrossing Cultures." In *Crossing the Stage: Controversies on Cross-Dressing*, ed. Lesley Ferris (London and New York: Routledge, 1993), 162.

10. Herbert Cole and Chike Aniakor, *Igbo Arts: Community and Cosmos* (Los Angeles: UCLA Fowler Museum of Cultural History, 1985), 121.

11. Carma Hinton and Richard Gordon (directors), *First Moon* (Long Bow Group, 1987).

12. Ruth D. Lechuga, personal communication, April 12, 1997.

13. John Emigh, personal communication, June 13, 1997.

14. Janet Brody Esser, *Behind the Mask in Mexico* (Santa Fe, New Mexico: Museum of International Folk Art, 1988), 165.

15. Sherry B. Ortner, "Is Female to Male as Nature Is to Culture?" In *Women, Culture, and Society*, ed. M. Z. Rosaldo and L. Lamphere (Stanford, California: Stanford University Press, 1974), 67–87.

16. Ortner, 72–73.

17. Bullough and Bullough, 24.

18. Bullough and Bullough, 24.

19. Barbara Walker, *The Crone: Woman of Age, Wisdom, and Power* (New York: Harper and Row, Publishers, 1985), 23.

20. Cole and Aniakor, 125.

21. Joseph Mora, *The Year of the Hopi: Paintings and Photographs* (Washington, D.C: Smithsonian Institution Traveling Exhibition Service, 1979), 77–85.

22. Mora, 65.

23. Mora, 65.

24. Esser, 110.

25. Marilyn Houlberg, "Notes on Egungun Masquerades among the Oyo Yoruba," *African Arts* 11/3 (April 1978): 26.

26. *Entroida en Laza*, a film by Jesus Lozano (New York University Presents, 1987).

27. John Nunley and Judith Bettelheim, *Caribbean Festival Arts: Each and Every Bit of Difference* (St. Louis and Seattle: The Saint Louis Art Museum and University of Washington Press, 1988), 56.

28. Frederick Lamp, *Art of the Baga: A Drama of Cultural Reinvention* (Munich: Prestel-Verlag, 1996), 158.

29. Henry John Drewal and Margaret Thompson Drewal, *Gelede: Art and Female Power among the Yoruba* (Bloomington: Indiana University Press, 1990), xv.

30. Drewal and Drewal, 73.

31. P. J. Imperato, "Bamana and Maninka Twin Figures," *African Arts* 8/4 (1975): 52.

32. John Nunley, "Cover Story," *Journal of the American Medical Association* 276/22 (December 11, 1996): 1782.

33. Nunley, *Moving*, 194.

34. Claude Lévi-Strauss, *The Way of the Masks*, trans. Sylvia Modelski (Seattle: University of Washington Press, 1982), 64.

35. Lévi-Strauss, 90–91.

36. Mora, 19.

37. B. A. Wright, *Kachinas: A Hopi Artist's Documentary* (Flagstaff, Arizona: Northland Press with the Heard Museum, 1973), 17.

38. Wright, 18.

39. John Emigh, personal communication, June 10, 1997.

40. Tennyson, Alfred, Baron, *The Complete Poetical Works of Tennyson*, ed. W. J. Rolfe (Boston: Houghton Mifflin, 1898).

Chapter 5: Theater

1. Gajendra S. Tyagi, "Decorative Intricate Patterns in Indian Rock Art." In *Rock Art in the Old World*, ed. Michel Lorblanchet (New Delhi: Indira Gandhi National Centre for the Arts, 1992), 308.

2. Vishnu S. Wakankur, "Rock Painting in India." In *Rock Art in the Old World*, ed. Michel Lorblanchet (New Delhi: Indira Gandhi National Centre for the Arts, 1992), 324.

3. Chen Zao Fu, "Discovery of Rock Art in China." In *Rock Art in the Old World*, ed. Michel Lorblanchet (New Delhi: Indira Gandhi National Centre for the Arts, 1992), 368.

4. Bruce Kapferer, *A Celebration of Demons: Exorcism and the Aesthetics of Healing in Sri Lanka* (Bloomington: Indiana University Press, 1983); M. H. Goonatilleka, *Masks and Mask Systems of Sri Lanka* (Colombo, Sri Lanka: Tamarind Books, 1978); Alain Loviconi and F. Lontcho, *Masques et Exorcismes de Ceylon/Masks and Exorcisms of Sri Lanka* (Paris: Editions Errance, 1981).

5. Goonatilleka; E. R. Sarachchandra, *The Folk Drama of Ceylon*, 2d ed. (Colombo, Ceylon: Department of Cultural Affairs, 1962).

6. Yi Tu-hyon (Lee Duhyun), "Mask Dance-Dramas." In *Traditional Performing Arts of Korea* (Seoul: Seoul Computer Press, 1986), 35–80; Lee Duhyun, ed., *Masks of Korea* (Seoul: Korea Overseas Information Service, 1981).

7. Patricia Berger, "Buddhist Festivals in Mongolia." In *Mongolia: The Legacy of Chinggis Khan*, ed. Terese Tse Bartholomew and Patricia Berger, 149–84 (San Francisco: Asian Art Museum of San Francisco, 1995); Mario Fantin, *Mani-Rimdu, Nepal: the Buddhist Dance Drama of Tengpoche* (New Delhi: The English Book Store, 1976).

8. Wendy Doniger, *The Implied Spider: Politics and Theology in Myth* (New York: Columbia University Press, 1998), 318.

9. Pradyot Ghosh, "Gambhira: Traditional Masked Dance of Bengal." *Sangeet Natak* 53–54 (1979): 53–77.

10. I Madé Bandem and Fredrik Eugene deBoer, *Balinese Dance in Transition: Kaja and Kelod*, 2d ed. (Kuala Lumpur: Oxford University Press, 1995), 118–41; John Emigh, *Masked Performance* (Philadelphia: University of Pennsylvania, 1997), 60–104.

11. Clifford R. Jones, "Bhagavata Natakam: A Traditional Dance-Drama Form," *Journal of Asian Studies* 22, 2/3: 193–200.

12. Emigh, 35–60.

13. Asutosh Bhattacharyya, *Chhau Dance of Purulia* (Calcutta: Rabindra Bharati University, 1972); Pashupati Prasad Mahato, *The Performing Arts of Jharkhand* (Calcutta: B. B. Prakasan, 1987).

14. Juga Bhanu Singh Deo, *Chhau: Mask Dance of Seraikella* (Cuttack, Orissa, India: Srimati Jayashree Devi, 1973).

15. Richard Schechner, *Between Theatre and Anthropology* (Philadelphia: University of Pennsylvania Press, 1985), 155–211.

16. Bandem and deBoer, 65–74; Judith Slattum, *Balinese Masks: Spirits of an Ancient Drama* (San Francisco: Chronicle Books, 1992), 48–75.

17. Dhanit Yupho, *Khon Masks*, 4th ed. (Bangkok: The Department of Fine Arts, 1971); Jukka O. Miettinen, *Classical Dance and Theatre in South-East Asia* (Singapore: Oxford University Press, 1992).

18. Emigh, 105–206; Bandem and deBoer, 44–56; Slattum, 22–47.

19. Soedarsono, *Wayang Wong: The State Ritual Dance Drama in the Court of Yogyakarta* (Yogyakarta: Gadjah Mada University Press, 1990); Kathy Foley, "My Bodies: The Performer in West Java." *The Drama Review* 34/2: 62–80.

20. Fu Shin Shen, *The Masks of Anshun's Earth Opera* (Taipei: Shu Hsing Publishing, 1985); Yu Quiyu, "Some Observations on the Aesthetics of Primitive Chinese Theatre," trans. Hu Dongsheng, Elizabeth Wichmann, and Gregg Richardson, *Asian Theatre Journal*, 6/1 (1989): 12–30.

21. Donald Keene, *Nō; The Classical Theatre of Japan* (Tokyo and Palo Alto, California: Kodansha International, 1966); Samuel Leiter, ed., *Japanese Theatre in the World* (New York:

Japan Society, Inc., and The Japan Foundation, 1997), 37–45.

22. Kyôtarô Nishikawa, *Bugaku Masks*, trans. and adapt. Monica Bethe (New York and Tokyo: Kodansha International Ltd. and Shibundo, 1978).

23. J. Thomas Rimer and Yamazaki Masakazu, eds. and trans., *On the Art of the No Drama: The Major Treatises of Zeami* (Princeton, New Jersey: Princeton University Press, 1984); Leiter, ed., 46–58; Keene; Rebecca Teele, ed., *No/Kyogen Masks and Performance* (Claremont, California: Mime Journal, 1984).

24. Samuel Taylor Coleridge, *Biographia Literaria*, vol. II, ed. J. Shawcross (London: Oxford University Press, 1939), chapter XIV.

25. Quoted in Guthrie Theatre season flyer, 1995.

26. William Archer, *Masks or Faces?* (New York: Hill and Wang, 1957), 103.

27. David Wiles, *The Masks of Menander: Sign and Meaning in Greek and Roman Performances* (Cambridge, England: Cambridge University Press, 1991), 77.

28. Wiles, 80.

29. Wiles, 130.

30. Lesley Ferris, *Acting Women: Images of Women in Theatre* (London: Macmillan, 1990), 38–46.

31. Allardyce Nicoll, ed., *The World of Harlequin: A Critical Study of the Commedia Dell'Arte* (Cambridge, England: Cambridge University Press, 1963), 208.

32. Quoted in Sears Eldredge, *Mask Improvisation for Actor Training and Performance: The Compelling Image* (Evanston, Illinois: Northwestern University Press, 1996), 13.

33. Susan Valeria Harris Smith, *Masks in Modern Drama* (Berkeley: University of California Press, 1984), 1.

34. Smith, 126.

35. Quoted in Eldredge, 50.

Chapter 6: Offense | Defense

1. Hans Plischke, "Das Gewand eines tungurischen Schamanen," *CIBA-Zeitschrift* 4/38 (October 1936): 1322–23.

2. Guenter Krauss, "Kefu Elak." In *Traditionelle Medizin in Oku (Kamerun)*, ed. Dr. M. K. Ramaswamy (Göttingen, Germany: Edition Re, 1990), 33–34.

3. Alfred Irving Hallowell, *Bear Ceremonialism in the Northern Hemisphere* (Menasha, Wisconsin: American Anthropologist, 1926), 11–12.

4. Charles Wilkes, *Narrative of the United States Exploring Expedition During the Years 1838, 1839, 1840, 1841, 1842*, vol. 5 (Philadelphia: Lea and Blanchard, 1845), 47–48, 55.

5. Richard Lattimore, ed., *The Iliad of Homer* (Chicago: University of Chicago Press, 1961), Book 17, lines 210–14, 359–60.

6. Robert Burawoy, personal communication, October 1998.

7. "A number of different cultures were examined and of the 15 societies in which warriors changed their appearance, 12 were high on the index of 'killing, torturing, or mutilating the enemy', while only one of the 8 with unchanged appearance was so aggressive." Philip Zimbardo and Richard Gerrig, *Psychology and Life*, 11th ed. (Glenview, Illinois: Scott Foresman, 1985), 615, 617.

8. Robert P. Ingalls, *Hoods: The Story of the Ku Klux Klan* (New York: G. P. Putnam's Sons, 1979), 86.

9. Bernie Parrish, *They Call It a Game* (New York: Dial Press, 1971), 62.

10. Michael C. Cutler, *Hockey Masks and the Great Goalies Who Wear Them* (Montreal: Tundra Books, 1977), 3, 5.

11. Karl B. Raitz, "The Theater of Sport: A Landscape Perspective." In *The Theater of Sport*, ed. Karl B. Raitz (Baltimore: Johns Hopkins University, 1995), 9.

12. Douglas E. Bradley, personal communication, December 1998.

13. Douglas E. Bradley, *Life, Death and Duality: A Handbook of the Rev. Edmund P. Joyce, C.S.C. Collection of Ritual Ballgame Sculpture*. The Snite Museum of Art Bulletin, vol. 1 (Notre Dame, Indiana: University of Notre Dame, 1997).

14. Michael Starr, "Arms Like Lead! Hit 'Em in the Head!" *Newsweek* (December 1, 1997), 70–71.

15. Reggie White, *In the Trenches: The Autobiography* (Nashville: Thomas Nelson, 1996).

16. Tara Weingarten, "Crashing to Earth," *Newsweek* (August 3, 1998), 47.

17. Lillian Kozloski, *U.S. Space Gear: Outfitting the Astronaut* (Washington, D.C.: Smithsonian Institution Press, 1994).

KING ALFRED'S COLLEGE
LIBRARY

BIBLIOGRAPHY

Chapter 1: Prehistory and Origins

Bacon, Edward. *Vanished Civilizations of the Ancient World*. New York: McGraw-Hill, 1963.

Brody, J. J. *Mimbres Painted Pottery*. Santa Fe, New Mexico: School of American Research, 1977.

Brooks, Robert, and Vishnu Wakankar. *Stone Age Painting in India*. New Haven, Connecticut: Yale University Press, 1976.

Cole, Herbert M., ed. *I Am Not Myself: The Art of African Masquerade*. Los Angeles: UCLA Fowler Museum of Cultural History, 1985.

Davidson, Robert, and Ulli Steltzer. *Eagle Transforming: The Art of Robert Davidson*. Seattle: University of Washington Press, 1994.

Fienup-Riordan, Anne. *The Living Traditions of Yup'ik Masks*. Seattle: University of Washington Press, 1996.

Furst, Peter T. "Jaguar Baby or Toad Mother: A New Look at an Old Problem in Olmec Iconography." In *The Olmec and their Neighbors: Essays in Memory of Matthew W. Stirling*, ed. Elizabeth P. Benson. Washington, D.C., and Cambridge: Dumbarton Oaks Research Library and Collections, and Trustees for Harvard University, 1981.

Garlake, Peter. *The Hunter's Vision: The Prehistoric Art of Zimbabwe*. Seattle: University of Washington Press, 1995.

King, Barbara J. *The Information Continuum: Evolution of Social Information Transfer in Monkeys, Apes, and Hominids*. Santa Fe: SAR Press; Distributed by the University of Washington Press, 1994.

Lechuga, Ruth D. *Mask Arts of Mexico*. London: Thames and Hudson, 1994.

Lhote, Henri. "The Rock Art of the Maghreb and Sahara." In *The Art of the Stone Age: Forty Thousand Years of Rock Art*, ed. Hans-Georg Bandi, et al., trans. Anne E. Keep. New York: Crown Publishers, 1961.

Lommel, Andreas. "The Rock Art of Australia." In *The Art of the Stone Age: Forty Thousand Years of Rock Art*, ed. Hans-Georg Bandi et al., trans. Anne E. Keep. New York: Crown Publishers, 1961.

Marshack, Alexander. *The Roots of Civilization: The Cognitive Beginnings of Man's First Art, Symbol and Notation*. Mount Kisco, New York: Moyer Bell, 1991.

————. "Evolution of the Human Capacity: The Symbolic Evidence." *Yearbook of Physical Anthropology* 32 (1989): 1–34.

Martynov, Anatolii Ivanovich. *The Ancient Art of Northern Asia*. Urbana: University of Illinois Press, 1991.

Maurer, Evan M. *Visions of the People: A Pictorial History of Plains Indian Life*. Minneapolis: Minneapolis Institute of Art, 1992.

Nunley, John. *Moving with the Face of the Devil: Art and Politics in Urban West Africa*. Urbana: University of Illinois Press, 1987.

Opler, Morris E. *Apache Odyssey: A Journey Between Two Worlds*. New York: Irvington Publishers, 1983.

Rousselot, Jean-Loup, Bernard Abel, Jose Pierre, and Catherine Bihl. *Masques Eskimo d'Alaska*. Saint-Vit, France: Editions Amez, 1991.

Shelton, Anthony. "Fictions and Parodies: Masquerade in Mexico and Highland South America." In *Masks and the Art of Expression*, ed. John Mack. New York: Harry N. Abrams, Inc., 1994.

Sieveking, Ann. *The Cave Artists*. London: Thames and Hudson, 1979.

Thackeray, J. F. "New Directions in the Study of Southern African Rock Art." *African Arts* (January 1993).

Thompson, William Irwin. *The Time Falling Bodies Take to Light: Mythology, Sexuality, and the Origins of Culture*. New York: St. Martin's Press, 1981.

Thybony, Scott. *Rock Art of the American Southwest*. Portland, Oregon: Graphic Arts Center, 1994.

Chapter 2: Rites of Passage

Berrin, Kathleen, and Esther Pasztory, eds. *Teotihuacan: Art from the City of the Gods*. New York and San Francisco: Thames and Hudson and Fine Arts Museums of San Francisco, 1993.

Cameron, Elisabeth. "Ancestors and Living Men Among the Batak." In *The Eloquent Dead: Ancestral Sculpture of Indonesia and Southeast Asia*, ed. Jerome Feldman. Los Angeles: UCLA Fowler Museum of Cultural History, 1985.

Geary, Christraud M. "Elephants, Ivory, and Chiefs: The Elephant and the Arts of the Cameroon Grassfields." In *Elephant: The Animal and Its Ivory in African Culture*, ed. Doran H. Ross. Los Angeles: UCLA Fowler Museum of Cultural History, 1992.

Hahner-Herzog, Iris, et al. *African Masks from the Barbier-Muller Collection, Geneva*. Munich: Prestel-Verlag, 1998.

Herreman, Frank, and Constantijn Petridis, eds. *Face of the Spirits: Masks from the Zaire Basin*. Gent, Belgium: Snoeck-Ducaju-Zoon, 1993.

Kasarherou, Emmanuel. *Le Masque Kanak*. Marseille, France: Editions Parenthèses, 1998.

Lamp, Frederick. "Cosmos, Cosmetics and the Spirit of Bondo." *African Arts* 18/3 (May 1985): 28–42.

Nunley, John. *Moving with the Face of the Devil: Art and Politics in Urban West Africa*. Urbana: University of Illinois Press, 1987.

Ross, Doran H. *Elephant: The Animal and Its Ivory in African Culture*. Los Angeles: University of California Press, 1992.

Schele, Linda, and Mary Ellen Miller. *The Blood of Kings: Dynasty and Ritual in Maya Art*. Fort Worth: Kimbell Art Museum, 1986.

Schlegel, Alice, and Herbert Barry. "The Evolutionary Significance of Adolescent Initiation Ceremonies." *American Ethnologist* 7/4 (1980): 696–715.

Stierlin, Henri. *Art of the Maya: From the Olmecs to the Toltec-Maya*. New York: Rizzoli, 1981.

Turner, Victor Witter. *The Ritual Process: Structure and Anti-Structure*. Chicago: Aldine Publishing Company, 1969.

Van Gennep, Arnold. *Rites of Passage*. London: Routledge and Kegan Paul, 1960.

Wolinski, Arlene. "Egyptian Masks: The Priest and His Role." *Archaeology* 40/1 (January/February 1987): 22–29.

Yoshida, Kenji. "Masks and Secrecy among the Chewa." *African Arts* 26/2 (April 1993): 34–45, 92.

Chapter 3: Festivals of Renewal

Adkins, Lesley, and Roy A. Adkins. *Handbook to Life in Ancient Rome*. Oxford: Oxford University Press, 1998.

DeMott, Barbara. *Dogon Masks: A Structural Study of Form and Meaning*. Ann Arbor, Michigan: UMI Research Press, 1980.

Griaule, Marcel. *Masques dogons*. 2d ed., No. 33 of *Université de Paris, Travaux et mémoires de l'Institut d'Ethnologie*. Paris: Institut d'Ethnologie, 1963.

————. "Les Symboles des arts africains." *Présence africaine* 10–11 (1951): 12–24.

Hammoudi, Abdellah. *The Victim and Its Masks: An Essay on Sacrifice and Masquerade in the Maghreb*. Trans. Paula Wissing. Chicago: University of Chicago Press, 1993.

Imperto, Pascal James. "Contemporary Adapted Dances of the Dogon." *African Arts* 5, no.1 (1971): 28–33.

James, Edwin Oliver. *Seasonal Feasts and Festivals*. London: Thames and Hudson, 1961.

Lewis, Naphtali, and Meyer Reinhold, eds. *Roman Civilization, Vol. 1: The Republic and the Augustan Age*. 3rd ed. New York: Columbia University Press, 1990.

Mora, Joseph. *The Year of the Hopi: Paintings and Photographs*. Washington, D.C.: Smithsonian Institution Traveling Exhibition Service, 1979.

Nunley, John W., and Judith Bettelheim. *Caribbean Festival Arts: Each and Every Bit of Difference*. St. Louis and Seattle: The Saint Louis Art Museum and University of Washington Press, 1988.

Poppi, Cesare. "The Other Within: Masks and Masquerades in Europe." In *Masks: The Art of Expression*, ed. John Mack, 190–215. London: British Museum, 1994.

Thompson, E. A. *The Goths in Spain*. Oxford: Clarendon Press, 1969.

Van Beek, Walter E. A. "Enter the Bush: A Dogon Mask Festival." In *Africa Explores: Twentieth-Century African Art*, ed. Susan Mullin Vogel, 56–73. New York: The Center for African Art; Munich: Prestel-Verlag, 1991.

Chapter 4: Men as Women

Bullough, Vern L., and Bonne Bullough. *Cross Dressing, Sex and Gender*. Philadelphia: University of Pennsylvania Press, 1990.

Cole, Herbert, and Chike Aniakor. *Igbo Arts: Community and Cosmos*. Los Angeles: UCLA Fowler Museum of Cultural History, 1985.

Drewal, Henry John, and Margaret Thompson Drewal. *Gelede: Art and Female Power among the Yoruba*. Bloomington: Indiana University Press, 1990.

Emigh, John. *Masked Performance: The Play of Self and Other in Ritual and Theatre*. Philadelphia: University of Pennsylvania Press, 1996.

Esser, Janet Brody. *Behind the Mask in Mexico*. Santa Fe, New Mexico: Museum of International Folk Art, 1988.

Ferris, Lesley. *Acting Women: Images of Women in Theatre*. New York: New York University Press, 1989.

Haag, Herbert, et al. *Great Women of the Bible in Art and Literature*. Grand Rapids, Michigan: Eerdmans, 1994.

Hinton, Carma, and Richard Gordon (directors). *First Moon*. Long Bow Group, 1987.

Houlberg, Marilyn. "Notes on Egungun Masquerades among the Oyo Yoruba." *African Arts* 11/3 (April 1978): 56–61, 99.

Imperato, P. J. "Bamana and Maninka Twin Figures." *African Arts* 8/4 (1975): 52–60.

Lamp, Frederick. *Art of the Baga: A Drama of Cultural Reinvention*. Munich: Prestel, 1996.

Lévi-Strauss, Claude. *The Way of the Masks*. Trans. Sylvia Modelski. Seattle: University of Washington Press, 1982.

Mora, Joseph. *The Year of the Hopi: Paintings and Photographs*. Washington, D.C.: Smithsonian Institution Traveling Exhibition Service, 1979.

Nunley, John. "Cover Story." *Journal of the American Medical Association* 276/22 (December 11, 1996): 1782.

———. *Moving with the Face of the Devil: Art and Politics in Urban West Africa*. Urbana: University of Illinois Press, 1987.

Nunley, John, and Judith Bettelheim. *Caribbean Festival Arts: Each and Every Bit of Difference*. St. Louis and Seattle: The Saint Louis Art Museum and University of Washington Press, 1988.

Ortner, Sherry B. "Is Female to Male as Nature Is to Culture?" In *Women, Culture, and Society*, ed. M. Z. Rosaldo and L. Lamphere. Stanford, California: Stanford University Press, 1974.

Ovid. *Pygmalion*. Trans. Rolfe Humphries. Bloomington: Indiana University Press, 1955.

Phelan, Peggy. "Crisscrossing Cultures." In *Crossing the Stage: Controversies on Cross-dressing*, ed. Lesley Ferris, 155–70. London and New York: Routledge, 1993.

Smithsonian Institution. *The Year of the Hopi: Paintings and Photographs by Jo Mora, 1904–06*. Washington, D.C.: Smithsonian Institution, 1979.

Walker, Barbara. *The Crone: Woman of Age, Wisdom, and Power*. New York: Harper and Row, Publishers, 1985.

Wright, B. A. *Kachinas: A Hopi Artist's Documentary*. Flagstaff, Arizona: Northland Press with the Heard Museum, 1973.

Chapter 5: Theater (Asian)

Bandem, I Madé, and Fredrik Eugene deBoer. *Balinese Dance in Transition: Kaja and Kelod*. 2nd ed. Kuala Lumpur: Oxford University Press, 1995.

Berger, Patricia. "Buddhist Festivals in Mongolia." In *Mongolia: The Legacy of Chinggis Khan*, ed. Terese Tse Bartholomew and Patricia Berger, 149–184. San Francisco: Asian Art Museum of San Francisco, 1995.

Bhattacharyya, Asutosh. *Chhau Dance of Purulia*. Calcutta: Rabindra Bharati University Press, 1972.

Chen Zao Fu. "Discovery of Rock Art in China." In *Rock Art in the Old World*, ed. Michel Lorblanchet. New Delhi: Indira Gandhi National Centre for the Arts, 1992.

de Zoete, Beryl, and Walter Spies. *Dance and Drama in Bali*. Singapore: Oxford University Press, 1973.

Doniger, Wendy. *The Implied Spider: Politics and Theology in Myth*. New York: Columbia University Press, 1998.

Eliade, Mircea. *Shamanism: Archaic Techniques of Ecstasy*. Princeton, New Jersey: Princeton University Press, 1964.

Emigh, John. *Masked Performance*. Philadelphia: University of Pennsylvania Press, 1997.

Fantin, Mario. *Mani-Rimdu, Nepal: The Buddhist Dance Drama of Tengpoche*. New Delhi: The English Book Store, 1976.

Foley, Kathy. "My Bodies: The Performer in West Java." *The Drama Review* 34/2 (1990): 62–80.

Fu Shin Shen. *The Masks of Anshun's Earth Opera*. Taipei: Shu Hsing Publishing, 1985.

Ghosh, Pradyot. "Gambhira: Traditional Masked Dance of Bengal." *Sangeet Natak*, 53–54 (1979): 53–77.

Goonatilleka, M. H. *Masks and Mask Systems of Sri Lanka*. Colombo, Sri Lanka: Tamarind Books, 1978.

Heppell, Michael. *Masks of Kalimantan*. Melbourne: Indonesian Arts Society, 1992.

Holt, Claire. *Art in Indonesia*. Ithaca, New York: Cornell University, 1967.

Ivanov, S., and V. Stukalov. *Ancient Masks of Siberian Peoples*. Text in English and Russian. Leningrad: Aurora Art Publishers, 1975.

The Japan Foundation: Asian Traditional Performing Arts Project, eds. *Dance and Music in South Asian Drama: Chhau, Mahakali Pyakhan, and Yakshagana*. Asian Traditional Performing Arts Project. Tokyo: The Japan Foundation, 1983.

Jones, Clifford R. "Bhagavata Natakam: A Traditional Dance-Drama Form." *Journal of Asian Studies* 22, 2/3 (1963): 193–200.

Kapferer, Bruce. *A Celebration of Demons: Exorcism and the Aesthetics of Healing in Sri Lanka*. Bloomington: Indiana University Press, 1983.

Keene, Donald. *Nō; The Classical Theatre of Japan*. Tokyo: Kodansha International Ltd., 1966.

Hsu, Tao-Ching. *The Chinese Conception of the Theatre*. Seattle: University of Washington Press, 1985.

Indira Gandhi National Centre for the Arts. *Man and Mask*. New Delhi: Indira Gandhi National Centre for the Arts, 1998.

Lee Duhyun, ed. *Masks of Korea*. Seoul: Korea Overseas Information Service, 1981.

Leiter, Samuel, ed. *Japanese Theatre in the World*. New York: Japan Society, Inc., and The Japan Foundation, 1997.

Loviconi, Alain, and F. Lontcho. *Masques et Exorcismes de Ceylon/Masks and Exorcisms of Sri Lanka*. Paris: Editions Errance, 1981.

Mahato, Pashupati Prasad. *The Performing Arts of Jharkhand*. Calcutta: B. B. Prakasan, 1987.

Miettinen, Jukka O. *Classical Dance and Theatre in South-East Asia*. Singapore: Oxford University Press, 1992.

Napier, David A. *Masks, Transformation, and Paradox*. Berkeley: University of California Press, 1984.

National Research Institute of Cultural Properties, ed. *Masked Performances in Asia: International Symposium on the Conservation and Restoration of Cultural Property*. Tokyo: National Research Institute of Cultural Properties, 1987.

Newton, D., and J. P. Barbier, eds. *Islands and Ancestors: Indigenous Styles of Southeast Asia*. New York: Metropolitan Museum of Art, 1988.

Nishikawa, Kyôtarô. *Bugaku Masks*. Translated and adapted by Monica Bethe. New York and Tokyo: Kodansha International Ltd. and Shibundo, 1978.

Pani, Jiwan. *World of Other Faces: Indian Masks*. New Delhi: Ministry of Information and Broadcasting, 1986.

Rimer, J. Thomas, and Yamazaki Masakazu, eds. and trans. *On the Art of the No Drama: The Major Treatises of Zeami*. Princeton, New Jersey: Princeton University Press, 1984.

Sarabhai, Mallika. *Performing Arts of Kerala*. Ahmedabad: Mapin Publishing Pvt. Ltd., 1994.

Sarachchandra, E. R. *The Folk Drama of Ceylon*. 2nd ed. Colombo, Ceylon: Department of Cultural Affairs, 1962.

Sarkar, Sabita Ranjan. *Masks of West Bengal*. Calcutta: Indian Museum, 1990.

Schechner, Richard. *Between Theatre and Anthropology*. Philadelphia: University of Pennsylvania Press, 1985.

Singh Deo, Juga Bhanu. *Chhau: Mask Dance of Seraikella*. Cuttack, Orissa: Srimati Jayashree Devi, 1973.

Slattum, Judith. *Balinese Masks: Spirits of an Ancient Drama*. San Francisco: Chronicle Books, 1992.

bibliography

Soedarsono. *Wayang Wong: The State Ritual Dance Drama in the Court of Yogyakarta.* Yogyakarta: Gadjah Mada University Press, 1990.

Teele, Rebecca, ed. *Nō/Kyōgen Masks and Performance.* Claremont, California: Mime Journal, 1984.

Tyagi, Gajendra S. "Decorative Intricate Patterns in Indian Rock Art." In *Rock Art in the Old World,* ed. Michel Lorblanchet, 303–318. New Delhi: Indira Gandhi National Centre for the Arts, 1992.

Varapande, J. M. L. *History of Indian Theatre: Loka Ranga, Panorama of Indian Folk Theatre.* New Delhi: Abhinav Publications, 1992.

Vatsyayan, Kapila. *Traditional Indian Theatre: Multiple Streams.* New Delhi: National Book Trust, 1980.

Wakankur, Vishnu S. "Rock Painting in India." In *Rock Art in the Old World,* ed. Michel Lorblanchet, 319–37. New Delhi: Indira Gandhi National Centre for the Arts, 1992.

Yi Tu-hyon (Lee Duhyun). "Mask Dance-Dramas." In *Traditional Performing Arts of Korea,* 35–80. Seoul: Seoul Computer Press, 1986.

Yu Quiyu. "Some Observations on the Aesthetics of Primitive Chinese Theatre." Trans. Hu Dongsheng, Elizabeth Wichmann, and Gregg Richardson. *Asian Theatre Journal,* 6/1 (1989): 12–30.

Yupho, Dhanit. *Khon Masks.* 4th ed. Bangkok: The Department of Fine Arts, 1971.

Chapter 5: Theater (Western)

Appel, Libby. *Mask Characterization: An Acting Process.* Carbondale: Southern Illinois University Press, 1982.

Archer, William. *Masks or Faces?* New York: Hill and Wang, 1957.

Brockett, Oscar. *History of the Theatre.* Boston: Allyn and Bacon, 1995.

Coleridge, Samuel Taylor. *Biographia Literaria.* Vol. II. Ed. J. Shawcross. London: Oxford University Press, 1939.

Duchartre, Pierre Louis. *The Italian Comedy.* Trans. Randolph T. Weaver. New York: Dover Publications, Inc., 1966.

Eldredge, Sears. *Mask Improvisation for Actor Training and Performance: The Compelling Image.* Evanston, Illinois: Northwestern University Press, 1996.

———. *Masks: Their Use and Effectiveness in Actor Training Programs.* Ph.D. diss., Michigan State University, 1975.

Ferris, Lesley. *Acting Women: Images of Women in Theatre.* London: Macmillan, 1990.

Leabhart, Thomas. "The Mask as Shamanic Tool in the Theatre Training of Jacques Copeau." *Mime Journal* (1995): 82–113.

Levi-Strauss, Claude. *The Way of the Masks.* Trans. Sylvia Modeleski. Seattle: University of Washington Press, 1982.

Lommel, Andreas. *Masks, Their Meaning and Function.* New York: McGraw Hill, 1972.

Napier, A. David. *Masks, Transformation, and Paradox.* Berkeley: University of California Press, 1986.

Nicoll, Allardyce. *Masks, Mimes and Miracles: Studies in Popular Theatre.* New York: Cooper Square Publishers, 1963.

———. *The World of Harlequin.* Cambridge: Cambridge University Press, 1963.

Prosperi, Mario. "The Masks of Lipari." *The Drama Review* 26, no. 4 (Winter 1982): 25–36.

Rolfe, Bari. *Behind the Mask.* Oakland, California: Persona Books, 1977.

Saint-Denis, Michel. *Training for the Theatre: Premises and Promises.* Ed. Suria Saint-Denis. New York: Theatre Arts Books, 1982.

Smith, Susan Valeria Harris. *Masks in Modern Drama.* Berkeley: University of California Press, 1984.

Sorell, Walter. *The Other Face: The Mask in the Arts.* London: Thames and Hudson, 1973.

Wiles, David. *The Masks of Menander: Sign and Meaning in Greek and Roman Performances.* Cambridge: Cambridge University Press, 1991.

Chapter 6: Offense | Defense

Berkowitz, Leonard. *Aggression: Its Causes, Consequences, and Control.* Philadelphia: Temple University Press, 1993.

Bernal, Ignacio. "The Ballplayers of Dainzú." *Archeology* 21 (1968): 246–251.

Bradley, Douglas E. *Life, Death and Duality: A Handbook of the Rev. Edmund P. Joyce, C.S.C. Collection of Ritual Ballgame Sculpture.* The Snite Museum of Art Bulletin, vol. 1. Notre Dame, Indiana: University of Notre Dame, 1997.

Brodzky, Anne Trueblood, et al., eds. *Stones, Bones and Skin: Ritual and Shamanic Art.* Toronto: The Society for Art, 1977.

Burch, Jr., Ernest S. "War and Trade." In *Crossroads of Continents: Cultures of Siberia and Alaska,* eds. William W. Fitzhugh and Aaron Crowell, 227–240. Washington, D.C.: Smithsonian Institution Press, 1988.

Coe, Michael D. *The Jaguar's Children: Pre-Classic Central Mexico.* New York: The Museum of Primitive Art, 1965.

Dean, Bashford. *Helmets and Body Armor in Modern Warfare.* New Haven, Connecticut: Yale University Press, 1920.

Diószegi, Vilmos, and Mihály Hoppál, eds. *Shamanism in Siberia. Selected Reprints.* Budapest: Akadémiai Kiadó, 1996.

Eliade, Mircea. *Shamanism: Archaic Techniques of Ecstasy.* Princeton, New Jersey: Princeton University Press, 1964.

Ffoulkes, Charles John. *The Armourer and His Craft from the Twelfth to the Sixteenth Century.* New York: Benjamin Blom, 1967.

Ingalls, Robert P. *Hoods: The Story of the Ku Klux Klan.* New York: G. P. Putnam's Sons, 1979.

Karcheski, Jr., Walter J. *Arms and Armor in the Art Institute of Chicago.* Chicago: Art Institute of Chicago, a Bulfinch Press Book, 1995.

Kozloski, Lillian. *U.S. Space Gear: Outfitting the Astronaut.* Washington, D.C.: Smithsonian Institution Press, 1994.

Krenn, Peter, and Walter J. Karcheski, Jr., *Imperial Austria: Treasures of Art, Arms and Armor From the State of Styria.* Houston and Munich: Museum of Fine Arts, Houston and Prestel, 1992.

Lattimore, Richard. *The Iliad of Homer.* Chicago: University of Chicago Press, 1961.

Leyenaar, Ted J. J. *Ulama: The Perpetuation in Mexico of the Pre-Spanish Ball Bame Ullamaliztli.* Leiden, The Netherlands: Rijksmuseum voor Volkenkunde, 1978.

Linton, Ralph. *Ethnology of Polynesia and Micronesia.* Part 6 of the Department of Anthropology Guide. Chicago: Field Museum of Natural History, 1926.

Maude, H. C., and H. E. Maude. "Tioba and the Tabitevean Religious Wars." *Journal of the Polynesian Society* 90/3 (1981): 307–36.

McCarty, Cara. *Modern Masks and Helmets.* Pamphlet. New York: Museum of Modern Art, 1991.

Munroe, Alexandra., ed. *Spectacular Helmets of Japan: 16th–19th Century.* New York: Japan Society, 1985.

Nickel, Helmut. *Warriors and Worthies Arms and Armor through the Ages.* New York: Atheneum, 1969.

Norman, A. V. B., and G. M. Wilson. *Treasures from the Tower of London.* Norwich, United Kingdom: Sainsbury Centre for Visual Arts, University of East Anglia, 1982.

Oliver, Douglas L. *Oceania. The Native Cultures of Australia and the Pacific Islands.* Vol. 1. Honolulu: University of Hawaii Press, 1988.

Parrish, Bernie. *They Call It a Game.* New York: Dial Press, 1971.

Raitz, Karl B., ed. *The Theater of Sport.* Baltimore: Johns Hopkins University, 1995.

Rubin, Arnold. "Accumulation, Power and Display in African Sculpture." In *Arts of Africa, Oceania and the Americas: Selected Readings,* ed. Janet Berlo and Lee Anne Wilson, 4–21. Englewood Cliffs, New Jersey: Prentice-Hall, 1993.

Schele, Linda, and Mary Ellen Miller. *The Blood of Kings: Dynasty and Ritual in Maya Art.* New York and Fort Worth: George Braziller and Kimbell Art Museum, 1986.

Sims, Patsy. *The Klan.* Lexington: University Press of Kentucky, 1996.

Stone, George Cameron. *A Glossary of the Construction, Decoration and Use of Arms and Armor in All Countries and in All Times, Together with Some Closely Related Subjects.* New York: Jack Brussel, 1961.

White, Reggie. *In the Trenches: The Autobiography.* Nashville: Thomas Nelson, 1996.

Wilkinson-Latham, Robert. *Phaidon Guide to Antique Weapons and Armour.* Oxford: Phaidon, 1981.

Zimbardo, Philip, and Richard Gerrig. *Psychology and Life.* 11th ed. Glenview, Illinois: Scott Foresman, 1985.

PHOTOGRAPHY CREDITS

Introduction frontispiece Photos courtesy The Art Institute of Chicago; Chapter 1 frontispiece Photos © Colorphoto Hans Hinz, Allschwil; 1.1 Photo courtesy John Nunley; 1.2a, b, c. Photo courtesy Alexander Marshack, after Marshack, Begouen, and Breuil; 1.3 Photo © Ruth D. Lechuga; 1.4 Photo © Bildarchiv Preussischer Kulturbesitz, Berlin; 1.5 Photo © Amon Carter Museum, Fort Worth, Texas, Bequest of Eliot Porter, P1990.51.2070.1; 1.6 Photo © Peter Garlake; 1.7 Photo courtesy Minneapolis Institute of Arts; 1.8 Photo © The Saint Louis Art Museum; 1.9a Photo © Brian Forrest; 1.9b Photo courtesy John Bigelow Taylor, N.Y.C.; 1.10 Photo © Fred Hirschmann; 1.11 Photo © Fred Hirschmann; 1.12 Photo © Grahame L. Walsh; 1.14 Photo © Ulli Steltzer, Vancouver; 1.15 Photo © Peter T. Furst; 1.16 Photo © Alice Marriott Collection, Western History Collections, University of Oklahoma, Norman; 1.17 Photo © Syndey Byrd; 1.18 Photo © David Sams and Stock, Boston; 2.1 Photo courtesy John Nunley; 2.2 Photo by Hillel Burger, © President & Fellows of Harvard College, Peabody Museum of Ethnology and Anthropology, Harvard University; 2.3 Photo © Mrs. Lucille Opler; 2.4 Photo © Frederick Lamp; 2.5 Photo © Royal Museum for Central Africa, Tervuren, Belgium; 2.6 Photo courtesy Dimitar Bistrini; 2.7 Photo © Gilbert Schneider; 2.8 Photo © Christopher D. Roy; 2.9 Photo © Arlene Wolinski; 2.10 Photo courtesy Merle Green Robertson; 2.11 Photo courtesy Merle Green Robertson; 2.12 Photo by D. Graf, © Staatliche Museen zu Berlin, Preussischer Kulturbesitz, Museum für Völkerkunde; 2.13 Photo © Trustees of The British Museum; 2.14 Photo by Claire Holt, courtesy New York Public Library; 2.15 Photo © Anthony JP Meyer, Paris; 2.16 Photo © Kenji Yoshida; 3.1 Photo © Syndey Byrd; 3.2 Photo © Trustees of The British Museum; 3.3 Photo © Christopher D. Roy; 3.4 © National Museum of African Art; 3.5 Photo by Jacques Lessard, © Musée de la Civilisation, Quebec; 3.6 Photo © Kunsthistorisches Museum, Vienna; 3.7 Photo courtesy John Nunley; 3.8 Photo courtesy Istituto Superiore Regionale Etnografico; 3.9 Photo © Judith Bettelheim; 3.10 Photo © National Library of Jamaica; 3.11 Photo courtesy John Nunley; 3.12 Photo by David Ulmer, © The Saint Louis Art Museum; 3.13 Photo by David Ulmer, © The Saint Louis Art Museum; 3.14 Photo by David Ulmer, © The Saint Louis Art Museum; 3.15 Photo by David Ulmer, © The Saint Louis Art Museum; 3.16 Photo by David Ulmer, © The Saint Louis Art Museum; 3.17 Photo by David Ulmer, © The Saint Louis Art Museum; 3.18 Photo courtesy John Nunley; 4.1 Photo © Henry Drewal, courtesy National Museum of African Art; 4.2 Photo © G. I. Jones and the UCLA Fowler Museum of Cultural History; 4.3 Photo courtesy Scala, Art Resource, New York; 4.4 Photo © Syndey Byrd; 4.6 Photo © The Metropolitan Museum of Art, Museum Excavations, 19-22-23; Rogers Fund, 1923. (23.3.1) All rights reserved; 4.7 Photo by Ian Logan, courtesy Museum of International Folk Art, Santa Fe; 4.8 Photo © Marilyn Houlberg; 4.9 Photo by Jean-Michel Arnaud, © Musée d'Aquitaine Bordeaux; 4.10 Photo © Frederick Lamp; 4.11 Hastings photograph, photo by Dr. Frang, American Museum of Natural History neg. no. 336106; 4.12 Photo © Stefan Frischknecht; 5.2 Photo © Young-eun Kim; 5.3 Photo courtesy John Emigh; 5.4 Photo courtesy John Emigh; 5.5 Photo courtesy John Emigh; 5.6 Photo courtesy John Emigh; 5.7 Photo courtesy Kedar Nath Sahoo; 5.8 Photo courtesy John Emigh; 5.9 Photo © Tom Ballinger; 5.10 Photo © The Horniman Museum & Public Park Trust, London; 5.11 Photo © Alid Djajasoebrata, photographer and Museum voor Volkenkunde, Rotterdam; 5.13 Photo © Trustees of The British Museum; 5.14 Photo courtesy of the Japan Society; 5.15 Photo © Martin von Wagner Museum, Wurzburg; 5.16 Photo © J.Paul Getty Museum, Los Angeles, California; 5.17 Photo by Bruce White Photography, © Trustees of Princeton University; 5.18 Photo © Glasgow Museums: Art Gallery and Museum, Kelvingrove; 5.19 Photo © Foto Biblioteca Vaticana; 5.20 © The Bodleian Library, Oxford University; 5.21 Photo © Deutsches Teatermuseum, Munich; 5.22 Photo © Drottningholms teatermuseum, Stockholm; 5.23 Photo © Nationalmuseum, Stockholm; 5.25 Photo by Martha Swope, © Time, Inc.; 5.26 Photo © New York Public Library-Performing Arts; 5.27 Courtesy Stratford Festival Archives; 5.28 Photo © 1999 Oskar Schlemmer Theatre Estate, 28824 Oggebbio, Italy; 5.29 John Vickery as Scar, Sam Wright as Mufasa, photo by Joan Marcus, © Disney; 5.30 Photo courtesy Warner Bros., BATMAN AND ROBIN © 1977 Warner Bros., a division of Time Warner Entertainment Company, L.P. All Rights Reserved; 5.31 Photo courtesy the Everett Collection; 6.1 Photo © Christian Schweizer; 6.2 Photos by Lynton Gardiner, courtesy Institut für Ethnologie der Universität Göttingen, Abteilung Völkerkundliche Sammlung; 6.3 Photo by David Ulmer, courtesy Charles and Kent Davis; 6.4 Photo by Anne-Marie Bouttiaux, © Royal Museum for Central Africa, Tervuren. Belgium; 6.5 Photo © Z. S. Strother; 6.7 Photo © Trustees of The British Museum; 6.8 Photo courtesy Robert Burawoy; 6.9 Photo by David Ulmer, © The Saint Louis Art Museum; 6.10 Photo by Hillel Burger, © President and Fellows of Harvard College, 1988; 6.11 Photo courtesy Ellis Library, University of Missouri, Columbia; 6.12 Photo © Micha Bar'Am and Magnum Photos, New York; 6.13 Photo © Arthur Grace; 6.14 Photo © Mitchel Osborne Photography; 6.15 Photo © P. & M. Marechaux; 6.16 Photo courtesy the Boston Bruins; 6.17a-d Courtesy Hockey Hall of Fame Archives; 6.18 Photo © Shaun Paul Gabbard; 6.19 Photo by Paula G. Leyenaar-Plaisier, © Rijksmuseum voor Volkenkunde, Leiden, The Netherlands; 6.20 Photo © The Cleveland Museum of Art, 1998, Dudley P. Allen Fund, 1969.29; 6.21 and 6.22 Photos © Johnson Space Center, NASA